MW01493783

IBOS: Hebrew Exiles From Israel Reprinting

Copyright © 2013 by Dr. O. Alaezi and Ibos Book

ISBN-13: 978-1494764180
ISBN-10: 1494764180

DEDICATION

This book is dedicated to all Ibos, African Americans and all Oppressed people anywhere in the world.

Dr. Martin Luther King Jr. speaking at the Civil Rights March on Washington, D.C.
The prophecy in his "I have a dream " speech has materialized.
The activities of the African American Civil Right Leaders instigated the struggle for Africa's Independence. For Africa's Independence and other mutually beneficial efforts, we are grateful.

ACKNOWLEDGEMENT:

As regards acknowledgement, it is unfortunate that the sheer weight of numbers precludes my mentioning all the people who contributed to this book in one way or the other.

Eze Ufere, the Traditional Ruler of Amankalu Alayi, in Abia State for logistic support.

Owelle Ndigbo, Rochas Okorocha for his financial support for the initial research work on this project.

Mr. Kingsley Njionye. Dr. Harold Ugochukwu Nwosu of the University of Port Harcourt Nigeria.

Prince Okonkwo-Uzor, Tel Aviv, Israel for their immense moral and logistics support as well Mr. Okoro Kalu and Mr. Eke Onuma all in Nigeria for sharing with me their Biblical knowledge of the subject.

Mr. Kenneth Onwuka Njoku, Atlanta, U.S.A, whose idea it was to write this American edition, for his immense literary and logistic contributions to the production of this book.

TABLE OF CONTENTS

Page

INTRODUCTION
By
Dr. Jerry Ekwulugo

With immense delight and pleasure, I introduce this great treatise on the Hebrew origin of the Ibos. The author's in-depth research into the many facets of Ibo history has made him a distinct and outstanding scholar of our times.

My father was a clergyman of the Anglican faith, known in Nigeria as The Church Missionary Society (CMS). He was converted to Christianity at a tender age of twelve (12), and ran to stay with the white missionary at Onitsha, three miles away from my hometown, Obosi. He eventually became a headmaster for fifteen years, before going to Divinity College after which he was ordained a reverend minister.

He worked very closely with the famous Dr. Basden of the Anglican Mission who wrote the book entitled THE NIGER IBOS. Dr Basden was a missionary scholar whose intense research and findings acclaimed him an international scholar and was recognized by King George V of Britain. He gave my father over twenty of his books, which he distributed to those who could read and understand English. I was always reticent and bashful about the photographs in this book that had ten naked Ibo virgins with bangles on the legs and arms. When I complained to my father about these pictures, he simply told me that it was exactly what he (the writer, Dr. Basden) saw. My father reminded me, of the terms and contents of God's curse on Hebrews, in Deuteronomy 28. "In nakedness shall we serve other gods". Brief, Dr. Basden established that the Ibos are Jews.

The author of this book, Ibos: Hebrew Exiles from Israel, Professor Alaezi, has vividly pointed out authentically the inscriptions in ancient Hebrew language in the palace of Eze Eri in Agulueri in 1997 and again in 2001 by both the Ibo and the Jewish researchers - inscriptions that had been there long before the arrival of the white colonial masters in Nigeria. It is also salient to mention here the archaeological British finding at Agulu, 500 feet below the soil, of "The Star of King David in bronze"! The British colonial rulers engraved it in the old West African coin, penny and half a penny, as a memorial. Any inquiry into this or effort to obtain these coins will confirm the above.

In 1948 when we were young boys in Dennis Memorial Grammar School, Onitsha, something dramatic took place. Our then principal from Oxford

England, Reverend E. D. Clarke, rallied all the 300 boys to the Assembly Hall for an important announcement. We rushed to the Hall.

He announced that the state of Israel had been born. We leaped with wild joy, and ran out of the hall, while he was still standing. He seemed to have been delighted as well. But the non-Ibos among us, including the Millers from the north, all stood like lampposts, motionless, and quite bewildered at our reaction.

Then we had seven British tutors - some English, some Welsh, and others Scottish. Amongst them was Rev. Birch, our phonetics master, who called me and another boy and asked: "Why are you jubilating?"

"Because the state of Israel is established," I answered.

Rev. Birch looked at Rev. Thompson, our Science master, from same place as him, and retorted, "They must be Jews."

Soon the celebration invaded the famous OTU Onitsha market. All sales stopped abruptly, and drinking and dancing spread all over the market. It spread all over other Ibo towns.

What about the color of the skin of the Jews vis-à-vis the Ibos? Color of the skins can never be the basis of Jewry. Israel can never be complete without the black Jews. In Numbers Chapter 12 verse 1 "Miriam and Aaron spoke against Moses because of the Cushite (now Ethiopian) woman whom he had married: "for he had married a Cushite woman". God reacted angrily against these two and made Miriam leprous on account of their antagonism to Moses' marriage. It is noteworthy that all the American translators removed the word Ethiopian and substituted Cushite. This is found in Amplified Bible, Living Bible, and New International Version. Actually, the kingdom of Cush was established in the middle of the Nile in Sudan. The kingdom thrived for many centuries. In 5 A.D., the fanatical Arab Moslems attacked it from the north and overran it. Today, the Cushites of Sudan are still proud of their past. Although they are blacks, they are different from Ethiopian Jews. As for the Ethiopian Jews, over 30,000 of them have been taken back to Israel, thus confirming Ezekiel's prophecy. It also establishes God's statement, "I am the LORD, I change not; therefore the sons of Jacob are not consumed" (Malachi Chapter 3 verse 6 -K.J.V)

The author's figure of 370,000 Ibos sold as slaves under the curse of Deuteronomy 28 is extremely accurate. Indeed, Jamaica, the largest Island in West Indies, has in its history book clearly stated that 60% of the black people there are of Ibo origin.

Why were the Ibos, not converted to Islam, by the violent Arab Fulani Moslems, of the northern region of Nigeria? They had overrun Ilorin and advanced to Oyo, where they were eventually stopped. They Islamized the areas they conquered. Coming to the eastern part of the country, the Fulani Arab Moslems fought fifteen battles with the Ibos in the northern fringe of

Ibo land. And they were defeated fifteen times. They eventually gave up the Ibos as unconquerable people.

My father described to me in minute details how the battles were fought. The Ibos had an incredible system of communication, and installed a permanent vigilante group monitoring the movements of enemies at the flanks of Ibo land. At the slightest information, the Ibos prepared for war in this wise:
(1)   The Awka blacksmiths were massively engaged to produce locally or native made guns and gunpowder in hundreds.
(2)   Builders were engaged to produce or build high-rise structures with wooden pillars, wooden floor and wooden walls with only one opening for shooting out. A steep ladder was attached to each structure as the steps. These structures were arrayed all along the boundaries.
The Bende professional Ibo soldiers, notably, the
     Ohafia, Abam and Item, were mobilized in readiness.
These were highly trained, articulate, athletic and sharp soldiers. On the way to war, each one had a young leaf of a palm tree (omu) in the mouth as a symbol of seriousness, not talking to anybody as long as the battle lasted. At war, each high-rise structure had two people up stairs, (a) one shooting and (b) one refilling the guns. In combat therefore, the front lines of the Ibo camp were these structures, and the professional soldiers massed on behind them, hidden by the tall grassland. The Fulani Arabs were now sighted; they came in hundreds on their horses, each carrying bows and poisoned arrows. Their commanders kept the camp silent until the enemy came within the range of the Awka made native guns. Then a signal of a hollow metal instrument (ogele) was given. Then shots went out to gun them down. The Fulani Arab arrows were released onto the Ibo war structures, but were caught by the wooden walls. The operation lasted for hours - about 8 to 10 hours. As the horses now not ridden by the dead Fulani Arabs ran helter-skelter, the Ibo soldiers advanced in what can be described as mopping up operation. Ironically, the confused horses gave a grand cover to the soldiers. Each Ibo soldier went in for about 10 heads of the enemy soldiers and left.
Finally, one could see the enemy retreating back home. The Ibos had won. This was done fifteen times over the stretch of many years. Eventually, at the fifteenth defeat, the Fulani Arabs gave up the Ibos as unconquerable people.
The Ibos and Israelites. There are certain facets of Ibo life that are identical with that of Israel. Every Ibo male is circumcised on the eighth day of his birth. It is a serious matter in Iboland. My father told me that I was circumcised at Iyienu Hospital, Ogidi, near Onitsha, in the missionary hospital ran by the white people from Britain. When I was brought home,

7

the elders of my family insisted that I was not properly circumcised. They therefore re-circumcised me. My father advanced two reasons for my re-circumcision: (1) that I would blame him when I grew up for not doing it correctly as in the traditional Ibo way of circumcision; and (2) more importantly, that God would be annoyed with him.

The author of this book narrated a similar experience to me about his two boys who were born in Gabon, Central Africa. After the Biafran war, a war of genocide, against the Ibos, in Nigeria (1967-70), they returned home, the elders of the family again insisted that they were not properly circumcised, and therefore were re-circumcised.

As an obstetrician, when I returned to Nigeria after many years of sojourn in Britain, I instituted male circumcision after three days of birth. It is almost bloodless, and painless because the nerves were not yet fully developed. Healing was between six to seven days. Generally, it was untraumatic. Then came a strong Ibo women delegation to my office. They were polite but pointed out to me that they wanted their male children circumcised on the eighth day according to the law and custom of their fathers and not on the third day. They did not want to annoy God, but to be at peace with Him. I, therefore, stopped the practice of circumcision on the third day and reverted back to the eighth day.

What about ajo ohia (evil or bad forest) of the Ibos? Every Ibo town has a piece of land set aside for disposal of everything evil in the town. It was called ajo ohia, evil or bad forest. No other people or tribe in Africa has this, but perhaps with the exception of the people of Jewish descent like the Ethiopian Jews. It is a replica of wilderness in Israel where the scapegoat is released by the high priest to atone for the sins of Israel. Today most of the ajo ohia are now left fallow and people are still hesitant to buy or cultivate it.

What about the forbidden meat, food and things in Ibo land as in Israel? Almost 95% of Ibos do not eat pork. Some of them rear pigs and breed them, but sell them to the neighboring states where they are readily bought for slaughter. Only in big Ibo townships where other communities other than the Ibos also inhabit are pork sold in the markets.

When we were children, A swam of locusts used to invade Nigeria especially the Eastern parts where the Ibos inhabit. They came from the horn of Africa in the direction of Ethiopia, Egypt and Israel. The Ibos (unlike the other tribes of Western and Northern Nigeria) went en masse in open fields with containers at night called calabash to collect these locusts for food. They made a feast of them in different forms. They also ate the beetles. When I enquired from our elders why they ate these two types of insects, while other ethnic groups in Nigeria did not, they replied that their

8

great grand fathers ate these from where they came. They knew not the exact place, but they knew it was
 a distant place. Now on maturity, I discovered in Leviticus Chapter 11 verse 22 that God permitted the children of Israel to eat them.
Even these of them ye may eat; the locust after its kind, and the bald locust after its kind, and the cricket after its kind, and the grasshopper after its kind. No wonder John the Baptist lived on locusts and wild honey.

The Osu caste system, in Ibo land.
The origin was a quasi attempt at Levites; but instead of dedicating men to God, the Ibos (Jews in exile in Nigeria) dedicated them to their newfound false "gods of wood and stone, gods unknown to their fathers" in line with God's curse on them in Deuteronomy 28. They later on feared to touch such people because they belonged to the gods, had nothing whatsoever to do with them so as not to incur the anger of the gods, and then later discriminated against them even as it is today. This is of the devil; it is null and void in the eyes of God Almighty. It is idolatry and must be discarded. The above points and many more have been treated in this book. It is therefore pertinent and salient for every Ibo {African American}, man, woman, boy and girl to read this most important book. It is relevant and inspiring for everyone to know his or her origin as revealed by the Almighty God to the author through his indomitable research work. As over 70% of the Ibos have gone back to their Jehovah, the Holy One of Israel, the God Almighty, these things have been revealed for the prophecy of his famous prophet Ezekiel to be fulfilled. In Psalm Chapter 89 verse 34, God said, "My covenant will I not break, nor alter the thing that is gone out of my lips". Most Ibos get intuitively depressed at any adverse report on Israel; but get elated on any favorable report on Israel. Why? Can all the overwhelming similarities between the Ibos of Nigeria and the Jews in Israel and in the Diaspora be a matter of chance or accident? What about the archaeological and religious evidences of the Jewish origin of the Ibos that abound in this book? For these and many more, I advise every Ibo {African American} to read this book. I also recommend it to every Jew irrespective of where he resides now.
Finally, I charge the Ibos and all Americans with the words of Sheridan: Can the quick temper of a patriot heart, thus stagnate in cold and weedy converse; or freeze in a tide less inactivity? No rather, let the fountain of your valour, spring through each stream of enterprise, each channel of conducive daring; till the full torrent of your foaming wrath overwhelms the flats of sunk hostility
Signed:
Dr. Jerry (Jeremiah) Ekwulugo, MB, BSCal, DRCOG, MRCOG (London).

CHAPTER ONE

HISTORICAL EVIDENCE OF IBO POPULATION (PERCENTAGE) IN AMERICAN SOCIETY

"This place is the wholesale market for slaves as not fewer than 20,000 are annually sold here; 16,000 of whom are natives of one nation, called Heebos (Ibos), so that this single nation has not exported a less number of people, during the last twenty years, than 320,000; and those of the same nation sold at New and Old Calaber, probably amounted to 50,000 more, making an aggregate amount of 370,000 Heebos. The remaining part of the above 20,000 is composed of the natives of the Brass country called Allokoos and also of Ibibios or Quaws (Ibibios Kwa).

Fairs, where the slaves of the Heebo nation are obtained, are held every five or six weeks at several villages, which are situated on the banks of the rivers and creeks in the interior...

The Heebos, to judge by the immense number annually sent into slavery (in chains, with 'iron yoke on their necks') inhabit a country of great extent, and extremely populous..., and it is very probable that the towns at the mouths of the rivers along the coast including New Calabar and Bonny, were peopled originally from the heebo country; in fact , Amacree (Amakiri)the King of New calabar, and Pepple, King of Bonny, are both of Heebo descent, as well as many of the principal traders at both these places (Adams, 1975:231-232).

TO BE SOLD, on board the
Ship *Bance-Island*, on tuesday the 6th
of *May* next, at *Ashley-Ferry*; a choice
cargo of about 250 fine healthy

FINE HEEBOES,

just arrived from the
Windward & Rice Coast.
—The utmost care has
already been taken, and
shall be continued, to keep them free from
the least danger of being infected with the
SMALL-POX, no boat having been on
board, and all other communication with
people from *Charles-Town* prevented.

Austin, Laurens, & Appleby.

N. B. Full one Half of the above Negroes have had the
SMALL-POX in their own Country.

BY THE PRESIDENT, OF THE UNITED STATES OF AMERICA.
A PROCLAMATION.

WHEREAS, on the twenty-second day of September, in the year of our Lord one thousand eight hundred and sixty-two, a Proclamation was issued by the President of the United States, containing, among other things, the following, to wit:

"That on the first day of January, in the year of our Lord one thousand eight hundred and sixty-three, all persons held as slaves within any State or designated part of a State, the people whereof shall then be in rebellion against the United States, shall be then, thenceforward, and forever, free; and the Executive government of the United States, including the military and naval authority thereof, will recognize and maintain the freedom of any such persons, and will do no act or acts to repress such persons, or any of them, in any efforts they may make for their actual freedom.

"That the Executive will, on the first day of January aforesaid, by proclamation, designate the States and parts of States, if any, in which the people thereof, respectively, shall then be in rebellion against the United States; and the fact that any State, or the people thereof, shall on that day be in good faith represented in the Congress of the United States, by members chosen thereto at elections wherein a majority of the qualified voters of such States shall have participated, shall, in the absence of strong countervailing testimony, be deemed conclusive evidence that such State, and the people thereof, are not then in rebellion against the United States."

Now, therefore, I, ABRAHAM LINCOLN, President of the United States, by virtue of the power in me vested as Commander-in-chief of the Army and Navy of the United States, in time of actual armed rebellion against the authority and government of the United States, and as a fit and necessary war measure for suppressing said rebellion, do, on this first day of January, in the year of our Lord one thousand eight hundred and sixty-three, and in accordance with my purpose so to do, publicly proclaimed for the full period of one hundred days from the day first above mentioned, order and designate as the States and parts of States wherein the people thereof, respectively, are this day in rebellion against the United States, the following, to wit:

Arkansas, Texas, Louisiana, (except the parishes of St. Bernard, Plaquemine's, Jefferson, St. John, St. Charles, St. James, Ascension, Assumption, Terre Bonne, Lafourche, St. Mary, St. Martin, and Orleans, including the city of New Orleans,) Mississippi, Alabama, Florida, Georgia, South Carolina, North Carolina, and Virginia, (except the forty-eight counties designated as West Virginia, and also the counties of Berkeley, Accomac, Northampton, Elizabeth City, York, Princess Ann, and Norfolk, including the cities of Norfolk and Portsmouth,) and which excepted parts are for the present left precisely as if this Proclamation were not issued.

And by virtue of the power and for the purpose aforesaid, I do order and declare that all persons held as slaves within said designated States and parts of States are and henceforward shall be free; and that the Executive government of the United States,

12

including the military and naval authorities thereof, will recognize and maintain the freedom of said persons.

And I hereby enjoin upon the people so declared to be free to abstain from all violence, unless in necessary self-defense; and I recommend to them that, in all cases when allowed, they labor faithfully for reasonable wages.

And I further declare and make known that such persons, of suitable condition, will be received into the armed service of the United States to garrison forts, positions, stations, and other places, and to man vessels of all sorts in said service.

And upon this act, sincerely believed to be an act of justice warranted by the Constitution upon military necessity, I invoke the considerate judgement of mankind and the gracious favor of Almighty God.

In witness whereof, I have hereunto set my hand and caused the seal of the United States to be affixed.

Done at the city of Washington this first day of January, in the year of our Lord one thousand eight hundred and sixty-three, and of the Independence of the United States of America the eighty-seventh.

ABRAHAM   LINCOLN

Frederick Douglas. The Ibo abolitionist, whose influence and persistence achieved the abolution of Slave Trade and may have instigated the American civil war.

PRESIDENT ABRAHAM LINCOLN.
HE ABOLISHED SLAVE TRADE AND AMERICA
BECAME THE REAL LAND OF THE FREE.

CHAPTER TWO

ISRAEL AND THE REALITY OF THE TORAH/BIBLE.

In this book, I have sort of established or re-established the fact that the Ibos of Nigeria, the Tutsis of East Africa, the Bamilikis of Cameroon and a few thousands of other Africans scattered in South Africa, Ghana and over 25% of all African Americans, are of Jewish origin. If I have to say this aloud, general laughter, mockery, abuses and harassment from certain quarters would be the response. Maybe, in a few years' time, certainly around the soon-coming 3rd World War, when, in keeping with the Almighty's unchangeable divine plan for the conclusion of the present earth's cycle, the gathering back of the scattered Jews from all the four corners of the earth and restoration of their fortunes will assume a global and final dimension, everybody in the world, including the Israeli authorities whose heart had hitherto been hardened to accept the reality of colored or black Jews will recognise this fact.

Israel and its branches scattered to all the four corners of the Earth – The challenge reality from The Torah/Bible

*The fact from the Scriptures that all living things such as fish, birds, mammals including man, came forth according to their kind (Genesis 1:21) is in perfect harmony with what today's scientists have found in natural creation that every living thing comes from a parent of like kind.

*According to Science, "all the chemical elements that make up living things are also present in non-living things. Therefore, the statement in Genesis 2:7 that "the LORD God formed the man from the dust of the earth" is true since all the basic elements that make up living organisms are also found in the earth itself.

*The fact that the earth is circular, round, global is contained in the Hebrew Scriptures. "He (the Almighty) sits enthroned above the circle of the earth..." (Isaiah 40:22). Thousands of years after the book of Isaiah was written, people continued to believe that the earth was a flat, rigid platform.

*Thousands of years before science discovered the law of gravity by which the Earth remains suspended on nothing, the Torah/Bible had it that

the Almighty God of Israel "suspends the earth over nothing" (Job 26:7). Actually, Newton published his findings in 1687 (that is over 2000 years after the book of Job was written) that the Earth hung on nothing in the space but was held in relation to the other heavenly bodies by mutual attraction to each other, by the law of gravity.

*The reality of a "Book of Life" in Daniel 12:1 and Revelation 20:15 that can keep names of the peoples of the world, a book that is capable of containing the records of what each of these peoples did during his or her life time (Revelation 20:21) can now be conceptualised or appreciated in the light of today's modern computer that can store billions of information and produce any of the information needed in a matter of seconds. If ordinary man can invent an equipment to keep such records for him, what about his maker?

*Above all, over 98 percent of the prophecies in the Holy Scriptures of Israel, the Torah/Bible, have been literally fulfilled today; the remaining 2 percent is about the last days. And of these last days' prophecies, virtually all are beginning and/or are sure to happen as exemplified in the miracles of modern Israel punctuated with the certainties and uncertainties of crises in the Holy Land which started 3,500 years ago with the birth of Isaac's twins, Esau (the forerunner of the present day Palestinians) and Jacob (Israel), the heritage which Esau handed over to Jacob (Genesis Chapter 25) and the tribal disputes and wars for centuries after - wars between Israel and the Palestinians supported by the Arabs, the descendants of Ishmael, with a promise of a war to end all wars in the world as prophesied in the Holy Scriptures and the hand of God or the Rock (Jesus Christ) descending from heaven to save Israel from total destruction by the combined forces of the Gentile nations.

Meanwhile today's events in the Middle East have shown that Israel is not just a Jewish foothold in the Middle East, is a place destined to produce events that will have world-shaking consequences and influence the future of humanity. Already, Israel, as very small as it is, is a bone of contention in world politics, presenting problems that world powers dread to attend to. Israel is prophetically and historically unique. It is the only nation that has its citizens also as citizens of other nations in all the four corners of the earth or rather in all the continents of the world. They include the American Jews (black and white) who are also full-fledged Americans, the European Jews, the Russian Jews, the Ibos of Nigeria, the

17

Tutsis of East Africa and the other African Jews in Ghana, Cameroon and South Africa yet to be identified. These Jews, the world over, are equally progressive and equally persecuted and hated by their neighbors, the non-Jews of the same nationality. Israel's history, witnesses to the truth of God's, words in the Torah, and the Bible in all their ramifications. The miracles of today's Israel are certainly of God.

Hundreds and thousands of tourists go to Israel each year to witness these miracles or rather God's prophecies being fulfilled - desert being turned into fertile land with water everywhere, tiny army of a few thousands of people of Israel defeating amalgamated fierce armies armed to the teeth of millions of Arabs even when Israel is completely surrounded at all ends by these enemy Arab countries and the Palestinians that have vowed to exterminate Israel from the face of the Earth. Three major highlights of these miracles of today's Israel - a witness that God of Israel is a reality - are as follows:

-        In the beginning of the chequered history of Israel, 3500 years ago, when after the death of Moses, Joshua had to lead the people to go and settle in the Promised Land, the land that God promised to give Israel for inheritance for ever or rather the present Holy Land in dispute between Israel and the Palestinians, the young nation of Israel then had to fight a war against seven nations "greater and mightier" than it (Deuteronomy 7:1). Again, when Israel was re-established as a nation in 1948, the young nation again had to fight against seven nations "greater and mightier" than it at that time. What a coincidence! These seven nations include Egypt, Iraq, Jordan, Lebanon, Saudi Arabia, Syria and Yemen. These invading Arab nations with professional soldiers, more money and better armed with sophisticated weapons had a total population of 40,000,000 (forty million) whereas young Israel had a population of 600,000 (less than one million). Yet small Israel won the war and the new state was formed to the astonishment of the whole world.

-        The people of Israel, the Jews, are the only people to have been scattered throughout the world, bitterly persecuted by most of the other nations of the world wherein they find themselves for over 3000 years, and yet miraculously gathered back into one of the smallest yet strongest nations of the world, to the total bewilderment of their enemies. And so miraculously too, the small Israel that is rightly one of the oldest countries in the world is now one of the youngest or rather the youngest with more historic and religious sites, more expansion and development in all facets of human endeavor than the other older and larger countries of the world.

Of all the dead languages of the ancient world, Hebrew, the language of the Jews is the only one that is surviving today, not only as a language of a tiny group of people called Jews, but as a virile, modern language that hundreds of millions of people in the Christendom the world over are very anxious to study in a bid to better understand their Bible.

Therefore in Israel we witness the miracles of God and see the truth in His words, in the words of the Holy Scriptures of Israel concerning world events of yesterday, today and tomorrow.

General Colin Powell as then Chairman of the Joint Chiefs of Staf.(1987–89) and Chairman of the Joint Chiefs of Staff (1989–93). Colin Luther Powell, was the 65th United States Secretary of State. Serving from January 20, 2001 to January 26, 2005. Powell became the first highest ranking African American government official in the history of the United States.

CHAPTER THREE

THE IBO EXPLOITS

This American Edition of the book, Ibos: Hebrew Exiles from Israel - Amazing Facts and Revelations, is an outgrowth, or if you like, the second volume of the first edition. However, only 20% of the information in the said first edition has been selected to go into this volume. This book contains lots of inspiring information on the exploits and progress of African Americans and Black American Jews most of whom originate from the Ibos of Nigeria as well as the untold story of a cluster of some lost tribes of Israel "scattered to the most distant part of the earth" in one of the big jungles of Africa South of Sahara over 2000 years ago. It is a story unparalleled in the history of Israel - a story that highlights the discovery of dark-skinned and sometimes fair-skinned Hebrews (Ibos) who in the first instance called themselves 'Ibrit' pronounced, 'Ivrit' as it is also pronounced in the ancient and modern Hebrew tongue – a name that today's World Jews or Hebrews call themselves. However, the name 'ivrit', was sometime corrupted as 'ifrit of ifite' by the Anambra Ibos or 'ihite' by the Imo/Abia Ibos. On realising their Jewishness, the British Colonial masters began to refer to the Nigerian Jews, the Ifites, as Hebrews (English version of Ivrite or Ifite) – a name that was corrupted as Heebo, Eboe and finally Ibo. The name Igbo, a name of a Nigerian Hebrew hero, as will be discussed in this book, is often confused with Ibo. Paradoxically, when the white man arrived on the scene and began to be seen as organised and as creative as the Ifite (now called the Ibo), the aborigines of Eastern Nigeria, the Kwas, the Allokoos, the Ituris and Pigmies who had earlier noticed the Ibos to be so creative and organised began to refer to the white people as oyibo, meaning Ibo person (if not in color, in behavior; and, in fact, they have seen lots of the Ifites, Ibos, with the skin color of the white man). Whether Hebrew, Heebo, Eboe or Ibo, one thing is clear: the name stands for one and the same people with the same origin, the same culture, the same destiny and the same fate, as will be made clear in this book.

In this book, the author has chosen to use the English version of the name for the Nigerian Jews, Ibo, instead of using the current indigenous version, Igbo or Ndigbo. Indeed, all the traits of Jewish character have cluttered up the Ibo fiction in Nigeria: the clever Ibo businessman, the unstable but shrewd Ibo politician, the brilliant Ibo doctor, the sneaky lawyer, the famous teacher, the careful money lender, the notable inventor, the highly prized sportsman and woman, and in fact, the highly world acclaimed Ibo as exemplified in the likes of Philip Emeagwali (an Ibo American) Bartholomew Nnaji, Eni Njoku (Jnr.) and many others dead or alive, too numerous to mention. Philip Emeagwali is now regarded (rightly or wrongly) as the greatest scientist in the world, having created the INTERNET and is working on billion dollar projects in America, Britain and IBM to make computers obsolete, having, in 1989, used 65,000 processors to perform what was then the world's fastest computation of 3.1 million calculations per second, solved one of the 20 hardest mathematical questions in the world today and is also working on how to achieve immortality by downloading and uploading the human brain using computer. There is also his fellow computer expert now resident in Nigeria, Leo Stan Ekeh, who assembled the first made-in-Nigeria computer. Many Ibo scientists are engaged in very complex research areas in American Institutions, research laboratories, and major projects all over the world. Dr. Eni Njoku (Jnr.) heads the geological section of the NASA Jet Propulsion Centre in California, coordinating the recent NASA exploration in Mars etc. Professor Nnaji is a Director of several engineering based laboratories and centres and an icon of international acclaim in automation and robotics. The Ibos, like their counterpart African American Jews, have made important inventions and discoveries, created great works of art, and excelled in science, music, literature, medicine and sports. They have played important roles in Nigeria's history, making the country proud in many cases, as a paradox of hatred for the Ibos by their neighbours, violence against them, indignities, torture, plunder and organised murder of their children, their men and women. However, while some of the Ibos retained as far as possible their purely Jewish character, rejecting even the foods, idols and aggressiveness of the aborigines of Nigeria, a vast majority of them consciously or unconsciously abandoned monotheism, the Judaic religion of their forefathers in Israel, immersing themselves deeply into the osu-idolatry of the aborigines, practising (as predicted in 2 Chronicles 33:6) sorcery, divination and witchcraft, and consulting mediums and spiritists in the shrines of ajoku, agwu, kamalu, ibini-ukpabi – small gods of the aborigines, etc., doing much evil in the eyes of the Almighty God of their ancestral home, Israel, provoking HIM to anger.

It is a perennial topic for debate as to how far we can claim that the Ibos of Nigeria were not part of the said Earth in the scriptural narratives. The discovery of the Hebrew writing on the floor of the ancient palace of Eze Eri in Aguleri by a combined research team from Israel and Nigeria led by the author – a writing that existed hundreds of years before the arrival of the white man in Nigeria; the archaeological British finding at Agulu in about 1917, 500 feet below the soil, of a Star of King David in solid bronze, indicative of a people that might have migrated from the ancient city of King David; the vast overwhelming evidence of cultural similarities, including the fact contained in the first edition of this book (with over 300 examples in a Table) that over 85% of the names of all Ibo towns and villages are Hebrew; and the inexplicable inner desire of the average Ibo man to associate himself with Israel at all times and under all conditions even during periods of great insecurity and tension as in today's Israel, fail to make any sense to these critics of the Hebrew origin of the Ibos. Instead, they prefer to hear that the Ibos of Nigeria are all of the Bantu or Negro race of West Africa who arrived in this part of the world 6000 years ago after falling from the sky where, according to Afigbo (2001:24), "(Ibo) man ate and gambolled and held discourse with God".

Conversely, there is now quite a significant number of works on the Ibos from pre-colonial to colonial days, and even now, that are very sympathetic to my thesis on Ibo Hebraism. Their notes fill out some points, which make discussions on the Hebrew origin of the Ibos worthwhile. The notes amplify my claims, vindicate and underline them. Prominent among them are those of Olaudah Equiano, Dr. Basden of the Anglican Mission, Adams, Rabbi Capers Funnye, etc., all of which have been discussed in this book.

What the Ibos (Hebrews) of Nigeria have done for the emancipation and development of the black race in Africa is akin to what their counterpart World Hebrews have done for the emancipation of the human race. For instance, the writings of the ancient Jews in the Torah (which includes all the books of the Old Testament Bible) shaped virtually all the today's major religions of the world such as Christianity and Islam, and formed the bedrock of today's best-known modern civilisations. Similarly, the Ibos, the Jewish exiles in Nigeria, who were later sold into slavery in America and who now constitute over 25% of all the African Americans were indisputably the foremost, if not the main contributors to the emancipation and development of the black race in America, in Africa and the world at large. Evidence of this can be seen in the roles of the Ibos in

22

Nigeria, in West Africa since 1500 AD as outlined in this book. Actually, "Captain Adams figure of 370,000 Ibo slaves sold in the Delta markets over a period of twenty years (and this slave trade flourished for 400 years!) – equal to about over a quarter of the total exports from all the African ports" gives us an idea of the number of Ibos sold as slaves to European slave traders for the American markets or of the number of Ibos of Nigeria who are now African Americans (Adams, 1975:49). Actually, according to Rabbi Capers Funnye, the only black Jew sitting on the Chicago Board of Rabbis, "there are about a quarter-million Jews of African descent living in America today" (The Jerusalem Post, April 2, 1999, page B4).

In 1804 the predominantly Ibo slave population of Haiti proclaimed the first sovereign state of freed slaves after having destroyed the Napoleon's best army in Haiti. These Ibo ex-slaves in Haiti did not only free their country, they went to war against the Spanish on the present day Dominican Republic, won and freed the slaves. Back here in Africa, the activities of the Ibos in the liberation, freedom and emancipation of slaved Africans were prominent. Bishop Turner, a freed Ibo slave was responsible for Liberia being a settlement republic for freed slaves. In the same manner, Olaudah Equiano, another ex-Ibo slave, was not only the first black slave to buy his freedom with his own hard-earned money in England and spearheaded for slave freedom in Europe, but also founded Freetown, a town for freed slaves, which later became the capital of Sierra Leone. Indeed, Olaudah Equiano and E.W. Blyden, all ex-Ibo slaves are known in history as the creators of the idea of pan Africanism, which another Ibo leader, Nnamdi Azikiwe otherwise known as 'Zik of Africa' carried forward to its successful end, earning for Nigeria its political independence in 1960.

Before independence, the Ibos provided the bulk of the human resources for the country, producing two out of every three commissioned officers in the Nigerian army, controlling the railway stations, the post offices, government hospitals, canteens, government bureaucracy, the public works departments both in the north and in the south. Indeed, by

Independence when the British were handing over, the Ibos were far more than any other tribe in Nigeria, very ready to take over from them. And since independence, the Ibos have played for Nigeria outstanding leadership and developmental roles in virtually all aspects of human endeavours. Dr. Nnamdi Azikiwe succeeded the last British Governor-General and then went on to become the country's first ceremonial president.   Another Ibo, J.T.U. Aguiyi Ironsi became the first indigenous army general and Commander-in-Chief of the Nigerian Armed Forces, with Dr. Nwafor Orizu, also an Ibo, as the first President of the Senate. The Ibos, now popularly referred to as the Japanese of Africa, were everywhere and into everything at the highest level of operation.

In the colonial days, the achievements and resilience of the Ibo system so baffled the colonial masters that they instituted various inquiries to know who really the Ibos were, why they were so organized, so achievement-oriented and progressive and at the same time so difficult to handle or "hard to govern" by the British, and what to do to checkmate them in Nigeria. From such inquiries "the British linked the Ibos to the Jews expelled by the Portuguese" (Onwukwe, 1995:25) or simply concluded that "the Ibos are a branch of Hebrews" (Basden, 1938). And so, right from Colonial Nigeria, the Ibos became a people to watch, study and subdue by the British colonial and the other country's rulers. And they made no mistake about it.

Indeed, the Ibos' Jewish origin would not allow them to accept any condition of servitude for too long. Apart from being the first tribesmen to challenge the excesses of the British colonial masters when all the other tribes in Nigeria accepted them without any question, Osuagwu (2000) recalls in his article entitled, "Ibo and Fulani factors in West Africa", in the Daily Champion Newspaper, October 23, 2000, that "Governor George Wallace of Alabama accused the Ibo in 1968 of causing the American civil war, because of their activities towards freedom for slaved Africans in North America (northern parts of the U.S.A)". This American governor's assertion on the Ibos may have been informed by certain considerations of things involving the Ibos as a group during that time, of the Nigerian Biafra War in which the rebellious Ibos fought for their freedom and held the whole country, Nigeria, all its allies in Europe spearheaded by Britain and the combined army of the Organisation of African Unity (OAU), to ransom for 3 years (1966 – 1970) before they eventually gave up. This is reminiscent of the Biblical fact on the Rebellious nature of the ancient Jews, the ancestors of the Ibos, in Ezra 4:11-19:

.....order a search…in the records…you will discover that this (Jewish) city has always been rebellious. Its people have always been very hard to govern…it has indeed been found that from ancient times Jerusalem has revolted against royal authority and that it has been full of rebels and troublemakers.

Anybody who knows the most typical and most representative Ibo town of Aba noted for rebellions and revolts from early times will very much agree that the picture of the ancient difficult-to-govern Jewish town described in the quotation above fits perfectly well into the above named town often said to be "the heart of Ibo land" but "full of rebels and troublemakers" and "hard to govern". For instance, the historic 1929 Aba Women Riot against the British colonial authority over disagreement in the payment of tax by Nigerian women to the British colonial government took place in the southern Ibo land city of Aba. Besides, various anti-government revolts, even during the infamous military regimes when popular revolts were most dangerous, took place in Aba. Though to a certain limit, the same can be said of some other Ibo towns like Onitsha in northern Ibo Land. The old Aba and parts of old Onitsha provinces recorded the first and virtually all the bloody revolts against the British colonial authority in Nigeria when no Nigerian tribe could dream of daring the British colonial authority.

Resilient as their counterpart world Hebrews or "regular" Jews, even in the face of their captors or enemies, the Ibos in the slave trade era would rather resort to mass suicide than be taken into slavery, and those who were eventually forced into it did all they could to regain their freedom either through coercion or negotiation, and went forth to fight for the freedom of other slaves. In her article entitled "Keeping Watch at the Ibo landing" in the Atlanta Journal and Constitution Magazine of October 30, 1799, Michelle Green notes that "The rebellious Ibo tribesmen ...re-enact a mass suicide that took place more than 150 years ago... these men had been sold into slavery in their native Nigeria...they were jammed into the hull of a slave ship and survived a torturous ocean crossing only to disembark at the night shrouded tidal creed and discovered that they would spend the rest of their lives toiling in the fields of a coastal cotton plantation. But the Ibo refused to submit to their captors. When they were led ashore, they turned, en masse, and linked by cumbersome iron chains, marched solemnly, slowly, into the deep water and drowned. And as they disappeared into the marsh, the men chanted: 'The water brought us... the water will take us away. The relevance of this book goes beyond stating the obvious fact that the Ibos are Jews in exile to that of being an instrument or vessel of honor in the holy hand of the Almighty God of Israel. By placing the Ibos alongside other lost tribes of Israel in history, serious effort is being made here at the Almighty's work, at helping to realize His word or promise of gathering back the scattered people of

Israel from the four corners of the earth, and of restoring their fortunes (see Deut. 30:3-5; Jeremiah 32:26-42).

Linguistic Groups

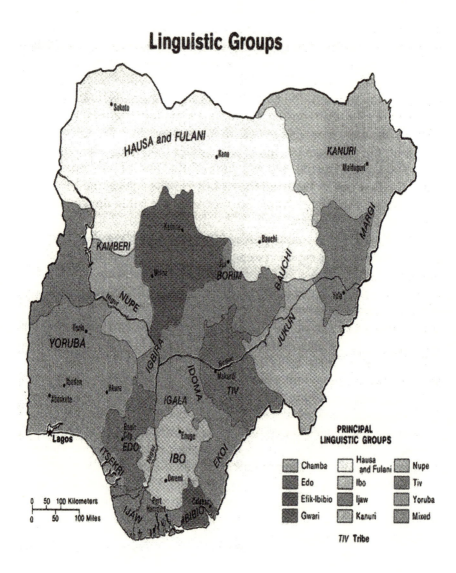

CHAPTER FOUR

THE IBOS (IGBOS?) OF NIGERIA

Several African tribes still consider themselves descended from Hebrew stock, including the Ibo of Nigeria, Tutsis of East Africa and the Bamilikis of Cameroon.

Black Jews in America trace their heritage back to those Jews who fled from Jerusalem into Africa after the destruction of the First Temple 2500 years ago... they intermarried with the local tribes as did Jews in most parts of the world, taking on new physical features (as in the case of the Ibo of Nigeria). Jews around the world tend to look like the communities in which they are found. Jews in China look Chinese, Jews in Poland look Eastern European, Jews in Ethiopia look Ethiopian. ("Black and Jewish in America," in The Jerusalem Post, April 2, 1999, page B4).

Concerning the origin of the Ibos, history books and contemporary writings on the subject confirm that the Ibos of Nigeria originated from Israel in the Middle East, that they were part and parcel of the "fall out" of the scattered Hebrews from their native land, Israel, around 597 BC and 70 AD respectively. The name 'Hebrew' is simply the English version of the Jewish word, 'Ibrit' pronounced as Ivrit, sometimes mispronounced as Ivite or Ifite or Ihite by the Ibos. In Hebrew, 'b' is pronounced as 'v'. For instance, Tel Aviv is written as Tel Abib in ancient Hebrew (see Ezekiel 3:15), but pronounced and now also written as Tel Aviv. Interestingly, 'b' is also pronounced as 'v' in some parts of Ibo land - for example, ibu (load) or ivu (load); ebule (ram) or evule (ram); abu (song) or avu (song). Ibrit means the one passed over, a wonderer - a name usually associated with Abraham, the father of Isaac and grandfather of Jacob whose name was later changed to Israel after his (Jacob's) encounter with the angel of the Almighty. Actually, the exiled Hebrews (Heebos, Eboes or Ibos as the British called them) into Nigeria originally referred to themselves as Ifite (corruption of Ivrit) in the Anambra Ibo areas. It is called Ivite in Agulueri

which is the first settlement area of the Ibo in Northern Ibo land or Ibo nation or Ifite in the other Anambra Ibo towns, or Ihite (corrupted as Ihie in some cases) in the Abia/Imo Ibo areas. In some parts of Iboland, 'f' is pronounced as 'h'. Examples include: Oraifite (Orifite), Ifiteukpo, Ifite, Ezinifite, Ihitenansa or Ifitenansa, etc., all of which are names of towns in Anambra State, or Ihite, Ezinihite, Ihite Uboma, Ihie, Ihieagwa Owerri. Ihiechiowa (Ihechiowa), Ihiemvosi Ihieoma (Iheoma), Ihie Ngwaukwu, Ngwa Ihiekwe (Iyekwe), etc. are names of towns in Abia/Imo Ibo areas. Without much corruption as in the other cases, we have Ivite Agulueri, that is, Ivrit Agulueri. In fact, even in places where it is written as Ifite, the old ones there would quickly remind you that the correct pronunciation is 'Ivite'.

Literally, Oraifite (Ora Ifite), a town in Anambra State, means community of Ifite or Ibrit or Hebrew as per the English version of the Jewish word, Ibrit. Ora or Oha is an Allokoo word for community. Hebrew equivalent of ora or oha is "am" now pronounced as "ama" by the exiled Nigerian Hebrew (Ibos). Today the Ibo use the two Allokoo and Hebrew words 'ora' or 'oha' and 'am' or 'ama' interchangeably. Hence names such as: Oraifite (Allokoo+Hebrew), or Amaigbo (Hebrew+Allokoo) each of which means community of Ibrit or Hebrew. Other examples of Ibrit - (Ivrit/Ibrit - Ifite or Ihite) related names in Ibo land abound, prominent among which are Ihieagwa Owerri, Ihiechiowa (Ihechiowa), Ihiemvosi, Ihieoma (Iheoma), Ihie Ngwaukwu, Ngwa Ihiekwe, and so on.

There is the other explanation for the word, Hebrew, in the Ibo context. The name "Eber" which is found in the "generation of Shem" (Genesis 11:15) is also used by the Ibos as name or part of the name of a town. Examples: Eber, Ebenebe, Eberiomuma, Ukebe, etc. Eber is an eponym from Ibrit (called Hebrew in English), like Romulus from Rome. The name Hebrew is found for the first time in the English version of the Bible in Genesis 14:13, where Abram was referred to as 'the Hebrew'. In some ancient books, 'Abram the Hebrew' is written as 'Abram the Crosser'. Hebrew is usually explained as those who crossed from the far side of the Euphrates, and applied by the other tribes to the Schematic family that crossed the Great River and settled in Canaan. The crossing of the Euphrates was epoch-making event, like Caesar's crossing of the Rubicon or Columbus' crossing of the Atlantic. As had been said earlier, Eber as a name in its undiluted form is still being borne by some Nigerian Hebrews (Ibos), as a name of person or place. Originally, the ancient Ibos, particularly those around Itam or Item ("Etam") areas of Ibo nation referred to themselves as Eber but more often as Ibrit (Ivrit or Ifite or Ihite). And in fact, in all essentials, the name Eber, Ifite or Ihite kept the early Ibos of Nigeria who bore them forever mindful of their Jewish origin. That name often humbled them and filled them with pride and gratitude in the days long before their humiliating encounter with the British Colonial masters. Actually, the forefathers of Oraifite, Ifiteukpo, Ezinifite, Ezinihite, Ihite Uboma, and their sister Hebrew towns bearing other names with or without Ifite or Ihite (Ihie) attached to them knew better what pride and gratitude that were associated with the appellation of the said names for the Nigerian Hebrews or Ibos. With equal pride and gratitude, the Hebrew (Ibo) people of Item ("Etam") from Abia State, Nigeria, often say 'Osari r'Eber', meaning 'it has always been like that right from our forefather's glorious times at Eber.' Indeed, that pride still lingers even in the memory and sub-consciousness of the descendants of the ancient Ibos everywhere they now find themselves in Nigeria.

Before now some writers on the origin of Ibos have come out with speculations only few of which can be supported either from evidence from empirical studies or from the Holy Scriptures, the Torah or the Bible, the acclaimed true history of the Jews regarding names of Ibo towns and people. For example, some claim that Aro is from the Igbo word, 'Aru', a forsaken person or thing. That 'Ndi Aro' means 'Ndi Aru' - a name for Igbo rejects. Arodi, or Aro for short is the name, of the junior brother of Eri. Aro is not Aru; it is the short form of Arodi, the sixth son of Gad and junior brother of Eri (see Genesis 46:16 - "The sons of Gad: Zephon, Haggai, Shuni, Ezbon, Eri, Arodi and Areli." From time immemorial, the Aros (now in Abia State) began to refer to themselves as Aro-Okeigbo meaning literally, 'Aro, the prominent son of great Igbo. Prominent indeed they are, for in them are represented in good measures most of the prominent and enviable attributes of the Hebrews: dynamism, tactfulness, cunning, fearlessness, business acumen, intelligence, etc. Even in their backslidden state of idol worshipping, having other god or gods or person called god, etc. before God, the Almighty Creator of the Universe, the Nigerian Hebrew (Ibo) exiles regarded and used Aro-Chukwu as their Jerusalem, the worship centre of the Jews in Israel. The Ibos did all that were done by the Jews in Jerusalem in Aro-Chukwu. During the Ibo-type of the Jewish Festival of First Fruit, the New Yam Festival called Ikeji in Aro-Chukwu Ibo dialect, going to Aro-Chukwu was like going to Jerusalem, the Holy Land for the ancient Jews or to Mecca, the Holy Land for the Arabs. At this time, once a year, food, money and merchandise flowed into Aro-Chukwu from all parts of Ibo land and from all the other twenty or more Aro colonies in Ibo land and beyond. To the shrine or deity of 'Tshuku' in Aro, and later 'Ibini-ukpabi' or 'long juju' and 'Uno-Nta', pilgrimages were made from all parts of Ibo Land. In the shrine of Uno-Nta, all ceremonies pertaining to Ibini-ukpabi - birth and death rites, marriage blessing, etc. - were conducted. The Ibini-ukpabi acted as the final Court of Appeal in the Ibo nation. Through a very formidable network of propaganda everybody was made to believe that Ibini-ukpabi or its priest could not tell lies; it was omni-potent and omni-science, and through it, the Aro man was respected and feared throughout the whole breadth and length of Ibo land and beyond. In the words of Onwukwe (1995:5). " Ibini-ukpabi was a stabilizing force which could by pronouncement, stop a war, condemn a criminal, banish a person into slavery and take life where appropriate." Just as it was in the ancient Israel that "no man should appear before the LORD empty-handed: each...must bring a gift" (Deuteronomy 16:16-17), no one was expected to go to Ibini-ukpabi or appear before the Tshuku or Chukwu in Aro-Chukwu empty-handed.

 The Aros all believe in an Almighty Being, omnipresent and omnipotent whom they call Tshuku, whom they constantly worship, and whom they believe to communicate with them through his sacred shrine at A'ro Baikie, "The Aro-Chukwu Oracle", in Hodgkin, T., Nigerian Perspectives, page 337). Arodi or Aro for short became permanently known as Aro-Chukwu because of the presence of the famous deity of Ibini-ukpabi' or "the long juju" (as the British nicknamed it) also called 'Tshuku' or 'Chukwu' in that area (see Alaezi, 1999).

When the Christians arrived in Ibo Land, the Kwa name Tshuku (or Chukwu) used originally for a shrine or oracle or deity was translated as God Almighty. Thus God the Creator was called 'Chukwu Okike' and in the same vein God of Abraham became 'Chukwu Abiama', etc. The Almighty God of Abram or 'Abiama' delegates power to rule to any one He chooses amongst His exiled Ifite or Ivite or Jews in Nigeria, and so any ruler over them is seen as a direct representative of God, a God's Regent. Hence the Ibo title, of 'Igwe' (of Heaven or the one sent from Heaven), for a titled chief or ruler in many parts of Iboland.

On leaving Uburu, the first port of call of the exiled Hebrews in Eastern Nigeria, the Arodis or Aros journeyed far and wide. They established their residence and trade posts in areas east and west of the Niger, in Yorubaland and Igalaland, and so on. In Igalaland, history has it that they (the Aros) found the other Hebrew exiles from the lineage of Eri who had earlier settled there on their way back to Onitsha from Benin.

It is necessary to mention here just in passing that 'Igbo' as a name is not the same as 'Ibo'. Igbo as a collective name for some Nigerian Hebrews had long existed before the advent of the white man in the colonial Nigeria who referred to all the identified exiled Ifite, Ihite or Jews in Nigeria as Hebrews, corrupted as Heebos, later as Eboes and finally as Ibos. Igbo, popularly referred to by the Arodis or Aros of southern Ibo nation as Okeigbo or Great Igbo was one of the descendants of Eri, the founder of Agulueri now in Anambra State of Nigeria. Igboukwu, for example, is an Ibo town named after this very Igbo of a person whose influence and name overshadowed those of his other relations in the whole of Eri kingdom and beyond because of his great exploits in virtually all human endeavors, his sheer determination to deal with all obstacles of life even in the face of great danger, his great wealth, his overbearing nature which sometimes resulted to exhibition of certain detestable traits of character. Today, we have Ama Igbo (Amaigbo) in today's Imo State of Nigeria, Obi Igbo (Obigbo now corrupted as Oyigbo for some political reasons) in Rivers State, Igbo Etiti (Igboetiti), Anambra State, Ezeigbo (name of person in all Iboland), Igbokwe (name of person in Iboland), Azigbo (or son of Igbo) in Nnewi, etc. Some Ibos still give their son the name, Igbo, which makes that name more likely a name of a person than that of a group of people or a nation. We do not see individuals, answering Yoruba or Hausa or Ibibio as a name.

Agulueri was the oldest of the Eri descendants in Nigeria. Eri himself was the fifth son of Gad, and Gad the seventh son of Jacob or Israel (see Genesis 46: 15-8. Numbers 26:16-18, Exodus 1: 1-5). Nri was the most prominent but the last born of Agulueri, just like Enugu-Agu was the last born of Nri, but most prominent among all his brothers. For some interesting historical accidents, the "Ofor Eri" had been held interchangeably between Agulueri, the first born, Nri or Enugu-Agu, each of who was ironically the last-born. What concerns us here, however, is the evidence of lineage, not heritage. In all essentials, whoever holds the Ofor Eri or the staff of office or symbol of authority of Eri also takes the following title: THE PARAMOUNT RULER OF IGBOLAND AND THE HEAD OF ERI KINGDOM...HOLDER OF OFOR ERI ... This is simply because Eri's presence is just overwhelming and most consistent in all Iboland. Indeed, in virtually all Iboland, where the name Eri is not used to coin the name of a place, it is used as a direct name or additional name to coin the name of person. Examples: Erimma (name of a person in virtually all Iboland) or Mbieri (name of a town in Imo State). Arodi (Aro, for short or Aro-Chukwu), as the descendant of the sixth son of Gad was bound to accept the rulership of Eri, the descendant of the fifth son, and therefore the senior brother. Other exiled Hebrew descendants (e.g. Judah and Zebulun) are not as many and have been swallowed up by the Eris. Besides, Judah, the third son of Jacob, who ought to have been considered head before Gad, the seventh son, who has his descendants cut across Ibibio, Iboland, Rivers, Benue, and so has no prominence or logical claim to rulership in Iboland, where comparatively only a small number of his descendants live as minority.

In his own version, Ofili (2002:139-140) holds:

Eri had followed his father Gad... to Egypt from Canaan when famine ravaged the land. After the death of his grandfather, father and uncle, Joseph, who was one of the rulers of Egypt... a new king who did not know Joseph assumed power in Egypt and oppressed the Jews. Consequently, Eri fled from Egypt and travelled southwards to Sudan. He raised a family with many children. The Israelites were too concerned with the burden of hard labor placed on them daily by the new Pharaoh in Egypt to bother themselves about one of them that had eloped. Moreover, the original family of Israel was polarized because of its polygamous nature. Gad's only brother from the same mother was Asher and so he did not have much influence. To worsen matters, he was the son of a slave woman named Zilpah, the maidservant of Jacob's head wife, Leah. The polarisation in the family accounts for the hatred of Joseph and Benjamin by their other brothers and the plot to sell one into slavery and kill the other. In ancient Jewish attitude, offspring of slave women are hardly accorded honor. Eri's descendants finally settled in the Niger area of present day Iboland and scattered at various locations in the area to establish a new nation. As the last Jew, at a time best known to and worked out by Yahweh, they (the Ibos) will not only be accepted but also be eagerly sought after by the other Jews.

Some of the Nigerian Hebrew exiles in Eri as in Aro, Itam or Item ("Etam"), etc. had and exhibited great mystical powers and were greatly patronised by both Jewish and non-Jewish nationals in ancient Nigeria. Indeed, there is the other popular legend that one of the descendants of Eri who first settled at Onitsha, at the bank of River Niger, near the domain of his relatives from the descendants of Zebulun (Ozubulu in Anambra State) had to travel across the Niger to the ancient Benin City or kingdom to prepare war medicine, (talisman or charm) for a prospective contender to the stool of Oba of Benin. The man who had the charm prepared by the Eri medicine man eventually won the battle and so became the Oba of Benin.

As a compensation for a work well done, the Eri medicine man was asked to stay back in Benin and given part of the ancient Benin kingdom to inhabit with his family and relatives and to control. In fact, the black man who was seen by the first Portuguese traders in the palace of Oba of Benin, teaching the children of the Oba how to read and write. a discovery that beat the imagination of the Portuguese and later historians alike may very well have been one of the descendants of Eri from the Onitsha group. But for some historical accidents, the stay of the Eri descendants in Benin kingdom was revoked after the death of the Oba who knew Eri or who benefited from his presence in Benin. So they were forced out of Benin back to Onitsha after a fierce battle. A section of the defeated Eri descendants went back to Onitsha through the Igalaland across the more shallow part of River Niger towards the North whilst the other section passed through the shorter route that now cuts across Agbor and Asaba, leaving behind on their different routes back to Onitsha remnants or descendants of Ibos in Igala near Nsukka (in Enugu State, and in Delta areas, Ika Ibos). Other Eri descendants on leaving Benin passed through the creeks of River Niger and finally settled in some parts of riverine Delta, Bayelsa/Rivers and from there some of them started again a journey that took them back to where their fathers had been before going to settle in Benin or rather in some Ibo hinterland regions where other exiled Jews in Nigeria had earlier settled. Hence we have the claim of the Ahoda (corruption of Yahoda or Judah), Bonny ("Bani"), some others in the Brassland, and many in the Delta and Rivers and Bayelsa including some people in the hinterland Ibo nation besides Onitsha people (e.g.: people of Ohafia in Abia State etc.) that they originated from Benin, not knowing their history beyond the Benin settlement. In all essentials, the focal point is Eri and his descendants, with Agulueri as a prominent and most historic Nigerian homeland of the exiled Jews into the country. With this in mind, I decided to carry out a more thorough research on the Jewish origin of the Ibos with emphasis on Agulueri for the purpose of writing this book.

CHAPTER FIVE

RESEARCH EVIDENCE ON THE ORIGIN OF THE IBOS – A REPORT

Judging by the information I received during my three research visits to Agulueri, I am in a position to categorically state that Agulueri is the pivotal town and traditional head of the Ibos of Nigeria. I visited the town three times in the year 2001. The town was just beginning to experience peace again after the devastating civil war with the sister town Umuleri (Umu-ulu Eri, or children of the second son of Eri - Ulu in Igbo means second child). Aguleri itself literally means the name sake of Eri, certainly a befitting name for a first son, as the ancient Jewish fathers often called their son after their names ('Agulu' in Igbo language means namesake). Let us recall to mind that the ancient Hebrews who were present at the occasion of the circumcision and christening of John the Baptist, on the eighth day of his birth, expressed great surprise that young John was not named after his father Zechariah (Luke 1:59). As for the Ibos, they also circumcise and christen their male child on the eight day of birth and often name him after the father (in which case the child is called Ogbonnaya or Ogbonna or Agulu (m), which in English means namesake). I could notice some cautious movements of people from the various Aguleri compounds as we drove pass with our police escorts. The just ended war between Agulueri and Umuleri had instilled fear into the minds of all first time visitors to the place; hence the need for police escort even for a research work such as this. Two Israeli teams had visited Aguleri and made some discoveries and positive statements regarding the Jewish origin of the people. One of the teams had actually established a basic Hebrew language class in the area before the devil struck with discord and war to halt the Almighty's plan for the furtherance of the in gathering of the Jews in this "distant part of the land under the heavens". Luckily for the Ibo as a whole, the people of Aguleri and Umuleri have decided to shame the devil and give peace a chance. My first visit to Aguleri brought me face to face with the Eze Eri, Ezedigbo, the paramount Ruler of the Igboland and the Head of Eri kingdom, and the members of Eze in Council. This visit was more of familiarization and it was very smooth from the beginning to the end. The second visit in the month of November 2001 during which a major discovery was made regarding the Hebrew writing on the floor just in front of the ancient stool of Eze Eri in the ancient traditional palace of Eri was rough, with our private vehicle, which was provided by His Royal Highness, Eze Ufere, the Traditional Ruler of Amankalu Alayi, Abia State, as one of his contributions to the on-going research, having an engine knock about two kilometres away from Agulueri town. This incident nearly marred the research visit. Again, I regarded this as the Satan's own plan to stop the discovery of the Ibos of Nigeria as a branch of the Hebrews. I became even more determined to continue. We were four in number - two research colleagues from Tel Aviv Israel, one video camera man and I. One was left behind to arrange for the recovery and safekeeping of our damaged vehicle at Otuocha Agulueri police station while three of us continued to Ivite (or Ivrit/Ibrit) Agulueri where the palace was situated.

The Eze Eri had traveled to Lagos, but Chief Anner Charles Ebogha was in the Palace to receive us, direct and answer all our questions, which he did very satisfactorily. We had chats with the other palace chiefs of Eze Eri, including a 115 year-old man. There was a lot to learn from this centurion who looked stronger and younger than a seventy-year old man. Inside the traditional palace of Eze Eri, which looked more like a shrine than a palace, we could see the wall adorned with paintings and strokes of white chalk in shaky handwriting. On the floor directly opposite the ancient stool made of mud we noticed strokes of ancient writing traced into permanence on the floor with white cowries in use in Nigeria before the coming of the white man. Elvis, my research colleague from Tel Aviv, Israel, quickly identified the writing to be Hebrew, and went on to give meanings to then, pointing out how one of them like an awkwardly written 7 of Roman figure could be turned this way and the other way to mean one thing or the other in Hebrew language. *"One thing is very clear now," he concluded, "this is Hebrew writing. It is a major discovery. The ancient Eri people who wrote this before the coming of the white man must have come from no other place other than Israel". The 115-year-old man told us that he knew when the first white man came to Ivite

(* The picture of the discovered Hebrew writing on the floor of the Palace of the Eze Eri can be seen on the last page of this chapter.)

Agulueri and that the Hebrew writing we saw on the floor had existed long before he was born and before his own father and grandfather were born too. He went on to tell us how special they had regarded themselves and had many laws of purity and decency to observe, sacrifice and purification rites, birth and death rites, and so on, to perform before the white man came and tore apart many of the customary things they held in esteem. He said that his father told him that his people came to Agulueri as strangers from a very far desert-like place.

It is forbidden for anyone to step onto the floor of the palace of Eze Eri with any shoes or footwear. We obeyed.

Conspicuously displayed on one side of the wall is a group picture of some members of the Eze in Council with a white man seated just beside the Eze Eri. I was later informed that the white man is called Mr. Yitzhad David Israel, the leader of the Jewish team that visited Agulueri in November 1997, or better, the International Director of King Solomon Shepherdic Federation who was said to have made the discovery of the Jewish ONYX STONE [Exodus 39: 6-7] of which I wrote about in the first edition of this book The said research team leader also highlighted the significance of Obugad, pointing out that the father of Eri is called Gad, the same name as in the Holy Scriptures of Israel (see Genesis 46:16). 'Obu' in Igbo language means Temple; so Obugad is simply the Temple of Gad. That Eri, the exiled in Nigeria built a Temple and named it after the founder of his tribe, Gad, is in conformity with Jewish custom. The 1997 Israeli team to Agulueri also noted the significance of the Agulueri stream of faith vis-à-vis the ancient River Jordan (of faith) in ancient Israel, and identified certain other Jewish artefacts. One of the Israelis in the 1997 team was said to have been moved to tears by what he saw, maybe by the way the Nigerian (Hebrews) Ibos, the Jewish exiles (the Ivrite, Ivite) in Agulueri had degenerated into such sorry state of existence.

I could hardly fix my eyes on one place in the traditional palace, as there were just too many things of interest to contemplate upon. The throne of the Eze (King) was really ancient. It was made of mud all through with side arm's length pillars to rest the two arms. This arrested my attention during my first visit to the palace. As the Eze Eri, the 31st, a fair-complexioned man with pointed nose, thin lips and near brown eyes, reminiscent of a typical Jew of the Middle East, arrived to sit on the ancient throne of his ancestors, two young virgins about 11 to 12 years old followed him, one carrying a big lump of white chalk on a tray and the other carrying a wooden saucer containing some kola nuts.

Two girls stood in front of the Eze, almost motionless, occasionally casting some shy glances at us, as long as our conversation with the traditional ruler lasted. At the beginning of our stay in the palace, the two girls were asked by the Eze either to serve us with the white chalk or the kola nuts. At the appropriate time both the while chalk and the kola nuts were given to the oldest man in the council of Ndieze who later passed them on to us. After the kolanuts had been taken round in the usual traditional manner of the Ibos in this part of Ibo nation, they finally got back to the traditional ruler for his blessing, and thereafter the nuts were broken into sizes for our consumption.

One remarkable thing was that all the members of the Eze Eri in Council greeted us in Hebrew with a shout of 'Shalom', and with a handshake that involved clapping of the upward extended right palm on the other person's palm three times, returning the hand and beating it gently on one's chest. With the big lump of white chalk that was actually presented to us before the kola nuts each of us in the palace drew four straight lines on the floor, following the example of the first palace chief who handled the chalk, and with utterances in different words evoked the holy spirit of God of the Universe for one good thing or the other in favor of everybody present, including the land of the Ibos as a whole, the town of Agulueri, the nation, Nigeria. Whereas some drew four lines, some added one or two other straight lines horizontally, while others added a curve to their vertical straight lines. One of the palace chiefs sitting next to me drew his own vertical lines and added one horizontal line and ended up making his own look almost like the star of King David that I had earlier seen on the official regalia of the Eze Eri. The whole things and structures in the palace appeared rugged and original in their first make. To my sense the whole place and atmosphere were very much charged with the aura of the ancients - ancient aroma and attire worn by the 115-year-old member of the Eze's cabinet who initially collected the kola nuts and white chalk meant for us from the two virgins in attendance; ancient stool of the King of Eri; pre-colonial ancient writing most interestingly in Hebrew language bearing a testimony of the place of origin of the people; ancient container of relics, the details of which I dared not ask for fear of not being dragged into discussions on the idolatrous practices of the people, and so on.

After the discussion with Eze Eri that lasted for about thirty minutes, he (the Eze) walked out in great majesty, behind the two virgins now followed by a young lad of about fifteen to sixteen years who later joined the girls in attendance, all dressed in white. As the Eze Eri, the paramount traditional ruler of the Ibos of Nigeria walked out, we all stood up as a mark of respect. Then we also took our exit.

As in the first visit, facilitated by Chief Rochas Okorocha, Owelle Ndigbo, who himself was also physically present for the occasion, the spokesman of the Cabinet of Eze Eri was Chief Ebogha, the chairman of the cabinet.

He led us to see the Obugad about 100 yards or a little less from the traditional palace. The Chief also took us to the burial place of the man Eri, the founder of Agulueri, who I was told was so handsome with very light skin, beautiful brown eyes and pointed nose that his name became a symbol of beauty, strength the respect in Iboland. This is exemplified in such Ibo names as Erinma (a child of beauty and great prospects) borne by some people in Ibo Land, especially females in southern Ibo Land.

Where is the extent of this Eri kingdom in Iboland? Are all the Ibos of Eri stock? I dared not ask this question aloud now for I did not want to interrupt the flow of the exciting stories of the pilot of our discoveries, the eloquent chairman of the cabinet of Eze Eri.

One of the cabinet chiefs with us seemed to have read my mind, and at an opportune moment, he told me that Eri kingdom stretched all through some parts of Abia, Imo and Ebonyi and all of Anambra and Enugu States down to the present Delta State.

I think that the Eri in question may not have been the same Eri, the direct son of Gad in Genesis 46:16, but his direct descendant who had borne the name as a name from his kindred, or as a family name as it is normal and common for the Jews over the ages to bear the same kindred or family names. Another school of thought holds that this Eri is the same Eri talked about in the book of Genesis, and that the first Hebrews in exile in Nigeria arrived the country some 3000 to 2500 years ago (see Ofili, 2002).

The track road in the bush leading to the burial place of Eri, the founder of Agulueri or rather Agulueri (namesake or first son of Eri) himself was almost covered by tall shrubs at both sides. It was unkempt and not motor able and so we had to make the whole journey of about five kilometers to and fro by foot. It was really exciting but exhausting.

All the people in the Temple of Eze Eri, including the chairman of the Town Union of Ora-Eri, a neighboring Eri town outside Agulueri, Chief R. O. Edozie, but excluding the Eze Eri himself and the oldest 115-year old man in the council, joined us in the long trek across the bush. I could see that we were in for an exciting journey. After trekking for about the first one and half kilometers inside the bush, the pilot,

Chief Ebogha, stopped and waited for every other person to get close to him for some information. "Over there", he said, pointing to two big trees, called ogulisi or ogirisi in Igbo language, apparently planted at a close distance to each other, "is the burial place of our great grand father Eri, the founder of Agulueri."

"Eri," he continued, "had some brothers and relations who arrived Nigeria with him, prominent among whom were: Arodi, Oreli and Igala. As he said this I quickly remembered the verse in the Holy Scriptures of Israel which recounted the names of the children of Jacob that later went into exile to Egypt with their father Jacob or Israel: The sons of Gad: Zephon, Haggi, Shuni, Ezbon, Eri, Arodi, and Areli (Genesis 46:16). "From the lineage of Eri, his sons and brothers came Edozie or Edozienu, Ogbe, Oba, Atta ("Attai"), Igbo, Ishi, Nri, Agu ("Agur"), etc, with settlements all located mostly in the present Anambra State but spread across all Iboland. For instance, Oba in Anambra State; Amoba in Akhaolo Okoko Item, Abia State; Atta - Aguata, Uratta Umuatta, etc, all across Iboland; Ishi Nnewi, Amaichi (Amichi), Ishi Agu (Ishiagu), Isiokpo, etc. They sometimes conquered, dominated ruled and established kingdoms in their names. Agulueri or namesake of Eri was the first son of Eri. Of all the relations of Agulueri, Igbo was the most stubborn and adventurous. He was so heady, rootless, intelligent, daring, and domineering that he overshadowed all his relatives to the extent of his name being used to refer to his descendants as well as the descendants of his brothers as a group by their non-Jewish neighbors in the then Nigeria."

Those Ibos who remembered the history of Igbo refused to answer the name, Igbo. Hence the situation in Onitsha area and some parts of Rivers, Delta and Bayelsa States where the people of Ibo descent derogatorily refer to the other Ibos as Igbo and refer to themselves either as Onitsha, Ubani, Ndoki, Ikwere, and so on, as a way of dissociating themselves from the bad records of Igbo. Igbo travelled far and wide and his descents spread widest, even to Yorubaland via Benin. His family name Igbo, eventually took over the names of his brothers' family names. And today, even among all Ibos, there is a big confusion between the two names: Ibo and Igbo, which must once again be made clear. As has been pointed out earlier, whereas Igbo is the name of the stubborn, aggressive and adventurous cousin of Agulueri who was sacked from the kingdom of Eri because of his bad behavior and who ironically later became more successful than all his brothers, Ibo on the other hand is the corruption of the English word Hebrew (corrupted as Heebo, Eboe and Ibo) the equivalent of the Jewish word Ibrit or rather the English version of Ibrit, Jewish name for the Israelites.

"Edozie and Ogbe migrated across the Niger via Onitsha to the present Edo State. Edo is the short form of Edozie or Edozienu just as Aro is the short form of Arodi. Ogbe in Edo State is the relation of Edo. Here in Agulueri we have a town called Umuogbe." As the narrator said this, I remembered that even in Item, another Jewish town in Abia State (called Itam in Akwa Ibom State, and "Etam" in Israel), we also have a town called Umuogbe. The popular praise-name for Item in Abia State is 'Item Ogidi'. Ogidi (now in Anambra State) is a popular town in the Eri region of Iboland. Note that one of the foremost generals of Israeli army is called General Etam, traceable to the same tribe of Judah as the Itemites or Itamites of Ibo nation of Nigeria..

"Igala", he continued, "is another brother of Eri. Igala and Edo people all migrated from this Agulueri to their present places of abode in today's Nigeria. In fact, uptil now, Igala people still come to Agulueri to pay homage to Eze Eri and perform certain traditional rites during the new yam festival. But Edo people are now so far away that they hardly even remember that they are a part of us, especially now that they have so many co-inhabitants from Yoruba and other smaller tribes across the Niger that lay claim to Edo as their ancestral home. I know that there are Yoruba and even some Hausa extractions in Igala too now placing doubts in the Hebrew (Ibo) or Eri origin of Igala. Igala is our people's name. Arodi or Aro now answer Aro-Chukwu".

"You see", continued Chief Ebogha, "we are very many all over Nigeria and only good research efforts such as the one you are now making can help to identify their exact places of abode in today's Nigeria. The bones of the great Eri, the founding father of the famous Eri kingdom and/or the big brother of all the Ibos in and outside Iboland are lying here. We know that for those Ibos now resident outside Ibo land whose language and culture have completely changed and remained very different, and even for some Ibos in Ibo Land, the story of Eri and/or the Jewish origin of the Ibos is a fairy tale. But very soon, I believe, they will come to understand. I believe God; I believe He will gather back all the Jews in His own time..." The pilot suddenly stopped talking and looked at me as if he now wanted my comment.

"How do you know that, that place is the burial place of Eri, since the death occurred many centuries ago", I asked, expecting to throw him into confusion with the question.

"You see, in this part of the country", came the pilot's subdued voice, "we usually plant ogulisi tree at the head side of a buried body. Once planted, the tree very hardly dies. Those two trees are as old as Agulueri itself and our fathers had always told us that this is the place of burial of their great forefather, who came to the place from Egypt. Soon after his burial those trees were planted, first to identify the burial place so nobody can mistakenly go to tamper with it, and secondly to show the position of the

40

head of the dead body. And since then till now nobody in Agulueri had ever dared to tamper with that portion of the land. We clear the place from time to time but nothing is ever planted very close to the burial place.

"That is exactly the tree that the oldest man in the palace talked to us about. According to the old man if you can remember, his grandfather informed him that his own grandfather who was extremely very old at the time narrated to people how the tree planted on the grave of his great grandfather, Eri, the founder of Agulueri, was cut down when it became overgrown and weak. In its very place another tree of its kind was planted in memorial of the great Eri. That tree does not just grow anyhow. Wherever you see it in Agulueri, it shows that somebody whose memory the people cherish and whose bones should not be tampered with had been buried there."

In the distance ahead of us less than one kilometer away, we could see the valley of a running stream. As we began to head towards it, the sky above us became very thick and dark with the threat of a heavy rain.

Soon big isolated drops of rain began to fall. That cut short our journey. However, the pilot, Chief Ebogha, told us that the aborted visit to the stream would have made a world of difference to our adventure. The water of the stream, he explained, provides cure for sick people from far and near. He proudly told us that the visiting Jew called Yitzhaq David Israel saw the stream and was quick to remark that it was a replica of River Jordan in ancient Israel, that the people of Agulueri looked upon it as the ancient Israelites regarded River Jordan, and that it was part of the Jewish mentality that the exiled Jews into Nigeria brought with them from Israel. "The best way to appreciate this remarkable water is to get to the place," the pilot continued. "Maybe we'll go there first when you come back here next time, concluded the pilot, with disappointment in his voice as we turned to walk or rather rush back to where our vehicles were packed to avoid being beaten by the impending heavy rain. The rainy season had not actually set in here in Agulueri. We did not anticipate any rain and so we had nothing to protect ourselves from the rain.

Back to the place where we took off, I could not but express my excitement to some of the people around and internally resolve to set aside a prominent place in this book to talk about this research visit to Agulueri with a view to bringing the small Ibo town into the limelight and perhaps turn Agulueri into an international tourist centre for the appreciation of Ibo Jewish origin, culture and civilization. This may have a special significance for all those who are currently involved in a research into the Jewish origin of the Ibos. Before now, I have read much about the views on the Jewish origin of the Ibos. Now I have come to Agulueri to see, touch and feel these things myself. Agulueri and the neighboring towns, for all intents and purposes should be the focal point of all Ibo-Jewish viewpoints. We appear to have no better Jewish sentiments and outlook anywhere in today's Ibo Land.

It has to be mentioned here that not all Igalas are of Hebrew (Ibo) descent. Many came from the stock of Oduduwa. Some of the Eri group that passed through the Igalaland route found it more convenient to settle at Igala where many inhabitants were also of Eri stock from Agulueri long before the Benin episode. Of this group those who continued tracing their way back to Onitsha were led by the most senior elder who by agreement and by right of birth would become the Oba or Obi of Onitsha if he arrived safely back to Onitsha and in good time. But because of the longer route he took, this most senior elder arrived Onitsha long after the group led by a junior elder had arrived and settled, using the short Agbor/Asaba route. So it was that the 'ought-to-be' Obi came back to Onitsha to meet an already duly installed and established Obi from his own kindred too. Rather than fighting and repeating the ugly incident that they witnessed in Benin, they settled for a kind of peace treaty whereby the 'ought-to-be' Obi was made a foremost, top-ranking chief of Onitsha, a ruler of a special rank, that would normally not bend or prostrate before the Obi of Onitsha to greet, give or receive a thing from.Hencethe title of, "Okwuoto ekene eze" in the present Onitsha chieftaincy arrangement. From this, the popular story that Onitsha people came from Benin as a fall out from the Benin stock is merely a legendary of half-truth. The people of Onitsha are purely Hebrews or Heebos (Ibos) of Eri stock from the tribe of Gad.

The Eri people who could not continue their journey to Onitsha together with their kith and kin who were already settled there from Agulueri, had to remain in the present Igalaland and formed the nucleus of the famous ancient Igala kingdom.

On the floor directly opposite the ancient stool of Eze Eri of Agulueri made of mud. One can notice strokes of ancient writing traced into permanence on the floor with white cowries in use in Nigeria before the coming of the white man, reminiscent of the *nsibidi* writing of the ancient Ibos in Aro-Chukwu. One thing is clear, namely that this is Hebrew writing. The ancient Ibo Eris who wrote this before the coming of the white man must have come from no other place than Israel.

OWELLE ROCHAS OKOROCHA

**A FOREMOST IBO PHILANTHROPIST. HE FINANCED THE
FIRST RESEARCH VISIT OF THE AUTHOR, TO THE PALACE
OF EZE ERI OF AGULERI IN ANAMBRA STATE OF NIGERIA.**

NSIBIDI WRITING OF THE OJAGHAM PEOPLE

EXAMPLES of A FEW TYPICAL NSIBIDI SYMBOLS
AND THEIR MANY SUBTLE VARIATIONS

LOVE, UNITY   HATRED, DIVORCE

WORD, SPEECH, MEETING, CONGRESS

MIRROR, REFLECTION

TABLE SET FOR DRINK AND MEAT

TREK, JOURNEY, VOYAGE, TRACKS

| NSIBIDI MIRROR | PREVENT/ DANGER | CLOSED SKIN | DEATH = FRIEND | MURDER WEAPON | SPEAR POINT | THIS LAND IS MINE |

Nsibidi (or Nsibiri) was a writing system of the ancient Ibos, particularly used by the Aro Ibos. It could be found on tombstones, secret society buildings, costumes, ritual fans, in gestures, body, ground and wall painting. We should not pay any particular attention to the interpretations of the symbols by the white authors, for the ancient Ibo elders lied to the colonial masters with regard to the actual meanings of the strokes of their writing or the symbols so as to fool them at the ensuing slave trade business in which the Aro Ibos were equal stakeholders. "Why," the Ibos reasoned, "would they unfold their secret and sacred writing to unknown strangers, the unbelievers and uninitiated?" One thing is clear, however. The writing was developed by combining the ancient Hebrew writing (as exemplified in the ancient Hebrew writing in the traditional shrine of Eze Eri in Isite Aguleri), which the Ibos brought with them from Israel, and the hieroglyphic writing of the ancient Egyptians to which the Ibos were also exposed during their long stay in Egypt before migrating to Nigeria.

CHAPTER SIX

THE IBOS AND THEIR JEWISH TRIBES

In fact, whereas most Ibo towns in Anambra, Delta and part of Enugu States are of the stock of Gad most towns in the South Eastern part of Nigeria spreading from Old Bende Division in Abia and Ebonyi down to Akwa Ibom, Cross River, Bayelsa, Delta and Rivers States of the present day Nigeria are virtually all of the tribe of Judah, with a few exceptions. My multi-dimensional stand on the tribal origin of the exiled Jews in Nigeria is informed by the fact that Jews give themselves names that are traceable in the particular kindred, as for example, the case of John the Baptist in the New Testament Bible.

And it came to pass, that on the eighth day they came to circumcise the child; and they called him Zechariah after the name of his father. And his mother answered and said, not so; but he shall be called John. And they said unto her, 'There is none of thy kindred that is called by this name' (Luke 1:59-61).

Therefore, by extension of the argument in the above quotation, Asa town in Abia State, for instance, is most likely to be originally made up of people from the kindred of Asa of the tribe of Judah. The same is true for Eri of the tribe of Gad. Agulueri means namesake of Eri. This confirms the earlier assertion that Agulueri town was founded by somebody named after Eri or the namesake of Eri from ancient Israel. In like manner we can safely talk about other stock of exiled Jews in Nigeria from the point of view of their tribal origin, e.g., the Gad stock, the Judah stock, the Levi stock, etc.

The Judah stock, for instance, among the exiled Nigerian Hebrews may be said to be flamboyant, daring, fearless, proud and intelligent as exemplified in the lives of, for example, the Ubanis ("Banis"), the Rivers Ibos. Prominent among the group of Judah in the South Eastern part of Nigeria are Item (Abia State) or Itam (Akwa Ibom State), Alayi ("Ahlai"), Ozuitem ("Uz Etam"), Akaeze ("Eker Ezer") Ugwueke (of "Eker"), Ohafia (of "Ophra" or Ofra, Afra), Edda ("Eldad"), and so on, in the former old Bende Division albeit with great mix-ups with the descendants

46

of the tribe of Levi, Reuben and Benjamin. Indeed, it is among this group of Judah descents that Aba in Ngwaland, Abia State, stands out most prominently, and so, like Onitsha of Gad descent, needs a special mention. Aba (of "Arba") is a Nigerian Hebrew town named after a famous Hebrew man, a relation of "Anan" with a close linkage with the people of the lineage of king "Ahab" and King "Abijah" (pronounced either as Abayi or Abia by exiled Nigerian Hebrews (Ibos), but more of the lineage of King "Ahaz", all of the tribe of Judah with whom the said Aba (Arba) or his descendants as it were went and settled at a place called Aba, having dropped the faint 'r' sound in Arba. The Hebrew ancestry of Aba, just like that of Onitsha and virtually all other Ibo towns and villages, is not in doubt. What is in doubt and for which effort is being made here to cast sufficient light on is the Aba/Allokoo/Kwa connections and the emergent new culture, names, words, sentence structures and meanings. Even at that, generalizations about these connections must be approached with caution, as there are some good pointers to the separate origins of the different items of culture in the emergent new culture (e.g., Igbo language of the Ibos). Equally, there are these pointers to both Hebrew and Allokoo origins of certain names of people and places in this part of Nigeria (e.g.. in the name of person, -'Ananaba', which Aba (Ngwa) people wrongly interpret to mean 'anunaba', but which really is a compound name coined from two Hebrew names: "Anan" and "Arba". The name of the town, 'Alauku' in the now Obingwa L.G.A. is merely an easy corruption of Allokoo, the original owners of Iboland before the Ibos, the Nigerian Jews, joined them some two and half thousand years ago or so. Another Allokoo town (now pronounced as Oluku) is found in Nkanu, Enugu State. It is pertinent to highlight here that virtually all the Hebrew related names in today's Aba in particular and Ngwaland and Mbaise in general have been traced to the tribe of Judah (e.g., Ahiaba from "Ahab", Ohazu from "Ahaz", Obikabia of "Abiah or Abijah (pronounced as Abiyah)", one of the sons of Solomon, Ahiara from "Ahira". Umuara of "Ara", one of the grand sons of Asher, Abida (corrupted as Obuda) descendant of Keturah, the black wife of Abraham after the death Sarah; also, Asa, Obete, Akwaete, Ogbaete of "Eter", Abayi, Araim Usaka of "Isachar". Actually, one can rightly say that Aba has not lost much of its attributes of Judah, although there are some negative modifications, additions and subtractions due to the Hebrew/Kwa/Allokoo aculturalization process. But in all, Aba and its people (the indigenes and the adopted inhabitants) are still, like all Judah descents, strong, influential and ever determined not to be subdued by other people's actions and events. For instance, all major

47

offensive and exemplary hard-line actions of the Ibos of Nigeria (e.g., the Aba Women Riot 1929; the famous Aba popular riots even during the infamous military regime in Nigeria in the eighties and nineties, Bakassi Operations for Aba Security Welfare and so on) have always started in Aba. Hence Aba is being popularly referred to as 'The Heart of Iboland' or 'The Elephant City'. True to its last nickname, Aba has always played the protective role of "big elephant" brother for the other smaller Hebrew (Ibo) towns in Nigeria. The indigenes of Aba, the Abaukwu, Obuda (from Hebrew name "Abida" - see Genesis 25:4", one of the sons Keturah, the black wife of Abraham), Umuokpoji, Eziukwu, Eziama, Akoli, Osusu, Ndiegoro, and the adjoining towns: Abayi (of Hebrew King Abijah, pronounced as Abiya, for 'j' is pronounced as 'y' in Hebrew), Ogbor, Umuola, etc., have always been very accommodative and understanding to their stranger elements or rather their Hebrew brothers from other parts of Nigeria. This is, however, in line with their Jewish heritage or Moses' injunction to the Jews as recorded in Exodus 22:21 - "And a sojourner (stranger) shalt thou not wrong, neither shalt thou offend him". In fact, Aba is one Hebrew (Ibo) town that accommodates the greatest number of indigenes of all known towns in the Heebo (Ibo) nation - Abia, Akwa Ibom, Anambra, Cross River, Rivers, Delta, Ebonyi, Enugu. .

Aba is in Ngwaland. The purest of all Judah settlements in Eastern Nigeria is perhaps in the northern Ngwaland from where Aba and the adjoining towns migrated to their present position. Here, there is hardly any trace of any other Hebrew town other than the tribe of Judah. However, as in the Gad dominated areas of Iboland, we still find traces of mix settlement of Hebrews (Ibos) from the other tribes of Israel in Ngwaland, particularly the tribe of Levi.

One is tempted to believe that the leader of the Judah group in Nigeria might have settled in the South Eastern part of Iboland or Ibo nation. For the traits of effective Hebrew leadership and kingship still present here as evidenced in the present domain and palace of Ezeukwu of Ngwaukwu, Eze B. O. Enweremadu, in the heart of the very two communities that bear the Hebrew royal names of Ahiaba or Ahaba (of King Ahab) and Abayi (corruption of Abia or Abijah - King Abijah, pronounced Abiya).

Apparently, as if in divine and/or providential confirmation of the above, Professor Muse Tetegne of the World Hebrew Organisation, leading a team of thirteen Hebrews or Jews from different parts of the world, including ex-president Jean-Baptiste Bagaza of Burundi, went to Ngwaukwu during their tour of Ibo (Hebrew) nation in Nigeria on 30th October 1999 to pay special homage on the Ezeukwu of

Ngwaukwu and then handed over to him the symbolic ark of Moses and candle - gift usually made to Hebrew kings in ancient Israel.

Whether from Aba, Onitsha or elsewhere in Ibo land, these Jews of different Israeli tribes called Hebrews, Heebos, Eboes and now Ibos scattered all over Nigeria now have different dialects and even languages, but their culture and norms are basically Jewish and the same in many cases. Take for instance, the practice of New Yam Festival, which in many aspects, is a replica of the Jewish Festival of First Fruits or Feast of Weeks. Moses emphasised the first fruit sacrifice, and even till today, the Jews do not joke with it. There is, for example, in agriculture, the first fruit in the literary sense of the terminology or first crop offerings and sacrifices to God (see Leviticus 23: 9 - 23), now translated into the popular tradition of new Yam festival by the Jews of Nigeria, the Nigerian Hebrews (Ibos); in commerce and industry, tithes from the profit of the first venture, in family dedication of the first child (e.g., Samuel in the Scriptures), and so on. Today, the New Yam Festival Ceremony is the most important aspect of Ibo culture all over Nigeria and in fact, their Jewish heritage. Just as in the years gone by in Israel, it affords us the unique opportunity to display to our people, moreover our young ones and neighbours, our rich cultural heritage in virtually all aspects of life - in youths and sports development, education and training; in agriculture and allied cottage industries; in settling quarrels and calling social deviants back to order; in music and dance; in dealing with complexities of human activities - marriage, birth, youth initiation into manhood, etc.; and in dealing with a wide variety of community realities such behaviours, attitudes, skills, etc. needed for effective living in society; in socio-cultural organisation and institutions in all their ramifications; in dispensing justice and fair play; and more especially in the revival and sustenance of the dignity of our people both at home and abroad.
It is in the Jewish-oriented ceremonies such as the New Yam Festival or Celebration that most critics even in the Colonial era see the uniqueness of the Ibo culture in Nigeria as a matter of concern, thereby really adding more impetus to the discrimination against the Ibos.

Actually, the history of biased treatment and discrimination against the Ibos began with the discovery by Basden that the Ibos are Jews in exile in Nigeria, which the British colonial masters did not feel comfortable about, as they remembered the Jewish conflict with the early Christians in Europe as will be discussed later, as well as the universal hatred for the Jews. The consequent abuse and violence against the Ibos assumed a disturbing dimension during the armed struggle between King Peppel of Bonny, a Heebo (Ibo) king and later King Jaja, another Ibo king, and the British. Again, almost at same time between the other Ibo kings in Aro Chukwu, Item, Mbaise, Obosi, to mention the best known examples and the British, in the course of which both Ibos (of course many more of the Ibos) and British citizens lost their lives - a situation that was absolutely absent and unimaginable in either Yoruba land or Hausa-Fulani land or in any other place in Colonial Nigeria. In the process of these struggles and after the defeat of the Ibos by the British, the Ibo kings were humiliated and sent into exile by the victorious British, and their subjects were henceforth to be seen in bad light. In fact, whereas it cost the British neither a bullet nor human life to subdue the whole of Yoruba and Hausa lands or rather the rest of Nigeria, it cost them lots of bullets and human lives to subdue the Ibo nation, the former Eastern Nigeria. Several British armed men and sometimes civilians were killed and their installations destroyed in many parts of Ibo land before the Ibos were eventually brought under British rule.

Even after this, the British colonial masters continued to have problems in the governance of the Ibos. For example, whereas women of all the other parts of Nigeria were made to join their male counterparts to pay income tax to the British colonial government in Nigeria, Ibo women all over Ibo land resisted every attempt to make them pay such tax. This was the cause of the famous 1929 Women Riot that started in Aba, and spread to the other parts of Ibo Land. The British Colonial government withdrew that tax policy, and so Ibo women were henceforth to be exempted from paying tax during the Colonial era until after Nigerian Independence (1960) when the Nigerian administrators reviewed the female tax policy. Consequent upon the perceived stubbornness of the Ibos and their suspected Jewish heritage or connection (particularly at a time when anti-Jewish sentiments were at their peak in Europe), series of anti-Ibo policies were unleashed in commerce, industry and politics. For example, of all the agricultural products of Nigeria, palm oil and kernel, the main agricultural products of the Ibo nation were deliberately priced lowest by the British in the European market so that the people remained very poor in comparison with the Yorubas of the West and Hausa-Fulani of the North whose products, cocoa, groundnut and cotton fetched much higher dividends.

Another prominent example is the political policy, of warrant chieftaincy as part of the general policy of indirect rule in the British colonial Nigeria. The policy of warrant chieftaincy took effect only in Ibo Land, not in any other part of Nigeria. The removed, exiled or killed Ibo kings were quickly replaced by warrant chiefs, most of whom were strangers to the land and knew little or nothing about the culture of the people they were supposed to rule. It appears that one major qualification for being a warrant chief was lack of knowledge of the culture of the people or alienation from the people so that there would be a disagreement between the ruler and the ruled - a situation that was expected to pave way for a continuous British intervention in the affairs of the people. Some Ibos understood this and protested. But their protest did not go far as the protesters or rather Ibo activists were quickly arrested and imprisoned or banished from their native land.

In some few cases, however, some of the Ibo activists or even chiefs who did not want to wait to be banished from their own land escaped and went to a completely new area to found yet another domain in the vain hope of gaining freedom from the British rule. This was the case with the Bani or Ubani man (real name unknown) called Dockyard by the British (corrupted as Dokiya and later called Ndoki) who, together with his immediate family and some extended family members, escaped the shores of Bonny to go and settle in the neighboring towns of Abala Ibeme, Ohambele, Azumini, Umuogo (of Jewish name of "Og" – see Deuteronomy 3:13), Obohia, Obunku, Ohanso, Akwete (of Jewish name, "Eter" – see Joshua 15:42), Ohanku, Ohuru or Ohahur (of Jewish name, "Hur" – see 1Chronicles 2:19), Akrika (of 'kalika", Hebrew word for waiting; also Umukalika, Abakalika, etc.), and the others. In Abala, for instance, the Dokiyas or Ndokis who were now advanced in the art of fabricating crude local guns for hunting in the thick forests of Abala - a skill they, like their counterpart Jewish exiles in Eri area, specifically in Awka (now in Anambra State), brought with them from their native home town in Israel - continued to disagree with the British as they earlier did in Bonny. The British finding it difficult to subdue the Ndokis of Abala in the face of their local "den" guns and potent talisman, (which the Ibos had as a collective group successfully used against the invading Fulani Arabs in Northern Iboland and earlier against the aborigines of Iboland, the Allokoos, the pigmies and the Kwas), abandoned Abala and went to settle in Aba in Ngwaland. As expected, the British, in anger moved out their trade post and in fact the entire British economy from Abala to Aba, with the consequent fall of the famous Orie Abala market and the rise of Ekeoha market of Aba.

Treatment such as this was part of the British grand design of undoing effective Ibo leadership and/or making a caricature of chieftaincy stool and leadership set-up in virtually all Iboland. Since then caricature has remained unabated with some Ibo chieftaincy and leadership arrangements even till date.

After this came the era of cultural imperialism against the Ibos in such a way that all traces of Jewish culture, artefacts, and so on in Iboland were targeted for destruction. For it was believed that the Jewish mentality of the Ibos was capable not only of causing further dangerous uprisings against the British as already evidenced in the said Ibo areas, but also of thwarting the spread of Christianity as was the case in the first century Europe when the Jews opposed the early Christians. Why did the Jews oppose the early Christians? One may ask at this point. Why would the Jews of Europe not hate the Christians? Why would European Jews want to identify with those who falsely accused and massacred them? The chapter that follows will deal with these questions and issues arising.

PROFESSORS (CHIEFS) ATHAN AND EVA MARY NJOKU
Prof. Njoku is a Renowned Professor of Economics at
Benedict College while Prof. Eva Mary is a Nationally Recognized
Professor of Social Work at South Carolina State University.

CHAPTER SEVEN

JEWISH ORIGIN OF THE IBOS; PERSPECTIVES FROM HISTORY AND DIVINE REVELATION

The first British explorers who met the Ibos of Nigeria were quick to identify them as "a branch of Hebrews" (Basden, 1938), and so simply referred to them as Hebrews (Heebos, Eboes and later Ibos). But during the time of the first documentation of the history of the Ibos, the early Ibos who knew very little or no English, following the pronunciation of the "new" version of their original name by their colonial masters deviated from the name Ivite as in Ivite Agulueri (from Ivrit) Ifite or Ihite and began to use the popular new and foreign language of the colonialists and so also referred to themselves as Heebo, a corruption of Hebrew or accepted to be called Heebo, Eboe or Ibo as a way of associating themselves with the emergent new culture of the colonial master. This corrupt version of the English word, Hebrew, remained unnoticed or was deliberately allowed to remain unchanged even when noticed by the British authorities so as to serve as a mark of derogatory distinction between the European Hebrews who are mostly whites and the Nigerian Hebrews who are mostly blacks, and henceforth all the early History works or books on the Ibos bore the corrupt version of Hebrew, that is Heebo or Eboe or Ibo (e.g.,"Heebo nation; Eboe slaves; Ibos of Eastern Nigeria", etc see Equiano1789; Basden, 1938; all other Colonial History books on Ibos).

In his own version of the historical evidence, Dr. Basden of the Anglican Mission pointed out in convincing details certain social and religious similarities between the Ibos and the Jews he saw in Europe, not withstanding the fact that unlike the European Jews, he (Basden) met the Nigerian Jews or Hebrews (Ibos) "in nakedness and dire poverty" and within a very hostile and pitiful environment. The striking similarities that Basden observed made him to conclude that "the Ibos are a branch of Hebrews" and that any European wishing to effectively deal with them should first of all go and acquaint himself with Mosaic laws. Specifically,

Basden pointed out similar social behaviours, rites, customs of circumcision and mummification, family life as well as identical sentence structures - the same findings that have always featured prominently in the reports of past and contemporary investigations into the origin of the Ibo.

The view of the origin of the Ibos in Israel by reasons of social behaviors and cultural similarities was first expressed in about 1789 by an Ibo ex-slave in London, Olaudah Equiano, in his writings, "The Interesting Narratives" and "Ibo Society in Mid-Century". Ethnographically and culturally, Equiano likened his people, the Ibos, to the Jews or Hebrews, succinctly highlighting what long struck him very forcibly, namely, "the strong analogy which even by this sketch, imperfect as it is, appears to prevail in the manners and customs of Ibos and those of the Hebrews, the Israelites - an analogy which induced him to conclude "that the one people had sprung from the other":

We practiced circumcision like the Jews, and made offerings and feast on that occasion in the same manner as they did. Like them also our children were named from some event, some circumstance or fancied foreboding, at the time of their birth.

Furthermore. Equiano recounted that in the Ibo society, adultery was punished with death or slavery - a practice that is also Jewish. Indeed, the sentence of slavery for an offence tantamount to death in the then Ibo land since it was believed that "slaves were purchased by the white people to be killed and eaten and that their blood was used to make red cloth" (Schon and Crowther. 1974:310).

Again, "the Ibo (like the Jews)", according to Equiano, "are almost a nation of dancers, musicians and poetry. Thus every great event, such as a triumphant return from battle, or other cause of public rejoicing, is celebrated in public dances, which are accompanied with songs and music suited to the occasion" (Equiano in Hodgkin, 1974:212). A clear illustration of what happens in a typical Ibo society with respect to music and poetry as described by Equiano can be seen in the Hebrew concept of poetry and music as recorded in the Holy Scriptures. The Hebrews had work songs (Isaiah 22:13); war songs (Joshua 5); wedding songs (Psalm 45); mocking songs (Numbers 21:27-30), as well as cultic or sacred songs; hymns; individual laments; collective laments (Joel 2:17; Psalm 44), etc. The Ibos in the same manner, have different songs and music suited to different occasions; they have war songs, ikperikpe ogu (e.g., Bende war dance); mocking song, iri ikpe (e.g., Ohuba song of Item people), wedding songs., individual laments, abu akwa; cultic or sacred songs, iri oboni, ekpe, aku or okonko, and so on, just as the World Hebrews.

Regarding the eating habit of the Ibos, Equiano wrote:
Before we taste food, we always wash our hand, indeed our cleanliness on all occasion is extreme, but on this, it is an indispensable ceremony.

After washing, libation: by pouring out a small portion of the drink...
(Equiano in Hodgkin, 1974:213).

Indeed, a visit to a typical Hebrew family at table will make one think that the ex-Ibo slave called Equiano was a real Jew. But was he not? Information such as the above might have led the famous Ibo scholar, Ogbalu, to link the Ibos with the Hebrews, maintaining in his work (1981) that the Ibos came from the Hebrews. The same view has been Shared by Arinze (1970), Ilogu (1974), Njaka (1974), Oraka (1984), Ezeala (1992), Ononoju (1996), Alaezi (1998, 1999, 2001), and so on. Alaezi (1999), for instance, devotes one full chapter on the cultural similarities between the Ibos of Nigeria, the Nigerian Hebrews and the World Hebrews, succinctly highlighting and discussing in details the following areas: status symbolism, thrift, hard work, spirit of adventure, tenacity of purpose, law and justice, competition, and so on. Certain "strange" customs seen among some of the Ibos in Nigeria are traceable to the Jews or other people of Jewish descent. For example, some Ibos, particularly those from Ohafia and Afikpo local government areas of Abia and Ebonyi states of Nigeria, unlike their neighbors, marry their cousins just as the Israelites do. From the Holy Scriptures the evidence is in the case of Eleazar who "had only daughters. Their cousins, the sons of Kish, married them (1 Chronicles 23:22)". Other examples abound.

Although these writers on the origin of the Ibos unanimously point to Israel as the ancestral home of the Ibos, they apparently disagree on their exact places or tribes of origin in Israel. For instance, the legendary and near scriptural view that the Ibos originated from "Schechenigbo, situated between Bethlehem and Hebron on the road that runs through Cairo in Egypt" started by the famous Stigmatist Innocent Okorie and popularized by Ezeala (1992) has now been seriously contested by the more recent Biblically supported ethno-linguistic view of the origin of the Ibos. This counter view holds that the Ibos of Nigeria are made up of Hebrews in exile from different tribal origins such as "Eri of the tribe of Gad" (Agulueri Oraeri. Umuleri, Mbieri, etc.), - Arodi of the tribe of Gad" (Aro or Aro Chukwu, Arodi Izuogu or Arondizuogu). "Etam, of the tribe of Judah," (Item, Ozuitem), "Zebulun of the tribe of Zebulun", (Ozubulu); "Ahab of the tribe of Judah" (Ahaba, Ahiaba). "Amok (Amorka), Amok),

"Asa" (Asa, Asaumuteke), "Ahiah" of the tribe of Benjamin (Umuahia), "Izhar of the tribe of Levi" (Izza)., etc., not from a particular one tribe or small town like Schechnigbo. It cannot, however, be ruled out that some of the Ibos might have come from Schechnigbo, but certainly not all the

Ibos. With this view of the multi-tribal origin of the Ibos from Israel, there seems to be no further much confusion with respect to the tribal origin of the Ibos. Jews generally do not answer names outside their family circles or tribal origin and the names mentioned above as examples reflect either those of the founder of the tribe (e.g., Zebulun) or tribal king (e.g., King Asa of Judah, King Ahab of Judah) or of prominent son of a particular tribe (e.g., Eri).

In his version of history, Adams (1975:232) states that

The Heebos, to judge by the immense number annually sent into slavery, inhabit a country of great extent, and extremely populous, the southern boundary of which may be comprised between Cape Formosa and old Calabar; and it is very probable that the towns at the mouths of the rivers along the coast, including New Calabar and Bonny, were peopled originally, from the Heebo country. In fact, Amacree (Amakri), the King of New Calabar and Peppel, King of Bonny, are both of Heebo descent, as well as many of the principal traders at both these places.
(Adams in Nigerian Perspectives, 1975:232).

Both King Pepple and King Amakri are Heebos or Hebrews (Ibos) who settled in the said riverine areas of Nigeria (Rivers State) from either Uburu or Aro Chukwu and quite much later from Benin after the sacking of the Eris from the Benin kingdom. The first name of King Peppel is 'Anna', a name from a Hebrew (Ibo) name, "Anan" (see Nehemiah 10:26). Actually, Peppel is a mere nickname, reflecting the dominant commodity, pepper, sold to European traders by his Bonny subjects. Hence the original name "King Anna Peppel" (later pronounced as Peppel) as recorded in history. Bonny is from Hebrew (Ibo) name "Bani" (see Ezra 10:29). The name Amakri is also from a Hebrew (Ibo) name Micri (see 1 Chron. 9:8). The name, 'Amakiri', is today still being borne by people of Nkwere, a typical Ibo town in Imo State.

History has it too that the other famous king who reigned in the Ubani (Bani) Hebrew (Ibo) areas of now Rivers State was incidentally King Jaja of Opobo, an ex-Heebo (Ibo) slave from Amaigbo (of Igbo, the famous son of Agulueri of the tribe of Gad) in now Imo State. In fact, the nickname of King Jaja, which took his real name, was Jiojo (which in Ibo means a yam that has been bought to be eaten by the buyer, but cannot be eaten) later pronounced as Jojo and finally wrongly pronounced as Jaja by the British. A prominent feature in God's dealings with the Hebrews at home and in the Diaspora has been that often the Hebrews themselves either as kings or ordinary citizens were used to inflict God's punishment on their fellow Hebrews. Hence the uncomfortable truism that Heebo (Ibo) traders from Aro Chukwu (Arodi), Nkwere (Nkwo Eri) and Amaigbo (Ama Igbo of Eri stock) were the chief actors in the notorious slave trade that had hundreds of thousands of Hebrew (Heebo or Ibo) people as victims in fulfilment of God's earlier curse of slavery among other calamities on their forefathers in Israel before their final gathering back to Israel. The fulfillment is now being witnessed by our present generation. There is also the ethno-racial lineage theory of the Jewish origin of the Ibos. This is somehow psychological in nature, and has to do with the negative attitude of some of the Ibos themselves towards their Hebraism and the arguments of those who strongly believe that a black man cannot be a Jew. Those who have this type of problem often say: 'We can't believe this. Can a black man be a Jew?' Many among them, even when there is a counter convincing evidence to make them believe or change their mind, are often gripped with the undercurrent fear of discrimination because of the color of their skin, referring to the case of the Ethiopian Jews as a case in point. However, this very fear has been drastically reduced by the knowledge and understanding expressed by some of the white Jews themselves like Donin in the following terms:

The universalism that permeates the faith of Israel is reflected not only in its theological formulation and in its vision of the future, but in the very composition of its people... these people (the people of Israel) include those whose skins range from the lightest to

the darkest in colors and within it a broad range of cultural diversity is represented. (Donin.1972:8).

After the establishment of the state of Israel in 1948, the efforts of gathering back the exiled Israelites by the World Zionist Organization and Aliya Bet, were focused on the Hebrew exiles in Arab countries, mostly in the Middle East, Iraq and Africa (in light skinned North Africa only, not in black Africa South of Sahara), forgetting that the unchangeable promise of the LORD God Almighty, through the mouth of virtually all the holy prophets of Israel to the Hebrews regarding their return from exile is to all, not just a section of the exiled ones, or some or many of them, in selected areas of the four corners of the earth where, they were scattered because they failed "to hearken unto the voice of the LORD, our God, to observe to do all His commandments and His statutes..." The promise simply is:

Behold, I will gather them out of all countries where I have driven them in My anger, in My fury, and in great wrath, I will bring them back to this place, and I will cause them to dwell safely... I will give them singleness of heart and action. For thus said the LORD, just as I have

58

brought this calamity on this people, so I will bring to them all the good that I have promised. (Jeremiah 32: 37-42).

Earlier on, from the mouth of Moses, the greatest of all the prophets of Israel, who first pronounced the curses of the "LORD in His furious anger and great wrath" on the erring Hebrews, the promise of total gathering back and restoration had been given in the following unmistakable terms: Then (after God's furious anger and great wrath shall have been turned away from the erring Hebrews in His own time) the LORD your God will restore your fortunes and have compassion on you and gather you again from all the nations where He scattered you. Even if you had been banished to the most distant land under the heavens, from there, the LORD your God will gather you and bring you back. He will bring you to the land that belonged to your fathers (Deuteronomy 30: 3-5).

And again through the mouth of Isaiah the prophet the LORD said: I will bring your descendants from the east and gather you, from the west I will say to the north, Give them up, and to the south, do not keep them back. Bring my sons from afar, and my daughters, from the ends of the earth everyone who is called by my name (Isaiah 43:5-6).

There is nothing whatsoever to suggest that the promise of gathering back and restoration of Israel and its people is only for a section of the Hebrews, say the white or fair-skinned Hebrews at the exclusion of the black or dark-skinned Hebrews, or for those living in one particular part of the world at the exclusion of those living in another part of the world. In fact, darkness of the skin of some Hebrews and the attempt by some of their brothers and sisters to downgrade them have remained the twin concepts that stand out as internal sensitive issues in the history of Israel since the days of King Solomon and beyond (see Song of Solomon 1: 5-6) I am black, but comely, O ye daughters of Jerusalem, as the tents of Keddar, as the curtains, of Solomon. Look not upon me, because I am swarthy (dark), because the sun hath scorched me. My mother's sons were incensed (angry) against me; they made me keeper of the vineyards; But mine own vineyard have I not kept.

In fact, the Holy Scriptures have it that black or dark-skinned people such as the Ethiopian Jews, the Tutsis of East Africa and the Ibos of Nigeria in Jewish lineage had come to be even at the very inception of the Jewish race. The establishment of the Jewish race began when God chose Abraham because of his righteousness and faith in Him, and called him (Abraham) out of his native country Shem, in the present day Iraq, separating him from his kith and kin and established him in the territory of Canaan, the son of Ham. Canaan was mostly dark-skinned or black people's territory in the Middle East. Other sons of Ham include Cush (now Ethiopia). Mizram (now Egypt), Put (now Libya), and Canaan (Palestine) (see Genesis 10:6).

Get thee now, the LORD has said unto Abram (Abraham), out of thy country and from thy kindred and from thy father's house, unto the land that I will show thee; and I will make of thee a great nation, and I will bless thee, and make thy name great; and be thou a blessing: and I will bless them that bless you, and him that curse you I will curse; and in thee, all the families of the earth will be blessed ... So

Abram departed as the LORD had spoken unto him... and into the land of Canaan they came. And the LORD appeared unto Abram and said to him your seed will I give this land (Genesis 12:I- 7).

In the new land, Canaan, after the death of Abraham's wife, Sarah, the mother of Isaac, Abraham was properly re-married to Keturah, a black woman from Ethiopia who bore him other legitimate children among whom was Midian who later went with his mother to settle in Ethiopia. Then again Abraham took a wife, and her name was Keturah. And she bore him Zimran and Jokshan and Medan, and Midian and Isbak and Shuah... All these were the children of Keturah (Genesis 25:1-4)

Indeed, it was the same Midian that was later to be used by the Almighty to properly establish the state of Israel through Moses. In Ethiopia, Midian being one of the sons of Abraham through his wife Keturah, zealously and faithfully applied the teachings in the book of Genesis and so raised his descendants to be priests and teachers of God of Abraham. And so in the fullness of time, God had to send Moses to a priest of Midian, "a descendant of Abraham through Keturah" to help him (Moses) fulfil his ministry and obtain the inheritance of the children of Israel (Exodus 18: 1-27; Numbers 10: 24-32).

A more direct case for the black Hebrews in Jewish history can be made when we consider that two of the maids of Jacob's (Israel's) wives, Bilah and Zilpah, who were given to him by his wives to bear children who actually became part and parcel of the twelve tribes of Israel that the Almighty chose for HIMSELF were all blacks. The children of these maids, the Scripture says, formed the nucleus of the tribes of Israel. Bilah, the maidservant of Leah bore for Jacob, Gad and Asher. The descendants of Gad and Asher are now traceable mostly in Eastern Nigeria and Ashanti areas of Ghana.

Another case in point is that of Moses. Moses married a Midian woman called Zipporah. This is besides the obvious fact that some Jewish people were intermarried with some Egyptians who agreed to marry a Jewish slave and more with the dark-skinned Cushites and Ethiopians during their 400 year-long period of slavery in Egypt.

Therefore, any Nigerian Hebrew (Ibo) that focuses his thoughts negatively on the color of his skin in actualizing his Hebraism is being unkind to himself; he s creating undue problems for himself and other black Jews.

Hagar would have been the first link with or source of the black or dark-skinned race in Israel if only Abraham had married her in the proper way as in the case of Keturah. Abraham's relationship with Hagar (Ishmael's mother) was based on a canal request made by Sarah who thought that she was too old to bear the God's promised child, Isaac. But God's plan cannot change, nor can man hasten His time. Something had to happen for God's plan to take its normal course. And so, on begetting her son, Ishmael, Hagar began to be too bigheaded to continue to respect her mistress as the madam of the house. She soon began to erroneously assume the role of the mother of the heir to her mistress and consequently, she (Hagar) was cast out with her son, Ishmael.

Wherefore she said unto Abraham, cast out this bond woman (Hagar) and her son for the son of this bondwoman (Ishmael) shall not be heir with my son, even with Isaac. (Genesis 21:10).

Of course, as Ishmael grew up his mother, Hagar taught him or made him to believe that Isaac had taken his birthright away from him. But by God's divine plan and promise, it was not his birthright, but Isaac's.

For the LORD had earlier said to Abraham: it is through Isaac that your offspring will be reckoned," (Genesis 21:12), not through Ishmael.

This erroneous thought cultivated in Ishmael's mind by her mother, without caring to know or ignoring the will of God concerning Isaac, had ever since remained impossible to correct. It hurtled Ishmael all through his life on earth and had gone deep down into the minds of all the descendants of Ishmael (now the Arabs) until date and has adversely affected the thinking pattern of the Arab twelve princes concerning Jacob or Israel and all its branches wherever they are in the world, the Ibos of Nigeria inclusive. This has perhaps led in no small measure to the incessant disagreements and wars between the two peoples wherever they find themselves, whether in the Middle East or elsewhere in the world.

There is finally, a third-wave argument to the theory of the Jewish origin of the Ibos which hinges on the much-talked-about contention of and/or revelation to the famous Stigmatist Innocent Okorie that the Ibos of Nigeria are of the Jewish race, that "the Igbos are descendants from Judea and they are Jewish people possessing knowledge and intelligence like the Jews" (Chukwukere 1985:13).

Innocent Okorie is reported to be a Stigmatist in the category of St. Francis of Assisi and of recent memory Padre Pio of Italy who enjoyed the gift of bi-location. In the book, The History of the Igbos as Revealed to Innocent Okorie, A Stigmatist, Innocent Okorie is portrayed as a Stigmatist who used to have profuse bleeding from the five Sacred Spots where Jesus was wounded on the cross during Easter Lents. In the lent of 1983, by about 7 a.m. on that Good Friday morning, at Owerre Ebeiri in Orlu, Imo State, Nigeria, Innocent Okorie was seen with the marks of flagellation all over his body "to the utter amazement of spectators and members of the Apparitions Investigation Association." In the afternoon of that Good Friday, Innocent Okorie profusely bled from the said five sacred spots in his body, and there was "also drops of blood from the nostrils, a sign of deep agony. From that moment till the following morning on Holy Saturday, Brother Okorie entered the state of coma." During the night, while members were keeping vigil, intermittent flashes in various colors were witnessed particularly in the room where Brother Okorie was lying. In the morning of Holy Saturday Innocent Okorie woke up "fit and smart looking, refreshed, with shining face, combed hair without a single drop of water, soap and towel supplied to him by any member of the Association keeping vigil over his body". And from that Holy Saturday to Easter Sunday Innocent Okorie released messages to the world, which he claimed were either from the Lord Jesus Christ or from the Blessed Mother of Jesus Christ. One of the most striking messages on this occasion was that our Lord Jesus Christ appeared to him while he was in a trance and revealed to him the following:

- "the Igbos and the Efiks arrived first into Nigeria in 638 B.C., after the exile of the Israelites in 718   B.C.".

- "the original native town of the Igbos, Schechenigbo in Judea, is surrounded by the following: Bethlehem to the north; a forest zone which extensively covers the area from Bethlehem southwards to Hebron; on the other side, towards the west are those living along the Mediterranean sea; length-wise is Joppa to the north, to the south is Azotus, continuing southwards are Ascalon and Gaza ... The road that runs through Jericho, turns out to two routes, one leads to Phasaelia and the other to Philadelphia and along the desert zone of Efikdonaelis, that place from which the people of Efik left for Nigeria" (Chukwukere. 1985: 11-12). Ordinarily, revelation or not, proof or not, the Ibos of Nigeria are simply and commonly referred to by the other tribes of Nigeria as Jews. For instance, during the recently concluded Oputa Panel's investigation into the various human rights abuses against the citizens of Nigeria by the successive military regimes and their civilian collaborators particularly during the infamous regime of the notorious dictator, late General Sani Abacha, an occasion arose when one of the counsels for the Arewa consultative forum, in a bid to disprove or cancel the claim of marginalization of the Ibos in Nigeria by the Ohaneze Ndigbo, the apex Igbo socio-cultural organisation, came up with a newspaper publication which quoted Dr. Nnamdi Azikiwe as telling

some Ibo students in America that "the Ibos are Jews, and so must strive to rule Nigeria or show that they are a special people in Nigeria".

At several other occasions one can hear other Nigerians refer to the Ibos living among them as Jews and they (the Ibos) accepting with deep satisfaction the Jewish tag on them even before the 2nd World War or the establishment of the state of Israel when it was extremely unpopular for one to be called a Jew anywhere in the world. It is common knowledge in Nigeria and beyond that another nickname for the Ibos of Nigeria is Jews of Africa.

The Hebrew lineage claim of the Ibo has gone beyond the shores of Nigeria and is now receiving international attention in the Western World including America, the Vatican and even in Israel among the orthodox and non-orthodox Jews. This is evidenced in the following two publications in the Newsweek magazine of April 16, 2001 page 52 and in the popular Israeli newspaper, The Jerusalem Post of April 2, 1999.

In The Jerusalem Post, Rabbi Capers Funnye, Jr., the only black Jew sitting on the Chicago Board of Rabbi told Sue Fishkoff in an interview that "several African tribes still consider themselves descended from Hebraic stock, including the Ibo of Nigeria and the Tutsis of East Africa. The Africans brought to the New World as slaves in the 18th and 19th centuries were mainly from areas where tribes with Jewish roots predominated.

"Funnye and other black American Jews view that horrific experience as the fulfilment of the Deuteronomy 28, he said, quoting, 'I shall bring you again into Egypt (slaves) in ships and you shall he sold for bondsmen and bondswomen.

"The questions we get are 'who are these black Jews? How many are they? Are they really Jews?

"It's that last question that causes the sharp break between black American Jewish community of whatever denomination. Most black Jews in the US have never gone through formal conversion to Judaism; they consider themselves already Jewish simply by virtue of having African ancestors who may have been descended from original Hebrews.

"We view ourselves not as converts, but as reverts to Judaism, Funnye explained." (The Jerusalem Post Friday, April 2, 1999, page B4.)

In another development, the joint reports in Newsweek of 16th April 2001 of Anne Underwood in New York, Robert Blair in New Delhi, Mahlon Mever in Hong Kong, Mac Margolis in Rio de Janeiro, Lara Santoro in Nairobi and Uche Ezechukwu in Abuja, have it that an Ibo, the former Archbishop of Onitsha and President of the Pontifical Council for Interreligious Dialogue, Cardinal Francis Arinze, "might become the first black pope... It will be a symbol that the church is color blind... This will make Arinze not only the first black pope but the first to claim a Hebrew lineage as well" (The Next Pope? Newsweek, April 16 2001, page 52).

Like the earlier Hebrew writing which was found on the floor of the palace of Eze Eri in Agulueri and reported in Chapter Two of this book, the Aros in the ancient Aro Empire evolved a kind of writing called "Nsibidi" which was between the form of ancient Hebrew writing as in the palace of Eze Eri and the hieroglyphics of the ancient Egyptians. This fact, together with the other discoveries akin to the ones made by Dr. Basden with regards the Eri stock, "made the Europeans to link the Aros to the Jews expelled by the Portuguese." (Onwukwe, 1995:25).

Despite all these revealing facts about the Jewish origin of the Ibos, the Ibo story has not changed neither has it received any significant attention in the World Jewry partly because of the disunity of ideas and purpose and dissenting voices of very few but powerful Ibo intellectuals and partly because the Almighty's appointed time for the treatment of Ibo case has not come but more because of the later, for whenever the Almighty's time is due, all other obstacles must give way. The said Ibo intellectuals' main counter argument hinges on the presumptions that Igbo as a Negro race is "a 'sky being' for he descended from the sky in the first place" (Afigbo, 2001:24), that "it was during this phase of Igbo experience (i.e., during the universalistic period) that the basic framework of what we know as Igbo culture and civilisation was laid" (p.25), that "the experience which makes a segment of the migrants of 6000 years ago Igbo was developed in situ in what is today Igboland. It was not brought in by them from wherever...Thus any similarities, real or imagined, found between their experience and the experience of any other population aggregate in any other part of the world is accidental... a fatal blow at the root of the hypothesis of Hebrew origin of the Igbo (p.9). Actually, the people being referred to in Afigbo's work are the same people that have been referred to elsewhere in this book as the aborigines of Iboland - the Allokoo, Ituri, Kwa and Pigmy races with whom the exiled Nigerian Hebrews (Ibos) lived and intermarried on arriving from the Lake Chad area. And, according to Jewish custom, as many of these aborigines as were properly married into the Nigerian Hebrew families and abided by the Jewish customs as practiced by the Ibos automatically became Jews too.

Highlights of Afigbo's narration of the Negro 'sky beings' (now called Igbos) who, on landing from the sky where they stayed and had discourse with God, migrated to Southern Nigeria about 6000 years ago, that is, 3000 years before the Nigerian Hebrews (Ibos) came from Israel to join them, run thus:

At a much deeper, that is esoteric, level which we are still to understand, and which we must strive to understand if we want to get to the root and meaning of Igbo experience... we should draw attention to certain figures which are central to Igbo enumeration and esoteric thought. First, we have the number otu (1 or unity) arising from the fact that in the beginning only God (Chineke/Chukwu) existed. It was only later out of Him (or out of it) there issued the primordial entities of the Igbo cosmos - man, sky and earth. Then came abua (2 or two), which captures the duality of the Igbo world. Thus in the beginning there were only two living entities – God and man, as well as, two entities, without life - the sky and the earth. There followed ato (3 or three)...

In the first place there was some kind of a divine coup d'etat with the earth becoming the dominant divine entity in Igbo culture. The sky God (Chukwu or Chineke) was thrown into splendid isolation as a result of which he or it was hardly worshipped. His feminine counterpart, Ala became the main object of worship throughout Igboland, as well as the guardian of the social order and morality. Omenala, the anchor point of Igbo law, jurisprudence and morality means that which Ala accepted, approved of and sanctioned. Ala also had a physical shrine, with each community having its own. At times, in an independent political community, mba (the village group), each village had its own shrine and priest of Ala. Another religious development in this period was the rise of a swarm of nature deities whose worship was as vibrant as that of Ala, if not more so on occasions. These were believed to dwell in a whole series of physical objects - trees, hills, rivers, streams, valleys, rocks and so on...(Afigbo, 2001:25-28).

The above narrative by a forefront Ibo intellectual at best portrays the Igbo as worshippers of many gods - gods of wood, stone, iron, rivers, streams and so on, and as a people who believe that they descended from the sky with the female counterpart of God called Ala, leaving her male counterpart, God or Chukwu, alone to live in the sky. Such a people as portrayed in the narrative cannot be called Jews at all. Whether this is so or not, and quite apart from its origin, the story is immensely important as an illustration of the low ideas, which are current amongst certain of Ibo intellectuals regarding the origin of the Ibos. We can understand the vehemence of the protagonists of the 'sky being' or Negro origin of the Ibos in opposition to their Hebrew origin when we realize the post Biafran War conceptions of many Ibos, especially those of them outside the Ibo central states of Abia, Anambra, Enugu and Imo. After the Biafran War, this group of Ibos felt it better to denounce their Iboness or their Ibo identity, change or distort their Ibo names (from Umuola to Rumuola, Obigbo to Oyigbo, Umuokoro to Rumuokoro, Umumasi to Rumumasi, Umueme to Rumueme, Ike to Iyk, and so on) to something beyond recognition, sound apologetic and even openly oppose everything Ibo so as to be better accepted as Nigerians for 'One Nigeria', and so join in the share of the spoils of war to the disadvantage of their kith and kin in the other Ibo states of the country. Even the belief of the great Northern Nigerian leader, Sir Ahmadu Bello, that "while recognizing the tribal affiliation of our constituencies, we should still always find a point of agreement in order to build a unified and great nation" has no meaning for this group of Ibos since they insist that the only way for the Ibo man to be properly forgiven for fighting the Biafran War and be fully reintegrated into the mainstream of the Nigerian society, economy and politics is to tear off his very Ibo heart, soul and culture and replace them with those of Hausa or Yoruba, if not English, and then proclaim loudest the universalism of the Ibo race hidden within a common national pool without any tribal affiliation, forgetting that there can still be national unity in cultural diversity.

On coming into contact with the Negro 'sky beings', with their claim of former coexistence with God in the sky but now in the worship of a swarm of nature deities or gods - gods of wood, iron, stone, etc., which the Almighty God of Israel warned His people not to have anything to do with, the exiled Nigerian Hebrews (Ibos) must have developed terrible fears, very anxious mind, despairing heart and felt very uncomfortable to live with the idolatrous Negro 'sky beings' or aborigines of Ibo Land. However, with passage of time, many Hebrews (Ibos) joined the idolatrous Negro 'sky beings' in worshipping these other gods as described by Afigbo, consciously or unconsciously dedicating themselves to the various man-made gods, and abandoning monotheism, the Judaic religion and tradition that are at the very soul of their Hebraism. To those exiled Nigerian Hebrews (Ibos) who held their heads while many others were losing theirs, these idolatrous people in Afigbo's narrative can at best be seen as an allusion of the people of whom the LORD Almighty God of Israel made the following derogatory mention in His course to the Hebrew parents in ancient Israel:

Then the LORD will scatter you among all nations, from one end of the earth to the other. There you will
worship other gods - gods of wood and stone, which neither you nor your fathers have known There the LORD will give you an anxious mind, eyes weary with longing, and a despairing heart...(Deuteronomy 28:64-65).

That the Negroes, their experience and their gods have been mentioned in this wise in Afigbo's narrative poses the challenge of fuller appreciation by the readers of this book of God's words in the Holy Scriptures of Israel, the Torah and the Bible. And behold His words can't change.

The challenge that the narrative pose for the author of this book is more emphasis on the fact that the Nigerian Hebrews (Ibos) migrated from Israel into Nigeria to live with and get assimilated into the culture of a group of Negroes who according to their mythology and religious belief fell from the sky and migrated into Southern Nigeria some 6000 years ago (Afigbo, 2001) - a story that all Jews in Judaism and Christianity alike will regard as an anti-scriptural African legendary of wild guess. Such a story is a serious antithesis to the Holy Scriptures of Israel, the Torah and the Bible. To ignore these Holy Scriptures is to ignore or even ignore God, the source, the origin and the fountainhead of all lives on earth. Furthermore, there is the need to clarify the fact that Igbo language which is the language of these legendary Negro 'sky beings' has been enriched by some words and names, like Ivite (Ivrit), Eri, Asa, Nebo, Nara, Uzzi, Ono, etc. (see the Table in Chapter Nine), which the exiled Nigerian Hebrews (Ibos) brought with them from Israel some three thousand years ago; and finally the need to further examine the Nigerian Hebrew (Ibo) case in the context of the World Jewry.

General C. Odumegwu Ojukwu
Former Biafran Head of State.

CHAPTER EIGHT

THE IBOS AND WORLD JEWRY; SAME PEOPLE, SAME DESTINY - THE UNTOLD STORY

There is more than Iboman's sense in his extraordinary quick recovery socially, politically and economically after the Biafran War or war of genocide against them between 1967 and 1970, and after each unprovoked attack on them, particularly from their neighbours in the Muslim North or Arab descents' dominated northern part of Nigeria. The history of the Ibos in Nigeria can be said to be a replica of that of the Jews in the Middle East (Alaezi, 1999).

Just as the world news constantly focuses the spotlight on the wanton destruction, animosities, violence and bloodshed that repeatedly erupt in the Middle East between the Israelites, the World Hebrews, and the Arabs, so also does the Nigerian national news repeatedly report the animosities, violence, bloodshed or wanton destruction of the lives and property of the Igbos, the proclaimed Nigerian Hebrews (Heebos or Ibos) in the Fulani/Hausa, the Arab descents' dominated parts of Northern Nigeria at the slightest excuse.

The sorry tale of the Nigerian Hebrews (Ibos) or the Ibos of Nigeria after their forced departure from Israel as revealed in the first edition of this book is in no way different from that of any other World Hebrews in Middle East, Israel, Europe, America, Russia or elsewhere in the universe. A close look at the history of the World Jews and the Nigerian Jews will reveal that the experiences of the World Jews in the hands of the Romans during the Roman Empire are replicated for the Nigerian Jews, the Ibos, during the slave trade era and to an extent in the British Colonial Nigeria. The story of these two sets of Jewish people in two different parts of the World can be summarized in the words of the prophecy of Daniel 11:40-45 confirmed by that of Ezekiel regarding how the power from the North (North of Nigeria, a land of exile for some Jews) or North of Israel in the homeland, Middle East, will at one time attack the people of God, Israel, for utter destruction.

One striking thing about the prophecies of the ancient prophets of Israel concerning the Jews is that they often have more than one occurrence and fulfillment albeit at different times and places but for the same group of people at home or in the Diaspora, in the same manner at different times, but at the same period in history. What a generation of exiled Hebrews in Europe experienced was in the same way repeated in the early and late 19th century for their counterparts in Africa and particularly in Nigeria. For instance, in Eastern Europe, Russia to be precise, the advent of the Jewish Pale of settlement can be seen as a repeat of the relocation of the exiled Nigerian Hebrews from Chad Basin area to their present settlement area in Eastern Nigeria. Although the Jews settled in Russia in the Crimea area as far back as the first century, the boundaries of the Pale were established only in 1804 as the only place in Russia where Jews could reside.

In the Nigerian case, although the Nigerian Jews or Nigerian Hebrews (Ibos) settled in Nigeria as far back as the first century or earlier than that (see Alaezi, 1999: Chapter 3) their discovery as a Jewish people by Dr. Basden of the Anglican Mission and the subsequent discriminatory treatment against them by the British Colonial authorities was only in 1846. The dates 1804 and 1846 are just within the same period in history. On discovering the Ibos in Onitsha areas in the present Anambra State, Dr. Basden, after sufficiently observing the people and their culture, was quick to conclude that the "Ibos are a branch of the Hebrews" (Basden 1938; Alaezi 1999).

The unique and uncompromising Jewishness of the Jews wherever they find themselves, their very Jewish mentality, is the most important factor that has kept them victorious over all the odds against them over the ages. The British colonial masters, who knew that the Ibos are Jews and have, for some other reasons stated earlier, came to regard them as stumbling block to their colonial adventurism and expansionism, have a good idea of the power of Jewish mentality. And so, in order to destroy the Jewish mentality of the Ibos, British colonial historians who were to come up with the history books on Nigeria were well instructed in the fable that the Ibos were part of the Bantu race who have their origin in Africa. Traces of Judaism among the Ibos by way of first fruit (new yam festivals, observance of traditional method of circumcision on the eighth day of birth of the male child and other new birth rites, new moon and burial rites, traditional marriage ceremonies, sharing of family inheritance, naming ceremony, avoidance of unclean animals and birds.

In the same way as the Jews did in Europe, were branded devilish, barbaric, uncivilized, unlawful or simply paganism or part of unholy rituals.

The ignorant peasantry in Hausa and Yoruba land was brainwashed to believe that the Ibos are barbaric and cannibals who also eat unclean animals and birds such as vultures. With such hideous campaign against the Ibos, the Hausa-Fulanis of Arab descent, who hitherto were looking at the Ibos as their brothers dropped their cloak of neutrality so that they could share in the coming spoils.

It is believed that the Arabs who came to Northern Nigeria centuries before the arrival of the British had some kind of friendly or rather brotherly relationship with the Ibos after their initial unsuccessful attempts to conquer and rule them (the Ibos). The Fulani led a jihad against the Hausa of Northern Nigeria because the Fulani leader, Usman dan Fodio, held that the Hausa had lapsed into paganism. The same was said of some parts of Yoruba of Western Nigeria. But in the case of Ibo land, the fact is different and includes some untold stories, which form part of the main object of this book.

The first untold story here has to do with the Ibo resistance of the Fulani invasion and the consequent freedom of the Heebo or Ibo (Hebrew) nation of Nigeria from Islamic conquest and denomination. Actually, the Fulani Arab invaders attacked the Ibos "fifteen times", according to Ekwulugo, and each time they (the Fulanis) suffered defeat in the hands of the Ibos. By virtue of the superior skill that the Ibos brought with them from the Middle East, they (the Ibos) were well able to perform this feat. They had, unlike the other primitive tribes of Nigeria, local craftsmen in the Awka and Abala regions of Ibo land who could fabricate "den" guns as well as men of great valor like the Eri medicine men and the magic warriors of Item, Abam and Ohafia who were also equipped with potential talisman of "gods of wood and iron" which they craftily used against the invading Arabs that were armed with bows and arrows, and seated on horse backs. Besides, the invading Arabs had earlier seen in the Ibos or Heebos, what Basden had just seen, some centuries after; namely: the spirit of the Jews and the practice of Judaism, the religion of the Jews, among the Ibos, and so thought it wise to rationalize surrender instead. Along this line of thought, the Fulani Arabs that had now conquered virtually the whole of Northern Nigeria and parts of Yoruba Land, particularly the Northern part of Yoruba Land, soon remembered that Abraham was the father of the Arabs as well as of the Jews. From Ishmael the cast-out son of Hagar,

the maidservant of Sarah or the Egyptian born wife of Abraham, came the seed of the Arabs. They knew that Moses, the Jews' great prophet and lawgiver, was also considered as chief prophet of the Koran. Even many of the great rabbis, including Jesus Christ, were looked upon as holy men in Islam. Again the Jews, in a bid to fight the early Christians, had been a potent factor behind the rise of Islam. Therefore, with all these vain attempts at subjugation and reassuring thoughts of brotherhood from the Middle East, since the Ibos had been identified as a branch of Israel in Nigeria, the Fulani Arabs soon abandoned the idea of subduing the Ibos and left them alone. Or, at least, they decided to henceforth approach the Ibos and the Ibo case with caution. And so, during those periods when the Hausas and Yorubas were being subdued by the Fulani Arabs, all those of Ibo descent in the Middle Belt (e.g., the Nok culture areas) and Eastern Nigeria knew times of peace and prosperity. And so the Ibos and the entire Ibo nation of Nigeria remained immune from Islamic contagion. And, in the words of Ojukwu (1967), the Ibos "came to stand out as a non-Muslim island in a raging Islamic sea."

One logical question here may be: 'How come that Abraham was the father of the Jews and the Arabs but the covenant blessings went to the Jews alone, and not to the Arabs and the other nations of the world, not until the time of John the Baptist when the "Kingdom of God suffered violence" and the real repentant, the true worshippers of God from the Gentiles, other nations of the world outside Israel, were allowed to be partakers in the salvation of Israel, though with the proviso that "Salvation is of the Jew first, and then the Gentile" (Romans 1:16).

The answer is simple. Abraham the father of Isaac and grandfather of Jacob (or Israel) was called out of Ur of the Chaldees in Mesopotamia, the present day Iraq (an Arab nation) where idol worshipping was and still is the rule rather than the exception. It was only Abraham and his family that worshipped God Almighty in truth and in spirit, without reference to another smaller god of any type or form. In fact, all nations of the world then were classified as being ungodly. They were idol worshippers until the call and separation of Abraham because of his proven righteousness - a separation that brought about the nickname 'Ibrit' for Abraham, pronounced as 'Ivrit' meaning a wanderer. On the other hand, the name 'Gentiles' was reserved for the people of the other nations of the earth (Deut.26: 5; Joshua 24:2; Ezek. 11:3). It will be recalled that it was the ungodliness of the nations of the earth, before "Noah found grace in the

eyes of the LORD" and before the separation of Abraham and his family that made God to regret ever creating man.

And GOD saw that the wickedness of man was great in the earth, and that every imagination of the thoughts of his heart was only evil (ungodly)

72

continually. And it repented the LORD that he had made man on the earth, and it grieved him at his heart. And the LORD said, I will destroy man whom I have created from the face of the earth... (Genesis 6:6-7).

But being God of mercy, He later decided to use Abraham as His instrument of bringing man (those who believe and do His will) back to Himself. Ever before the demonstration of God's love to Abraham, the pronouncement of the covenant blessings of Abraham from the Almighty, He set standards for Abraham to follow and Abraham diligently obeyed. Part of God's standards for Abraham was the sacrificing or dedication of first fruit to God. Refer to the story of Abraham and his first son Isaac whom God ordered to be used as a sacrifice to Him, as a test of Abraham's faithfulness (Genesis; Leviticus 23:15-21). Abraham faithfully kept this God's standard of first fruit sacrifice and so God blessed him and his descendants, that is, the descendants of the covenant child, Isaac, not Ishmael, the father of the Arabs, the son born for Abraham by the maidservant of his wife. Isaac's own son of covenant was Jacob, not Esau, and so the covenant blessings of Abraham and Isaac went to Jacob and his twelve children who later became the twelve tribes of Israel, not to Esau and his children, the present day Palestinians. Consider this from the Scriptures.

Two nations are in your womb, and two peoples from within you will be separated; one people will be stronger than the other, and the older (i.e., Esau) will serve the younger (i.e., Jacob) (Genesis 25:23).

The Ibo case in Nigeria is not different from that of their counterpart Jewish Pale in Russia. The establishment of the Jewish Pale was one notable event in the history of general discrimination against the Jews all over the world. In 1827 Jews were driven ruthlessly from the smaller villages in Russia into already overcrowded Jewish quarters in the larger cities. With the Czars fully in power, there were frequent wild mobs of Cossacks and peasants and students who all screamed for Jewish blood. As the Nigerian Jews (the Ibos), in the British colonial era were falsely accused of witchcraft and cannibalism to whip up sentiment against them for possible destruction, so also were the Russian Jews treated in Czarist Russia. The ignorant Russian peasantry was made to believe that "Jews

were magicians and witches who used Christian blood for their rituals". This actually gave rise to a series pogroms - anti-Jewish riots and expulsion of Jews from Russia. Pogroms and anti-Igbo riots based on such false allegations have been the same steady portion of the Nigerian Hebrews (Ibos) in Nigeria, leading to their expulsion at one time in 1966 from all other parts of the country and thereafter the Biafran War or war of genocide against the Ibos, and after and often times from certain other parts of the Hausa-Fulani (Arab) dominated Northern Nigeria such as Yola, Kaduna, Bauchi, Kano and Sokoto, to mention the best known examples of the persecutions and Ibos: Hebrew Exiles from Israel.

The Nigerian Hebrews (Ibos) as well as the World Hebrews are good metaphors of scapegoat syndrome in Nigeria and in the world at large. They are blamed and made to suffer the consequences of any major mishap in their place of dwelling even when they are not directly involved. In Poland and Russia for instance, incidences of inflation or any other type of socio-economic malaise were often attributed to the action of the Jews and thereafter they (the Jews) were singled out for attack and destruction of their lives and property.

Most of the attacks on the Ibos in the past and recent years have always been attributed to events for which the Ibos cannot be reasonably held responsible. For instance, the Bauchi massacre of the Ibos in 1987 started with a fight between a Bauchi indigene of Christian faith and his counterpart Muslim faithful over the selling of pork meat near the Muslim's meat stand in the open market. The fight spread to the city of Bauchi and in a twinkling of an eye the only victims of the small fight that began in the small town of Tafawa Balewa spread to nearby big city of Bauchi and environs where Igbos live. They were attacked and killed and their property plundered without mercy.

A year or so before in Yola, a fight between two different Muslim sects in the town had finally ended up with the indiscriminate looting of Ibo people's goods and property and the killing of their men, women and children. The same could be said of the killing of the Ibos in the other parts of Northern Nigeria and some other parts of Nigeria in recent years. Even some popular demonstrations in non-Ibo regions of Nigeria could end up and had, at times, actually ended up with the looting of Ibo people's property, and everybody is aware of this. Such is no longer news in Nigeria. For instance, quite recently in 1999, civil servants in Lokoja, Kogi State, went on strike to protest the Government's inability, to pay the

N3,000 minimum wage approved by Abdusalmi Abubakar's military regime. During the protest match, knowing very well that neither Abubakar nor his advisers were Ibos, "the demonstrators suddenly began shouting 'Igbo ole! Igbo ole!' meaning the Ibos are thieves, and then attacked and left hundreds of Ibo shops massively looted (Daily Champion 27/4/99 P. 5}.

In the neighboring African countries outside the shores of Nigeria, where the Ibos reside, the same fate very much awaits them there. The Ibos resident in the neighboring countries of Africa outside Nigeria have the same sorry story of scapegoatism to narrate about themselves. In 1996-7 during the peak of the Bakassi Peninsula problem between Nigeria and Cameroon, the Ibos in Cameroon were singled out among other Nigerians living in that country for attack; they were not only accused of supporting their motherland in the struggle that ensued but were, worst of all, falsely and maliciously accused of being responsible for "the disappearance of the male reproductive organs (penis) of certain victims that came across their way". For this, they (the Ibos) were hunted, brutalized and driven away over a crime they were later found not to be guilty of. In far away Sierra Leon and Liberia, after the agonizing civil wars in these countries - a situation in which Nigeria was said to be somehow involved - the Ibos in that country were particularly punished for the sin of their "father Land", Nigeria.

Again, in Charles Taylor's Liberia, for instance, the Ibos there, after being physically punished in various manners, were herded into refugee ships, deprived of all their possessions, back to Nigeria to begin life all over again. In these entire instances, the Ibos are clearly made the scapegoats, the guilt or sin-bearers for others just as in the case of their counterpart World Hebrews.

The latest development in the anti-Ibo sentiments of northern Nigerians of Arab descent is understandable yet it can be said to be a good case of scapegoat syndrome against the Ibos of Nigeria. Between 12th and 13th October 2001, Kano, the largest Muslim city in Nigeria was thrown into chaos as hundreds of Islamic fundamentalists took to the streets to protest the on-going US led strikes on Afghanistan. According to Sunday Champion newspaper, October 14, 2001 page 1, 3, "the protesters, who chanted anti-Bush slogans, overran the streets" burnt American flags and called on the US to stop running after Osama bin Laden, the principal suspect in the September 11 terrorist attacks on New York and

Washington DC. It had earlier been reported in all Nigerian dailies that Muslim youths in Zamfara and Kano States were publicly jubilating over the September 11 terrorist attack on the two American cities. They claimed it was an act of Allah against America and Israel for their anti-Muslim policies. When, later after the bin Laden's mayhem had died down, Israel had to invade some Palestinian territories for some obvious reasons of territorial safety, about 5000 Kano Muslims had to stage yet

75

another rally to protest Israel's invasion. "The protesters burnt an Israeli flag amidst the same shouts of 'Allahu Akbar' (God is great)" that usher in every previous anti-Ibo demonstrations and subsequent attacks by the Northern Nigerian Muslims.They also shouted "death to Israel" and condemned theUnited States of America (This Day April 8, 2002, page 1).

The northern Nigerian Muslims as the other groups in Nigeria seem to firmly believe that the Ibos are Jews and by extension of this belief, they (the Ibos) were ruthlessly joined in the "suit" against America and Israel in the bin Laden's show and the mayhem, with the looting or burning of their (the Ibos) shops and a call for death penalty for Israel and all its allies. Indeed, as the Kano Muslims boiled for Osama bin Laden, "property (of the Ibos) worth millions of naira had been destroyed or looted, scores (of people) injured with over 100 dead and yet the city was still counting its losses." (Saturday Punch, October 20, 2001, page 3).

This time around there was a serious face-up between the Ibo youths (apparently in support of Israel and America and/or in defense of their property) and the rioting Muslim youths shouting anti-Jewish and anti-American slogans in support of Osama bin Laden and the Muslim world. If the damage done to the Ibos in Kano this last time is added to that so recorded in the cities of northern Nigeria with heavy Hausa-Fulani/Arab descent presence - Yola, Bauchi, Kano, Kaduna, Jos, there would be enough wreckages from Ibo possessions to cover the whole of Lagos and Abuja. Yet there are no signs of serious concern on the part of the Nigerian Federal government for the plight of the Ibos in Nigeria, except for some few bemused headshakes and sighs among certain concerned citizens of the country.

The Ibos, as usual, this time through the mouth of the Deputy Secretary-General of the Ohaneze cried out against the injustice against them saying, "We are watching. We want to see how Mr. President deals with this ugly situation especially as we can't find a linkage between what is happening between America and Afghanistan that directly concerned Ndigbo (the Ibos). We shall need full explanation on the sins the Igbos have committed in this conflict (US vs. Afghanistan)" (Saturday Punch, October 20, 2001 page 2)

The Ibos, like the Ohanaeze scribe, who asked questions that hinged on the Ibo scapegoat victim syndrome in Nigeria and hope for solution may wish to recall that each time the Ibo lives and property are lost in similar unprovoked attack against them in Northern Nigeria in the past, the governors of such states would pretend to be annoyed at what happened and then promise to "deal decisively with all those behind the acts of violence… Every person in Nigerian knows that such governors are merely play-acting or playing politics of deceit and hypocrisy as nothing ever happened after.

In one Nigerian Newspaper story, Boniface Egboke (2001) laments, "Any time the Hausa-Fulani goes on his religious riot or the OPC wants to demonstrate their unholy behavior, these senseless individuals go after the Igbo, their shops and wares to maim, kill and loot! Many a time, they got away with these crimes against the Igbo. People know that our people import their products in large containers to clear them at Lagos or Port Harcourt. You only have to ask these importers to hear their sordid stories and severe manhandling meted out to them by officials before they can clear their goods from the wharves! Sometimes, the acts are programed to cheat and hurt the Igbo. Since the end of the Nigeria-Biafra war, the Igbo are still being punished for their genuine resistance to injustice and deprivation. Sometimes, our plights are made worse by our own people, the Igbo, who delight in playing the roles of sycophants and traitors to the Igbo course.

"The Igbo environment does go beyond our shores and borders to include all our sons and daughters in parts of the United States, Europe, Asia, Russia, South America, etc…(and like the other Jews in the Diaspora, very many). As at now, the Igbo are losing their cultural strength and drive as a people. We must look back to history and archaeology to find our bearing once more. We have variously and shamelessly swallowed all sorts of damaging cultures and religions that are now wiping out the great culture of our forefathers. The Igbo now dress like Yorubas or Hausas. The sad effect is that we are gradually becoming a no-people." ("Ohanaeze-Ndigbo and their debased environment" Daily Champion, Tuesday, September 11, 2001, page 6.).

I know the Ibos of Nigeria have taken this situation for too long, but I don't know if the future generation of the Ibos will continue to take the situation as the Almighty's divine will for them and so continue to suffer in silence like the present Ibos of Nigeria.

I often tell myself that the circle of the Almighty's curse on the Jews for disobeying Him was complete during the 2nd World War and that after that His (God's) anger subsided and the promise of forgiveness and restoration as predicted in the Scriptures was now to follow not only in the Jewish homeland, Israel, but in all parts of the nations of the world where the Jews are located even before their final gathering back to Israel.

The untold story about the Jewish sufferings during the holocaust of the Second World War can be read in the Biafran War or War of Genocide

(1967-70) against Nigerian Hebrews (Ibos). The experiences of the Nigerian Hebrews (Ibos) during the Biafran War may serve as a very good supplement to or a replica of the story of the Jews during the Second World War. Soon after the January 15 military coup in Nigeria which was mischievously branded an Ibo coup by the BBC, the British Broadcasting Corporation, London, there followed the genocide in which 50,000 Ibos were slaughtered in cold blood all over Nigeria and nobody asked questions, nobody showed regret, nobody showed remorse. And so Nigeria was suddenly turned into a jungle with no safety, no justice and no hope for the Ibos. Therefore, they (the Ibos) decided to found a new place, the state of Biafra for themselves, "a human habitation away from the Nigerian jungle" (Ojukwu, 1967). That was the origin of Biafra and the war of genocide that greeted the declaration of the independent state of Biafra by Ojukwu. And between July 6, 1967 and January 1970, during the Nigerian-Biafra War proper, hundreds of Ibos were killed daily through shelling, bombing, strafing and starvation advised, organized and supervised by a certain foreign power. In the end, over 700,000 Ibos perished in the war. Some reports say three million Ibos perished in the war. They were brutally murdered, their corpses dumped in mass graves and their property pillaged. Children and mothers saw their beloved husbands taken away in a most agonizing manner never to be seen again. Men saw their wives and daughters raped sometimes in their presence, and fetus gouged out of Ibo pregnant women. Ibo men, women and children were roasted alive or buried alive in the spirit of 'Operation Keep Nigeria One'. Here and there Ibo bodies were splashed with petrol and set ablaze, and so on (see Nwankwo, 1999).

Inside the Biafran enclave, fine concerts and groups such as Sony Oti group gave weekly concerts to the soldiers and some privileged civilians. Very few schools ran on irregular schedules. Biafran Radio was the only source of news and Biafran money became a legal means of exchange. Outside the Biafran military zones, civilians particularly in the evenings, when the risk of conscription into the Biafran Army was less gathered to argue and talk about the war. They argued about the many Biafran enemies and the saboteurs, that is the other Ibos who felt it better to support the Federal troops either for money or for food, and the foreign countries that failed to see the Biafran side of the matter or armed Nigeria to annihilate Biafra because they wanted the Nigerian oil.
Similarly, during the Second World War, while the Jews inside the ghetto (like the Ibos inside the Biafran enclave) had arguments as their great

pastime, inside the war zones, before entering into the German gas chamber for "final solution", the Jewish victims were tortured in the same manner as the Ibos during the Biafran war; they were driven insane, beaten and degraded, and every known atrocity conceived by man was committed against them.

Reporting the incidence of the said Biafran War in the Readers Digest of April 1969, David Reed, a British journalist, had this to say:

"For the second time in this century, the world is witnessing the destruction of a people. The first time, the victims were the Jews of Europe. This time, the victims are mostly Ibos (the Jews of Nigeria), members of a remarkable and progressive African tribe.

The industrious Ibos have boundless ambition and an avid passion for education. In just half a century, they have produced astonishing numbers of doctors, lawyers, scientists, engineers, clergymen and wealthy businessmen. Ibo country was a land of pride and near plenty... Now Ibo land - Biafra - is like a nightmare. At St. Mary's Mission in Obowo, we watched as 50 children were selected from among 90 every bad kwashiorkor (a protein-deficiency disease) cases to be flown to nearby Gabon. Hysterical mothers fought to have their children selected. Guards beat them back with switches...

At the root of Biafra's ordeal is now almost forgotten conference of European powers held in Berlin in 1884 and 1885. There, Africa was divided up, the chuck that became known as Nigeria going eventually to Britain. The British tried to make one country out of it - a policy that made sense economically - but Nigeria was dynamite from the start. Some 250 quarrelling tribal and linguistic groups were penned into the politically absurd boundaries.

Among the welter of tribes, three predominated. The northern part of Nigeria was peopled with Hausas, who had adopted an Islamic civilization from contacts with the Arabs. The south was divided between the Yorubas in the west and the Ibos in the eastern Nigeria. While the north stagnated as a medieval Muslim society, the southerners benefited from mission education and forged ahead.

Enterprising Ibos soon swarmed out of their homeland in search of new economic opportunities. Two million settled in the Hausa north. They got better jobs and soon dominated the small businesses. The Hausas finding economic control passing into Ibo hands, burned with tribal hatred the dynamite was finally detonated in 1966 after two rulers were murdered in successive military coup d'etat.

Then on May 29, 1966, mobs of Hausas attacked Ibos in the northern cities with guns, broken bottles, knives and bows and arrows. The pogrom continued for months. No one will ever know how many Ibos were slain - one estimate is 30,000. When it was over, nearly all the Ibos left alive had returned to their home area, penniless.

The Ibo-dominated eastern region proclaimed its independence on May 30, 1967, as the Republic of Biafra. Here was the most promising new nation in Black Africa. It had the largest pool of skilled manpower, vast oil fields, and nascent industries. With 14 million people, it was Black Africa's fourth most populous country. Its new head of state was 33-year-old Lieutenant Colonel Chukwuemeka Odumegwu Ojukwu, a career army officer with an Oxford degree in modern history...

When the fighting started... the Biafrans were fighting in defence of their homeland. In a daring thrust, they came within 135 miles of Nigeria's capital city of Lagos.

Meanwhile, in what rates as one of the finest humanitarian efforts of recent times, Catholic and Protestant churches, Jewish and non-sectarian groups supported the humanitarian relief operations.

Yet the tragedy and horror are always there. People roam the streets abjectly begging for food. And at times death suddenly comes screaming down from the sky. We underwent two air raids in one day. Coming in at rooftop level, two Migs fired rockets, cannons and machine-guns at the hospitals, crowded market places and churches. They left behind 20 dead and nearly 200 wounded...

Dotted around Biafra are some 700-refugee camps where the people of Africa's most industrious and educated tribe now live in the ultimate degradation.

The Biafrans vow that they will die fighting, or from starvation, rather than surrender... The Biafrans were helped by the French and Portuguese to acquire arms. Four countries all African, recognised the Biafran independence; while the rest of the world considered Lagos the "legitimate" government of Nigeria. The argument is that if Biafra succeeds in breaking away, it will encourage a disastrous "Balkanization" of other African countries..." (Reed. "Must Biafra Die?" Readers Digest April 1969 pp. 157-162).

Actually those who lived through the said Biafran war would be quick to point out that Reed's narration is a fair but a very big understatement of the war situation in terms human suffering and man's inhumanity to man. For instance, in the Ibo areas outside the Biafran enclave or rather in the

Nigerian Federal troops' held areas such as Asaba (Delta State) or Enugu or Nsukka areas of Biafra, the Ibos were routinely rounded up, taken to isolated areas and forced to dig their own grave, before being killed and dumped into such graves. And so the Heebo (Hebrew) nation in Nigeria was caused to exist without a future, and their lives were made bitter in hard bondage as exactly as it was for the world Jews just before and during the Second World War. The Ibo nation became a theatre of man's greatest inhumanity to man, of mass slaughter and most indecent mass burial and indecent abandonment of dead bodies of innocent children, women and men so that as predicted in the holy Scriptures of Israel, "their (the Jews') carcasses will become food for all the birds of the air and the beasts of the earth and there will be no one to frighten them away" (Deuteronomy 28:26). As soon as the Biafran war ended, the Biafran pound, the Biafran legal tender, was understandably declared illegal. In a deal of a well planned economic "coup d'etat" against the Ibos who had just come out from a most bloody war, all those in possession of the Biafran pound were advised "in their own interest" or rather ordered to go to certain Federal Military Government's designated areas in the Biafran (Ibo) enclave and deposit whatever amount of money they had for exchange for the Nigerian currency. All the Ibos who survived the war trooped out in their millions to these "Nigerian banks" and deposited their money in tens, hundreds, thousands and millions, with duly issued receipts for their deposits. The very old and the sick who could trek to the designated places gave out all thee money they had to their more able friends and relations to deposit for them in the hope of an equitable exchange in the end. And, to the utter disbelief and rude shock that sent many of the few surviving rich Ibos to their untimely death, the exchange rate, announced after it was certain that every Ibo had deposited the last penny in his possession, was twenty Nigerian pounds or forty naira irrespective of whatever amount of Biafran pound deposited; twenty pounds for one million Biafran pounds and the same twenty pounds for ordinary one Biafran pound deposit - a wicked and most cruel flat rate that impoverished all Ibos at a time when there was surplus oil money in the country, when there was too much money in the country and many Nigerians, especially in Yorubaland became millionaires, could buy or build industries of their own without even going for a bank loan. At a well calculated time, the Nigerian Military Government at the center passed a decree for the indigenisation of all foreign industries and called on all Nigerians who had money to buy shares in these industries. Twenty pounds or forty naira in the hand of a man who had just come out from a most dehumanising war with his family was not enough at all to meet his most basic needs of food, shelter and clothing, not to talk of buying shares. And here lies the root of the current quest for or habit among many Ibos to meet up financially, sometimes in an indecent haste so as to be like the other Nigerians. Having been dispossessed of his money and property, the only thing left for the Ibo man was to remain afloat through education. And when the Nigerian Military government realized this, it quickly introduced the quota system to checkmate another Ibo incursion into the country's educational sector, and distance the Ibos from power and decision-making in Nigeria. The Ibo youth who, by share grace of God, manages to scale through the difficult hurdles of the country's quota system and gain admission into the tertiary institution soon discovers that on graduation, he has no chance of getting employment or that his counterpart from the North or West who has an inferior degree or diploma or no degree at all has far better chances of getting employment before him, as most of the country's employment generating institutions built with oil money from his backyard are located in the West and in the North, not in the East, his homeland. And so in the face of the humiliating discriminations in finding white-collar jobs by the educated Ibo youths, those of them in the conventional school system dropped out and many of school age refused to attend school. Instead, they got into hazardous businesses of street trading, petty trading, etc.; they got into small, and in some few cases large-scale commerce and industry. Again the Nigerian government soon discovered this and littered the Ibo trade routes, particularly in the East with fierce-looking armed policemen at vindictive police check-points and customs officials who extort money at will from the Ibo traders, besides the multiple taxes levied upon them so as to render their commercial life "bitter with hard bondage". Yet the resilient Ibos continue to find their feet and are even making their impact felt not only in the economic life of the people of Nigeria, but also, as in the case of their World Hebrew counterparts, on the economic life of the world.

In fact, the Ibos and the World Hebrews in the theatre of war may be of different breed but they share so much in common - in misery, in endurance, in courage and determination to make the best out of life in the midst of odds. The style of and reasons for attacks on them by their neighbours are strikingly the same.

In the course of the war physical structures of the Ibos were destroyed and after the war their property in some parts of the country were seized and declared 'abandoned property', vividly reminding one of what the Head of Hitler's Gestapo, Heinrich Himmler said to his SS generals in October

1940 during his campaign of Genocide to exterminate the Jewish race at Pasha:

The extermination of the Jewish race... is one of those things it is easy to talk about... most of you must know what it means when 100 corpses are lying side by side, or 500, or 1000... I have issued a strict order that their wealth should be as a matter of course, taken from them and handed over to the Reich without reserve.

It may be correct to say that the same bad spirit that was permitted by the Almighty to dwell in Heinrich Himmer was also found in the Nigerian Military ruler who, in Rivers State of Nigeria after the Biafran war, branded Ibo buildings, lands, etc, "abandoned property", and ordered for their seizure and subsequent handover to "indigenes" of Rivers State "without reserve". These similarities are just overwhelming, and the events that brought them about are strikingly the same.

After the Biafran war, there was at least in principle, not in practice, the policy of "reconstruction, rehabilitation (relocation) and reintegration" of the Ibos, with Britain who openly helped Nigeria to prosecute the war against the Ibos coming to offer help in the rehabilitation of the displaced Ibos, the Nigerian Jews. It is most note worthy that Britain also played a very significant role in the establishment of the state of Israel after the Second World War, after the same Britain, with its concentration camps, had helped to prosecute the war of Genocide against the World Jews. But whereas the rehabilitation and relocation of the Ibos were limited to Ibo homeland in Eastern Nigeria and other places within the same country, that of their counterpart World Jews after the First and Second World Wars were considered outside the Israeli homeland.

The untold story here is about possible and impossible suggestions of possible new locations of Israel including that of an Israeli boy of 18 years in a black restaurant in Tel Aviv, though quite recently in 1997, over fifty years after the Second World War. "Shortly before 1947 when the state of Israel was recognized by the United Nation and given its independence". Cheche had told his audience in a book launch in Aba, Abia State Nigeria, "there was, a wide debate as to the desirability of relocating Israel from its present location to any other part of the World to avoid further World conflicts. Suggestions were made as to where it would be located. Africa was one of the prime choices. Some suggested Seychelles - a cluster of Oceanic Islands after South Africa. Majority suggested somewhere in Uganda. In 1997, a young Jewish boy of 18 years in a black restaurant in Tel Aviv, looking back at the events of the past in the location of the new state of Israel after its recognition by the United Nation, put a joke across and said, 'these Europeans who control the U.N. think they are smart. They should have given us oil rich Eastern Nigeria instead of dry Uganda or lonely Island of Seychelles instead of this desert where we are now. If they did, we would have conquered the World. " Can this be a joke, a wishful thinking or a divinely inspired statement or an utterance of a divine plan for two people of the same breed, root and destiny in two different distant lands of the earth. Your guess is as good as mine. Cheche the brilliant young Ibo lawyer who had spent quite sometime on pilgrimage to Israel and had lived and worked in Tel Aviv went further to narrate the story of an Ibo migrant who dared the Israeli government in court over his claim of Jewish origin. "In Tel Aviv, Israel", Cheche's story continued, "there is a man from Mbaise, Imo State Nigeria, called Chima, popularly called Rabbi Chima amongst Nigerians living in Israel. He is known to have migrated to Europe - Italy to be precise - before the Biafran war in search of the Golden Fleece. In Italy, he became involved in the religion of Judaism i.e., religion practiced by the Jews - (see Chapter 4 of Alaezi's book, Ibos: Hebrew Exiles from Israel... for a clear purview of this religion). In the course of this movement, he found out and was ultimately advised that the aims of the movement i.e., to establish that Ibos are Jews could be better pursued in Israel. He decided to leave Italy for Jerusalem. This he ultimately did abandoning albeit temporarily his wife and children. In Israel he continued and made out a strong case that gave him audience with the members of the KNESSET (Israeli Parliament) and a committee, was set up by the KNESSET. He had gone through all the hierarchies of the courts in Israel trying to establish a claim for us (the Ibos). As at 1998, the case was stuck at the Supreme Court of Israel. It is not easy to reach decision in such cases. It is one of the passivist instances where a court exhibits a passivist posture in the determination of conflicts between individuals or persons in law simply because the State policy is questioned. The Supreme Court will not give a decision that will lead to an influx of colored Jews especially in the wake of the conflict between orthodox Jews and non-orthodox Jews consequent upon a similar decision of the KNESSET to all Jews from the U.S.A., Asia, Russia and Australia. On the other hand, it will not also give a decision that will have the effect of debarring their brothers in distant land from entering Israel if ultimately their claim is sustained. Thus the stalemate." (Cheche, 2000).

This claim by Ibo activists like Rabbi Chima and the knowledge that there are some lost tribes in distant parts of the world yet to be discovered and integrated into the World Jewry are so strong that the government of Israel, at least in principle, appears to have allowed some Jewish individuals and groups such as the King Solomon Shepherdic Organisation and the World Hebrew Organisation led by Professor Muse Tetegne to travel to Nigeria for fact finding (see Alaezi, 1999) and air their views publicly.

Earlier in 1903, following the efforts of Zionism when an attempt was made to settle the Jews, the British came forth with a proposal. They offered the African territory of Uganda to the Zionists for Jewish colonization - an offer that would have made Israel one of the colonial masters of the period. But "the Zionist rejected the offer on the grounds that they could not find Uganda in the Bible" (Leon Uris. 1958: 223). How I wish that Eastern Nigeria were mentioned then, as did the Jewish boy in the black restaurant in Tel Aviv. The Zionists could have found hundreds of Jewish names of persons and towns including similar cultures in the Ibo homeland of Eastern Nigeria, more than enough Biblical evidence to make people believe that the Ibo homeland is another Jewish homeland. Maybe this would have prevented the present Arab-Israeli conflicts, and other Jewish related problems in the Middle East. But God Almighty did not permit that apparently beautiful situation and solution to the Jewish problem then. For that would have meant making the Almighty God of Israel a liar. The Almighty cannot lie. His plans, though they may tarry in the eyes of man, cannot be faulted or changed. He had said:

I will bring you back my exiled people Israel... I will plant Israel in their own land, (not in Seychelles or Uganda or Eastern Nigeria or any other land outside Israel) never again to be uprooted from the land I have given them, says the Lord your God (Amos 9:14-15)

It pains me to recall all these striking and sometimes ugly similarities between the World Jews or World Hebrews and the Nigerian Hebrews (Ibos), but they helped to manifest the untold true story about the Jewish origin of the Ibos of Nigeria, and to show why they (the Ibos) behave the way they do and why they are so much hated by their neighbors. Why they are often repaid with "cruel oppression" even for their developmental efforts in favor of their country. Why others, the people that they "do not know... eat what their land and labor produce", and why the Ibos (the Nigerian Hebrews), are often made scapegoats, "an object of scorn and ridicule" by their neighbors or fellow citizens of Nigeria (refer to Deuteronomy 28 for details of this curse). And so for the Nigerian Hebrews as other Hebrews or Jews in exile all over the world such as the Yemenite Jews, the Russian Jews or Jewish Pale in Russia, the following prediction in Deuteronomy 28:15-68 has a special meaning:

And it shall come to pass, if you do not obey the LORD your God and do not carefully follow all His commands... all these curses will come upon you and overtake you: the LORD will scatter you among all nations, from one end of the earth to the other (from Israel to Yemen to Russia, to Poland, to Germany, to North Africa, to West Africa, to Eastern Nigeria, etc.). The LORD will drive you and the king you set over you to a nation unknown to your fathers. Among these nations you will find no peace, nor resting place for the sole of your foot. There... you will become a thing of horror and an object of scorn and ridicule... A people that you do not know will eat what your land and labor produce and you will have nothing but cruel oppression...

In the above regard, the Yemenite Jews are a better comparative example to cite. These Jews were rendered tragic figures as they were gathered out of Yemen after the Second World War en route back to Israel after 3000 years of exile in Yemen. "They were dressed in rags, filthy and half dead from starvation and thirst" (Uris, 1958). Whereas Dr. Basden of the Anglican Mission discovered the Ibos of Eastern Nigeria as "a branch of Hebrews" and described them as "tragic figures, filthy, naked and badly fed (Basden. 1938), the Yemenite Jews, on being discovered, were also described in like manner (Uris, 1958).

The Yemenite Jews lived a life of misery in what can best be described as unenviable simple homes in Yemen. And as for the said Ibos, they also lived in simple homes, in shelters of raffia palm or grass roof matting. They sewed skins or frond from raffia palm tree into clothing. On occasion, they painted the body of their young girls. They also painted their houses and punctuated the painting with strokes of white chalk that mimicked some ancient Hebrew writing on their walls, giving people evidence of the existence of some kind of ritual life of the ancient Hebrews. In fact, their wall paintings, artifacts and excavated materials particularly in the Igboukwu, Agulueri and Afikpo areas in later years after Basden's initial contact with them indicate that there might have been some kind of strong relationship between the Ibos and the Jews of the Old Testament Bible. Surely, in their paintings on the wall, their pure Jewish names, in their rituals in connection with marriage, birth and death, in the practice of circumcision like the Jews, and in the discovery of solid bronze star of King David from one of the excavations by the British colonial workers at Agulu which later informed the inscription of the star on the colonial British West African coin of farthing, half-a-penny and one penny, one gets the strong impression of a people who together with the

Yemenite Jews once lived in an ancient city of King David fully and actively but who had much in common with the primitive life style of the "original" indigenes of Nigeria - the Allokoo, Ituri, Kwa and Pygmy races. As the ancient Hebrews, the Ibos in the traditional Ibo society still practice multiple marriages. As the Jews, some

Ibos particularly in the old Bende areas of Abia and Ebonyi States, to the distaste and surprise of their neighbors, marry their cousins. They still practise the law of Moses regarding farming, leaving the land fallow for seven years before returning to it, not taking home all the crops in the farmland after harvest but leaving some for the less privileged creatures (man or animals) who may be in need, observing the festival of the first fruit in the form of new yam festival though adulterated with Allokoo or Kwa pagan rituals, practising circumcision on the eighth day and making offerings and feasts on that occasion, setting their slaves or servants free after seven years of service, and so on. Also with the Ibos (especially in the traditional Ibo society) as with the Jews, there is the tradition of "a kinsman-redeemer", a tradition whereby a close kinsman of a dead man could "acquire the dead man's widow, in other to maintain the name of the dead man with his property" (see Ruth in the Bible). Today, this "kinsman-redeemer" tradition is still being respected among certain Ibos, especially in Anambra and Imo Ibos areas, although it can only hold where the widow is willing to accept the kinsman-redeemer.

The Basden-discovered Ibos' belief in Mosaic laws, in Judaism or Jewish way of life (or Omenala Igbo) was absolutely literal. Dr. Basden asserted that anybody "who wishes to deal effectively with the Ibos should first go and acquaint himself with Mosaic Laws" (see Alaezi 1999). Like the exiled Yemenite Jews or Jewish Pale in Russia, the exiled Nigerian Hebrews (Ibos) had been subjected to the miseries of wars (tribal wars in Nigeria) and slavery (from the British/American slave masters). They, more than their Yemenite or Russian counterparts, had been the proper witness to the, Almighty's curse on the Jews regarding "iron yoke on the neck" in the land of exile as the children of the Ibos were carried away into slavery to America during the infamous slave trade "with iron yoke on their necks". For these Ibos the following curses were most fulfilled in the 1700s and 1800s:

The LORD will strike you with wasting disease, with fever and inflammation... You will have sons and daughters but you will not keep them, because they will go into captivity... Because you did not serve the LORD your God joyfully and gladly in the time of prosperity, therefore in hunger and thirst, in nakedness and dire poverty, you will serve the enemies the LORD sends against you. He will put an iron yoke on your neck... The LORD will send you back in ships to Egypt (to America in the case of Nigerian Hebrews) on a journey I said you should never make again. There you will offer yourselves, for sale to your enemies as male and female slaves... (Deut.: 28:15 -68).

In Alaezi (1999:51), there is a reported case of an Eboe (Ibo) female slave who offered herself for sale so as to be with her only son who had been separated from her and sold away to a certain slave master, saying: "Buy, me too, mas'r for de dear Lord's sake!' - Buy me - I shall die if you don't," thereby fulfilling words of God's curse in the above quotation, namely: "There you will offer yourselves for sale to enemies as male and female slaves".

Other ethnic groups in Nigeria ,reading this may be quick to point out that it is not only Ibos that were taken away into slavery by the British in Colonial Nigeria. This is true. But captain Adams' figure of "370,000 Ibo slaves sold in the Delta markets over a period of twenty years - equal to about one quarter of the total export from the African ports" - reveals the fact that the Ibos were the main target of the African slave trade (Hodgkin, 1975:49). 370,000 Ibo slaves sold over one period of 20 years equals 18,500 each year. And the slave trade lasted over a period of 400 years, bringing the minimum number of Ibo slaves sold out into slavery for the whole period of the slave trade to a barest minimum of 4 million. Dr. Basden's narrative of the Ibos was that they were in nakedness, filthy and in dire poverty when he discovered them. Yet as the Yemenite Jews in Yemen, the ancient Ibos still carried with them their Jewish culture and identity in the form of omenala Igbo until the coming of the white man, the British, who put "a knife into the things that held us together" as Okonkwo lamented in Achebe's Things Fall Apart.

The Jews of Yemen would have seen in the Jews of Nigeria (the Ibos) a replica of themselves in many respects. In physical appearance (though not in the color of the skin

for the harsh equatorial sun had darkened the Ibos, in season and out of season) and in spirit, the Yemenite Jews could have been mistaken for the Ibos. Both the Yemenite and the Nigerian Hebrews (Ibos) had left the land of Israel some 2500 years ago during one of the Babylonian conquests of Israel and settled in Egypt hundreds of years before the fall of the First Great Temple in Jerusalem before the one group went and settled in Yemen and the other went and settled in Eastern Nigeria. But the same unchangeable curse of God followed them in equal measures and over took them. However, it is to be noted here that the Nigerian Jews, the Ibos, were made up of more of the disobedient groups, more like the warlike lost tribe of Jews in Hadhramaut in the Eastern Protectorate who fought their way to Aden after the Second World War. They (the Ibos) were more deep down in love with the forbidden Gentile ways of life, consequent upon their inter-marriage with the aborigines of Nigeria which led them much more into idolatry, "worship of other gods - gods of wood and stone", gods of these other Nigerians, "gods unknown to their forefathers". Consequently, these Ibos, unlike their Yemenite counterparts eventually fell more victims to the above quoted curses, and so apparently more than other Jews in exile, have until today "found no resting place for the sole of their foot" in perfect fulfillment of the Almighty's curse on them in the Holy Scriptures (Deuteronomy 28:65). Indeed, today, many Ibos of Nigeria seem to have found no resting-place for the sole of their feet, as they are neither at peace among themselves in their home land nor in their other places outside Ibo Land.

After their arrival at Lake Chad areas from Egypt, after their second temporary stay in Africa on coming from Israel, the early Ibos got integrated into the complexities of the Nigerian tribal life. But, they (the Ibos) still had the needed skills that they brought with them from Israel; they were the finest artisans and craftsmen of the then Chad Basin area. Unfortunately, they were, a very stubborn and disobedient breed of Jews. They disobediently mixed up with the aborigines of Nigeria in marriage and in food - marrying and eating many of the forbidden meat and food, and joining Gentile Nigerian juju men and witch doctors to practice sorcery, divination and witchcraft; to consult mediums and spirits of dead people and as the Holy books of Israel predicted and so "did much evil in the eyes of the LORD, provoking Him to (more) anger." (2 Chron. 33: 6). Do you know that some Ibos of Nigeria are still in the forbidden worship of gods of wood and stone and other gods in other forms other than the LORD God Almighty, God of Israel, God of their forefathers?

There can be no better way of painting the similar pictures of the exiled Jews of Nigeria, the Nigerian Hebrews (Ibos) on their discovery in colonial Nigeria and their counterparts in Yemen, Poland, Russia and in fact all the 120 nations of the world from where about 100 nations have now seen their return to Israel after three thousand years of exile, than by recalling to memory some of the earlier quoted words of Oluadah Equiano, an ex Ibo slave who became literate and ultimately purchased his freedom from his British master. Equiano was born in 1745 in "Essaka" (maybe from a town in Ikwuano Umuahia called Ariam Isaka. Refer to "Aram Issachar" see 1 Chronicles 7:3, Gen. 46:13; and Umu - "Ahiah", see Neh. 10:26). In his writings, "The Interesting Narratives", "Ibo Society in mid-century" and "The Interesting Narratives of the life of Oluadah Equiano…" (1789). The ex-Ibo-slave, Equiano, did give enough evidence in his narratives to convince his audience that the Ibos are of Jewish stock.

A description, of the traditional religion, of the Ibos that ran nothing short of Judaism, the religion of the Jews. "As to religion", Equiano continued, "the natives believe that there is one, Creator of all things... They believe he governs events, especially our deaths or captivity; but, as for the doctrine of eternity, I do not remember to have ever heard of it; some, however, believe in the transmigration of souls in a certain degree... I remember we never polluted the name of the object of our adoration; on the contrary, it was always mentioned with the greatest reverence, and we were totally unacquainted with swearing... They have many offerings, particularly at full moons; generally two, at harvest before the fruits are taken out of the ground; and when any young animals are killed, sometimes they offer up part of them as sacrifice. These offerings, when made by one of the heads of a family, serve for the whole... Some of our offerings are eaten with bitter herbs. Though we had no places of public worship, we had priests and magicians and wise men. I do not remember whether they were in the same persons, but the people held them in great reverence. I have before remarked that the natives of this part of Africa are extremely cleanly. This necessary habit of decency was with us a part of religion, and therefore we had much purification and washing, indeed almost as many, and used on the same occasion, if my recollection does not fail me, as the Jews. Those who touch the dead at any time were obliged to wash and purify themselves before they could enter a dwelling house, or touch any person, or anything we eat… They are totally unacquainted with strong or spirituous liquors; their principal beverage is palm wine. This is got from a tree of that name, by tapping it at the top; and fastening a gourd to it, and sometimes one tree will yield three or four gallons in a night. The same tree also produces nuts and oil. Our principal luxury is in perfumes: one sort of these is an odoriferous wood of delicious fragrance, the other a kind of earth, a small portion of which thrown into the fire diffuses a most powerful order" (Equiano 1789:3- 14). What Equiano had tried to describe to his British audience in the above quoted words tantamount to distorted account of the practice of Judaism by the early Ibos of Nigeria. Actually, the "bitter herb" which Equiano mentioned in his narrative represents the same bitter herb that the Jews eat during their Feast of Liberation or Feast of Unleavened Bread. In that feast, there are Matzos, the unleavened bread to remind the Jews that they had to leave Egypt so quickly their bread was unleavened. There is an egg to symbolise the freewill offering, watercress for the coming of spring and shank of lamp bone to recall the offerings to God in the Great Temple. Finally, there is a mixture of nuts and diced apples to symbolize the mortar the Egyptians forced them to mix for brick building, and manor, bitter herbs to symbolize the bitterness of bondage.

Ironically, Equiano sorry tale of Ibo slaves in the British slave ship to America is paradoxically similar to Uris' tale of discomfort of the Yemenite Jews on the 'eagle', the (aeroplane), that flew them back to Israel at the end of their three thousand years of exile in Yemen.

Before embarking the aircraft, "the women shrieked as doctors and nurses tried to remove their lice-filled rags in exchange for clean clothing. They refused to have their bodies examined for sores and diseases, and rebelled against shots and vaccination just in the same manner as the Nigerian Hebrew (Ibo) women who were too reserved or saw their body too sacred to be touched by strangers (and worst still by men who they were not properly married to) reacted to the treatment of European doctors during the great scabies, inflammation of the skin epidemics of early 1900s in Ibo Land. There was a continuous fight against the workers who tried to remove temporarily the infants who badly needed treatment for malnutrition...A hundred and forty-two (Jewish) Yemenites were packed into the craft...The stench hit his nostrils. Foster stepped in and closed and locked the door. Where upon the unventilated hundred-and-twenty degree heat began to work on the odors... He threw the window open to get air but instead got a blast of heat..he held his head out of the window and vomited... and finally, with the coming of cooler air, his stomach came under control... They're all complaining..." (Uris, 1958).

As for the comparative Ibo slaves in the slave ship to America, the "stench" was the same and very much there. In the words of Equiano: "The stench of the hold while we were on the coast was so intolerably loathsome, that it was dangerous to remain their for any time, and some of us had been permitted to stay on deck for the fresh air; but now the whole ship's cargo were confined together, it became absolutely pestilential. The closeness of the place and the heat of the climate, added to the number in the ship that was so crowded that each had scarcely room to turn himself, almost suffocated us. This produced copious perspiration, so that the air soon became unfit for respiration, from a variety of loathsome smells, and brought on a sickness among the slaves, of which many died - thus falling victims to the improvident avarice, (as I may call it) of their purchasers.

This wretched situation which was again aggravated by the galling of the chains ("the iron yoke on their neck"), now became insupportable and the filth of the necessary tubs, into which the children often fell, and were almost suffocated" (Equiano, 1789).

 The shrieks of Ibo women on a journey to slavery like that of their counterpart Yemenite women on a journey to liberty in Israel, and the groans of the dying and those in pains from discomfort or slavery have rendered the whole story of the two Jewish people in exile in Yemen and Nigeria an almost inconceivable similar but contrasting scene of horror for the same group of people under the
same curse by the same God of their forefathers albeit in two different parts of the earth where God had scattered them in keeping with His word as earlier quoted hereinafter, or in two opposing circumstances. Indeed, this similar example can be multiplied many times to fit in perfectly into any other two sets of Jewish people in exile in any two different places of the world.

In fact, right in their different places of exile, in slavery or in ordinary condition of man-made deprivation of the Jews in fulfillment of the ancient prophecies against them, the similarities of their life are equally striking. Take this other example. The slave master of the Nigerian Hebrew (Ibo) slaves was an absolute wicked master or ruler. He exercised almost unlimited power by virtue of gunpowder alone. The slaves were considered as legal goods and classed together with other agricultural livestock. They were inspected and assessed by their prospective buyers just as a farmer inspects a cow, a goat, or sheep for sale. Breeding was encouraged among the slaves as part of the commercial venture, since a slave's born-child belonged to the slave master and increases his "stock of slaves". British American documents only give a hint of the stack horror and tragedy of the slave trade in those days. In the ship they took to America from Nigeria, the slaves, mostly Ibos or Jews of Nigeria, remained enclosed under crated hardware between decks. "The space", according to Reverend Walsh, "was so low that they sat between other's legs and were stowed so close together that there were no possibility of their lying down at all or changing their 'position by night or day'. They were all branded like sheep with the owners' marks of different forms. These were impressed under their breast or on arms, and burnt with the red-hot iron" (Walsh, 1830, Notices of Brazil). And to all these human sufferings, the British/American slave masters were completely indifferent.

Actually, the LORD God Almighty hardened the heart of the slave masters just as He hardened the heart of Pharaoh of Egypt and much later, that of other masters or rulers of the Jews, including that of Hitler and his cohorts, so that His words concerning the Jews, their exile, their condition and eventual restoration could be fulfilled.

What the American or British slave master was for the exiled Jews of Nigeria albeit in slavery in America was exactly what the Imam of Yemen was for the Jews of Yemen. Like the slave masters, the Imam of Yemen, a relative of Mohammed, was an absolute wicked ruler. He scorned civilization and did all in his power to keep it away from his subjects. He provided no civil or social services for the Jews. "The Imam" according to Uris (1958), "sat in crossed-legged pompousness and dispensed justice according to his whims, ordering the noses of prostitutes cut off and the hands of thieves amputated".

All these are but a hint on the similarities between the Nigerian Hebrews (Ibos) and the World Jews in misery and in normal conditions. And even in misery, the two groups of Jewish people responded in like manner. The Ibo slaves who were much preferred to other African slaves "for their hardiness, intelligence, integrity and zeal" (Equiano. 1789) were so often characterized as "happy-go-lucky" and carefree because of their willing and cheerful acceptance of their servitude condition as evidenced in their singing and dancing while on their slave duty in America. Similarly, during the Second World War, Jewish prisoners who were 'enslaved' in the German and British concentration camps also exhibited the same 'gaiety in bondage' quality of their counterpart enslaved Nigerian Hebrews (Ibos), as they assumed a forced air of gaiety and even fraternized with the German guards they knew to be waiting to exterminate them. The same thing could be said of the exiled Jews or Jewish slaves in ancient Babylon or Egypt. It is as if these Jews in two different situations were saying with one accord: 'We know why; there is nothing we can do to change the Almighty's word or curse on us for the disobedience of our forefathers. The LORD has said it and it must come to pass; but equally our forgiveness and restoration are assured - why should we not accept all these conditions with joy?

Unlike the Ibos, the Jews of Nigeria, the Jews of Yemen held steadfastly to the LORD God Almighty, the God of Israel, the reason for which perhaps God has decided to deal with them first in these days of restoration, to grant them His favor of the promised restoration and return to Israel before their counterpart Jews of Nigeria, the Ibos. Actually, the same pressures that made the Ibos to succumb to the temptations of idolatry came but the Yemenite Jews resisted. During the years when the Nigerian Jews fell back into idolatry in their land of exile, the Yemenite Jews still held fast unto the Almighty and He who rewards people accordingly has made it so that they now serve as the most prominent witnesses of the Almighty, as the present perfect example of the fulfillment of the word of God concerning His people Israel in the last days, and of the truth of the Torah and the Bible as the word of God.

Narrating his story of the return of the exiled Jews to Israel after the declaration of the state of Israel in 1948, Leon Uris (1958) has this to say about the Jews of Yemen in addition: "That the Jews of Yemen remained Jews was incredible. For 3000 years, these people had no contact with the outer world. Their lives would have been much easier had they taken up Islam (or to paganism as in the case of the Ibos). Yet the Yemenite Jews kept the Torah, the Laws, the Sabbath, and the Holidays through the centuries of isolation…

"Direct pressure was often brought to make them convert from Judaism to Islam but they resisted… During the years, the Yemenite Jews never stopped looking toward Jerusalem. They waited through the centuries in patience and devotion for Him to send the word for them to "go up on eagle wings". From time to time small groups or individuals managed to get out of Yemen, and they returned to Palestine and established a small community there…

"The port of Aden was the goal of the Yemenite exodus… Under the agreement with the British, the Israeli Provisional Government had to get them out of Aden. So Arctic Circle Airways became Palestine central and Forster J. McWilliams unwittingly answered an age long prophesy by dropping from the sky with the first of the 'great eagles.' They (the Yemenite Jews) had diligently waited on the LORD and He, in keeping with His word that changed not, "shall renew their strength" and make them go up on eagle's wings or soar on wings like eagles.

They that wait for the Almighty shall renew their strength; they shall mount up with wings as eagles; they shall run, and not be weary; they shall walk, (as in the case of the Yemenite Jews who managed to get out of Yemen and returned, walked back to Palestine before the arrival of the prophesied 'eagle', aeroplane), and not faint (Isaiah 40:31).

The arrival of the plane created tremendous excitement... They saw the eagle, for the plane from afar looked like an eagle to them, and nodded their heads knowingly: 'God has sent it as He said He would'."

Yes, the fulfillment of lifting the exiled Israelites up on "eagle wings" back to Israel had literally been fulfilled and evidenced in the case of the Yemenite Jews and later in the case of the Ethiopian Jews.

Maybe because God reckoned with, their steadfastness with Him, and has decided to use them, as first examples for the demonstration of the truth and permanence of His word. The Yemenite Jews' return as well as that of other Jews from about 100 countries out of 120 where the Jews had been exiled into was soon after the re-establishment of Israel. Others have to wait even till date. Some people would say: 'If I were God, I should have delayed or even cancelled the return of those exiles who, during the 3000 years or less of exile (just three days or less in the sight of God!) disobeyed and continued in their iniquities'. But God's ways are not our ways. "My ways are not your ways...," said the LORD. Besides He had said:

I will gather all back. I will correct thee (those who continued in the sin of their forefathers, sin of idolatry, etc.) in measure (Jeremiah. 30:11).

The case of the Jews of Nigeria is a bad one with the additional burden of the color of their skin, but not a hopeless one. Indeed, those exiled Jews who continue in the sin of their forefathers will surely be corrected "in measure" before being saved "not for their sake but for the sake of their forefathers, Abraham, Isaac and Jacob", for the sake of the holy name of God whom they have profaned among the Gentiles of Nigeria.

There are surely other similar cases for the later gathering back phase of the Jews. But no matter what the condition, no matter what the added burden, "no Jew will be turned from the door of Israel" (Uris, 1958).

Meanwhile, out of 120 different nations of the world harboring the exiled Jews, only about 100 nations have shown good prospects of gathering back of the Jews. The others are still waiting for the Almighty's time. As at today, the Lord's early favor in the area of His return promise to the exiled Jews has reached quite a significant number of Jews from Kurdistan to India up to Argentina and Africa (north, east, west and south). God has kept His promise of return to Israel for the exiled Jews in Iraq and Turkey. Jews had gone back to Israel from France, Italy Yugoslavia, Czechoslovakia, Rumanian, Bulgaria, Greece and Scandinavia. They went back from China and India where they had settled 3000 years before, from Australia, Canada, England - some trekked back: some went back by car; some mounted on the prophesied "eagle wings" and flew; and many others including those of us in Nigeria are still anxiously waiting for their turn to go back to Israel within the framework of the Almighty's own plan, either to settle in or to visit their ancestral homeland at will and without any restriction.

Can the Ibos be sure of their eventual future in Israel given their present state of idol worshipping and disobedience to God of Israel? Having taken to the ways of the Gentiles in Nigeria (unlike their counterparts in the other parts of the world) and even surpassed them in some ways, can God still forgive and restore them? Do the Nigerian Hebrews (Ibos) have the survival techniques of their counterpart World Hebrews or Jews? For instance, the World Hebrews always bring to the public notice the nature and extent of atrocities committed against them and in so doing reduce the tendency of their enemies to continue acting against them. This is not the case with the Nigerian Hebrews (Ibos). One wonders why the pogrom committed against the Ibos of Nigeria prior to and during the civil war was allowed by the Ibos to be forgotten soon after the Civil War. I have always believed that if the Ibos have the survival technique of their counterpart Jews in Europe and America, if they behaved like the other World Jews, Nigeria would have been at peace with each other and the Ibos inclusive. Or at least the attackers of the Ibos from other ethnic groups in Northern Nigeria and some other parts of Nigeria would have left them alone by now. As for the World Jews, no week passes by these days without either a Radio Network or Television Station reminding the World of the atrocities committed against the Jews. But the Ibos, despite the numerous atrocities committed against them in Nigeria remain silent both in their Radio and Newspapers, although there are a few isolated and sustained voices like that of Arthur Nwankwo besides the usual voice of Ojukwu calling the attention of Nigerians and the World to the hideous crimes against the Ibos before, during and after the Biafran War. If the other World Jews had behaved that way, we may never have had any law known as "Crime against Humanity' and the perpetrators of these crimes would never have been tried and punished.

Some of them identified by the Jews are still being tired now. Of all, only the breed of Jews of Nigeria, the Ibos, has the capacity to forgive and forget and suffer in silence. However, they seem to exhibit their Jewish trait only in the trifle, in political disagreements amongst themselves, not in the real matter of

genocide and plunder against them. When you hear some Ibos say they cannot forgive the Yorubas for a perceived betrayal or breach of promise during the Biafran War, one wonders what would be their attitude towards those individuals who really committed atrocities against them in Hausa land or elsewhere in Nigeria?

Having deviated so much from certain basic ways of life of their counterpart World Jews, can the much talked about salvation of the Jews in the last days be of the Ibos too? Undoubtedly, God has not only given His words to the ancient prophets of Israel regarding the restoration and salvation of the Jewish people everywhere in the world, He has also supplied a witness verifying it in today's Israel, in all the modern miracles that today's world witness in Israel.

Say unto the house of Israel thus said the Lord; I do not this for your sakes, O house of Israel, but for Mine holy name's sake, which you have profaned, whither you went.... I will sanctify My great name, which was profaned among the nations, and they shall know that I am the LORD... for I will take you among the nations, and gather you out of all countries, and will bring you into your own land (Ezekiel 36:22-24)

Many Ibos who had discussed the ideas of their origin in Israel with me, after realizing from the facts in the Scriptures that the Jews include people of all colors - "from the darkest to the lightest in color" - have all almost asked the same questions. Can small Israel contain all the Jewish exiles now in all the four corners of the earth? Earlier, Jacob had been promised of increase in his descendants so much so that the Promised Land will not contain all of them, all the Jewish people at home and in the Diaspora. But God's promis,e of the establishment of a monarchy - "one king shall be king to them all..." (Ezekiel 37: 21-22) - cannot happen when the Jewish people are still scattered all over the world; it must be when they are all gathered back in the land as prophesied. Indeed, it had already been said in the Scriptures that the land is too small for the latter day Jews.

Though you were ruined and made desolate and your land laid waste, now you will be too small for your people... The children will say, This place is too small for us: give us more space to live in. (Isaiah 49: 19-20).

This shows that the LORD God of Israel has not ignored the important question of the small space available for the state of Israel, for the Israeli exiles that will eventually return in their millions in the last days to dwell in the land. In an apparent answer, the LORD had said to the Israelites that He could even give them other nations of the earth for inheritance on request.

Ask of me, and 1 shall give thee the nations for your inheritance, and the uttermost parts of the earth for thy possession (Psalm 2:8).

How can this be possible? What will happen to the inhabitants of these nations? And as in answer to these questions the LORD Almighty had said to Jeremiah:

Though I make a full end of all nations whither I have scattered you, yet will I not make a full end of you; but I will correct you in measure... all they that devour you shall be devoured, and all your adversaries, everyone of them, shall go into captivity; and they that spoil you will I give for a prey (and there former land will I give you) (Jeremiah 30:11; 16).

Besides, the Scriptures teach that in the last days, modern Israelites will recover the lands bordering Israel, "the mountains of Edom, the mount of Esau, Philista, Ephraim and Samaria, Gilead and Zarephath", to significantly increase the present size of their country (Obadiah v. 18). It is said that the last days Israelis in the recovery process will be like "fire" and "a flame" in getting back the said surrounding Arab lands and the Palestinian hide-out areas within and outside Jerusalem. In modern parlance, "the mountains of Edom, the mount of Esau, Philista, Ephraim and Samaria, Gilead and Zarephath" correspond with south Jordan, Gaza, the West Bank, north Jordan and south Lebanon - every place presently occupied by the modern Edom, the descendants of Esau, the Arafat's Palestinians. Of these lands yet to be recovered in order to extend the present territory of Israel, the LORD Almighty said that (before the Third World War, before the coming of Jesus Christ, the great Messiah of Glory) the last days Israelis "shall kindle and destroy them and no survivor shall remain of the house of Esau (Obadiah, v. 18)". It is frightening and difficult to imagine that "no survivor shall remain in the house of Esau" (the present day Palestinians). But because the LORD had said so, it must surely happen, for His word "change not". This will mean a very significant increase in the land available for Israel and the children of Israel that will eventually come back from exile.

Then they shall know that I am the LORD their God who sent them into captivity among nations, but also brought them back to their land and left none of them captive any longer (Ezekiel 39:28).

Events of the last days and the Almighty's purpose for the Hebrews at home, Israel and in the Diaspora, including Nigeria are treated in details in the last chapter of this book.

David Ben-Gurion, First Leader of Modern Israel.

CHAPTER NINE

THE IBOS AND THE BLACK AMERICAN JEWS

There is still one untold story or rather an unanswered question. The assertion of Rabbi Capers Funnye in the Jerusalem Post that "Africans brought to the New World as slaves in the 18th and 19th Centuries were mainly from areas where tribes with Jewish roots predominated" and "that there are about a quarter-million Jews of African descent living in America today" not only jolted my thinking but left me with one big unanswered question.

The historic fact that Ibo slaves were preferred to all other African slaves because of their intelligence, dedication and hardiness and that 370,000 of them were sold in the Delta markets over a period of 25 years within the whole period of the slave trade that flourished for over 400 years! And that "the number of Ibo salves equal to about over a quarter of the total exports from all African ports" (Adams, 1975) vividly show that the people being referred to by Rabbi Funnye are the Ibos of Nigeria, and that by extension of the argument, over 25% of all of today's African Americans are made up of the said Ibo slaves. The postulation of Alaezi in Ibos: Hebrew Exiles from Israel...(1999) with lots of evidences that Ibos are of the lost tribes of Israel and therefore Jews, the historic fact just cited above, and the assertion of Rabbi Capers Funnye lead to the conclusion that among the most intelligent and hardworking Black Americans and among the professed American Black Jews are mostly Ibos.

There must be some Iboness in such famous Black Americans as Booker T. Washington, who advised William Howard Taft and Theodore Roosevelt on civil rights matters. Washington was a teacher who founded the Tuskegee Institute to train African-Americans to become carpenters, farmers, mechanics, and teachers. Washington also became the main civil rights leader after the death of Frederick Douglass and the saying is that America would not be the same had it not been for Booker T. Washington. Other notable Black Americans include: Marian Anderson, William Christopher Handy, Martin Luther King Jr., Crispus Attucks, Matthew

Henson, <u>Phillis Wheatley</u>, <u>Langston Hughes</u>, <u>George Washington Carver</u>, <u>Mary McLeod Bethune</u>, <u>Frederick Douglass</u>, <u>Harriet Tubman</u>, Jan Ernest Matzeliger, <u>Rosa Parks</u>, Benjamin Banneker, <u>James Beckwourth</u>, Mary McLeod Bethune, <u>George Washington Carver</u>, Guion Buford, <u>W.E.B. Du Bois</u>, Maya Angelou, <u>Charles R. Drew</u>, Shirley Chisholm, Bessie Coleman, <u>Matthew Henson</u>, Jesse Jackson , Toni Morrison , Oprah Winfrey, Ralph Bunche, Lewis H. Latimer, and Sojourner Truth.

Marian Anderson became the first African-American soloist to sing with the Metropolitan Opera in New York City.

Dr. Martin Luther King Jr. was a leader in the Civil Rights Movement who won the Nobel Peace Prize for working in peaceful ways to get equal rights for Black Americans.

Crispus Attuks was an American hero and martyr of the Boston Massacrprior to the American Revolutionary War.

<u>Rosa Parks</u> was the Black American who refused to give up her bus seat to a white passenger in Montgomery, Alabama. This helped to start the Civil Rights Movement.

Benjamin Banneker was an astronomer, mathematician, inventor, surveyor, and the first African-American to receive a presidential appointment.

<u>Ralph Bunche</u> worked at the United Nations and was the first African-American to win the Nobel Peace Prize.

James Beckwourth was one of the known Mountain Men; he discovered a pass through the Sierra Nevada into California that was named after him.

Mary McLeod Bethune worked to help educate African-Americans and worked with four Presidents to further expand educational opportunities.

George Washington Carver was a scientist famous for agricultural research and for discovering the many uses of peanuts.

Guion Bluford was the first African-American to go into space.

<u>W.E.B. DuBois</u> was a Civil Rights activist and NAACP Founding Member.

Maya Angelou was a prize-winning poet; she recited one of her poems at President Clinton's first Inauguration.

<u>Charles Drew</u> (Duru in Ibo) fought against all odds to become a doctor.

Shirley Chisholm (Chisom in Ibo, meaning God with me) was the first African-American woman to become a member of the United States Congress.

Harriet Tubman led hundreds of slaves to freedom in the North through the Underground Railroad.

Matthew Henson, an African-American explorer, discovered the North Pole with Robert Peary.

 Toni Morrison was an author and winner of the Nobel Prize in Literature.

Dr. Andrew Young a Reverend Pastor, Civil Rights Leader, UN Ambassador and a Spearhead for African development.

Oprah Winfrey (Oparah in Ibo, is the name usually given to the first son in a family) is the most acclaimed Talk show host and a leading African American Philanthropist.

Collin Powell was the Generals General of the US Armed forces. He latter became the US Secretary of State under the amiable President George Walker Bush.

Dr. Philip Emeagwalli, who has earlier been listed as one of the Ibo scientists, is now an American citizen, having taken American citizenship. As an African American, he deserves a place here too. Dr. Emeagwalli invented the Internet and is now regarded as a foremost world scientist of great repute.

These Black Americans, most of whom are surely American Jews or Ibos, have made important inventions and discoveries, created great works of art, and excelled in Science, Music, Literature, Medicine and Sports Religion and Diplomacy. Their talents, perseverance and bravery has provided inspiration for others and has won for them the respect of all Americans. They have played important roles in America's history; they have excelled in an amazing variety of careers, triumphing over great handicaps of prejudice and discrimination to do so. They were the pioneers in their respective fields whose talents range from publishing to exploration, from painting to law – as doctors and artists, educators and inventors – these American Black men and women have led the way for the other gifted Blacks the world over to follow.

Actually, in some cases, the names of celebrated Black Americans in American history and Black Jewish names that are not English or European seem to be names of Ibo origin. They include, just to mention only few of them: Wynia, corruption of Ibo name, Nwana or Nwanna, an Aro Ibo name meaning the son of our father - another name reserved for a male relation, a name that portrays solidarity, singleness of purpose and action among a group of people in a certain setting. If an Ibo man meets another Ibo for the first time at home or abroad, what either of them will call the other, without caring or before asking to know the real name, is simply 'Nwanna' corrupted in America as Wynia. Iyke is the corruption of a popular Ibo name, Ike, short form of Ikechukwu or Ikenna, meaning God's power or God's will. Khanga (as in Ylena Khanga, the famous

102

Black Jew of Russian and African descent who chronicled her family) is the corruption of Ibo name, Ikenga, meaning right hand – a symbol of strength and uprightness. Other Ibo-based Black American names include: Dr. Ida (Ada) Gray – Ada is a popular Ibo name, usually borne by the first daughter in a family, just like the Jews; Ella (Ola) Josephine Baker – Ola, meaning precious ornament or a highly favoured child by God is a popular name borne by female children in Item and other areas in old Bende of Abia State; Dr. Charles Drew (Duru) – Duru is a popular name borne by titled men in Owerri (Imo State) areas of Ibo nation; and so on.

To deal with the question of the Jewishness or Ibonness in Black Americans, I have begun to do some extra research work, which must involve Black Americans themselves. This means talking to the intellectuals, seeking out Black Americans or Black American Jewish writers and scholars. A certain African American that I met at the 6th Leon Sullivan Summit in Abuja, Nigeria in 2003 had agreed to organise a joint-research project but apparently changed his mind on the matter for reasons unknown to me. I am, however, aware that there is a pool of notable American Black Jewish protagonists such as Michael Hudson, a convert (or should we say a revert) to Judaism, who maintains a Black and Jewish web page; Aaron Freeman, a Chicago-area comedian and columnist; James McBride, author of The Color of Water, a novel about his white Jewish mother who raised Black children; Robin Washington, A Boston-based journalist and co-founder of the Alliance of Black Jews; Yelena Khanga, a Black Jew of Russian and African descent who chronicled her family; Julius Lester, a Professor in the Judaic and Near Eastern Studies Department and adjunct professor in the English and History Departments at the University of Massachusetts, Amherst; Rebecca Leventhal Walker, daughter of author Alice Walker and civil rights lawyer Mel Leventhal; and Ketya Gibel Azoulay, a dual citizen of the U.S. and Israel, is the author of the rather academic Black, Jewish and Interracial. What I do not know is their idea about a study on the Jewishness or Ibonness in Black Americans.

Actually, the vision of Dr. Sullivan had built a bridge from America to Africa. Leading a group of African Americans (as Dr. Sullivan did) to return to Africa is a noble vision; but leading them to return with a knowledge of their exact tribe or race and ancestral origin is a wonderful added advantage, which makes for more self-realisation, self-awareness and self-rediscovery.

Most American Black Jews, out of the ignorance of the Jewish origin of the Ibos of Nigeria, the largest single group of slaves from Africa, think of

themselves only as descended from Ethiopian Jews (sometimes called "Falashas, strangers in Ge'ez"),
 who claimed to be descended from Solomon and the Queen of Sheba and Judaism has been recognised by mainstream white Jews as fully legitimate.

This has spurred the growth of Black Judaism and the claim of the Ethiopian descent by many Black Jews in America.

Many "educated" people outside Europe/USA, Black Americans inclusive, know a lot about Europe and Euro-America, but have less interest in peoples outside Europe/Euro-America, including their own people. Many African Americans know little of Africans on the other side of their continent. World knowledge of the Jewish Diaspora is no exception to the Euro-Americentric rule. Most White people (sadly including Black people) picture Jews as white Europeans. Actually, the Jewish communities of Africa and Asia had dominated the Jewish intellectual and cultural scene in antiquity. Before the modern age, Egypt of Africa, together with Iraq of Asia, were the world centers of Jewish learning and religious authority. The Septuagint, a Greek translation of the Bible, was produced in Egypt. Prominent religious leader and scholar Moshe ben Maimon, the Rambam (1135-1203), served as nagid for the Egyptian Jews. He spent much of his life in Cairo as a Jewish scholar and as chief physician to the sultan.

Israelite tribes first entered Egypt during the reign of Pharaoh Amen Hotep IV (1375-1358 BCE) and migrated from Egypt in the Exodus around the year 1220 BCE. During the time of the Babylonian conquest of Israel, many Jews who were not deported to Babylon fled to Egypt, as recorded in the book of the prophet Jeremiah. Large scale immigration began in 332 BCE when Egypt was under Greek rule, leading to the settlement of Jews from Egypt in Ibo (Heebo or Hebrew) land in Nigeria and some other parts of Africa south of Sahara. Although the Ethiopian Jewry represents one of the oldest Diaspora communities, yet it does not have the largest number of expatriate Jews; Nigeria, a much more conducive environment, hosting the fleeing Jews (who referred to themselves as Ifite (Ivrit) from Ibrit pronounced as Hebrew corrupted as Heebo, Eboe or Ibo by the British) does. It was pure Jews but mostly of dark colour who migrated to Nigeria after the fall of Egypt. According to one theory, Ethiopian Jewry had its origin in Jewish soldiers stationed in Ethiopia, who married local women and converted the people to Judaism. Another tradition holds that one of King Solomon's sons arrived in Ethiopia with his retainers and settled there. Christian and Jewish kingdoms fought in Ethiopia during the Middle Ages, and when Christians eventually gained the upper hand, many Jews converted to Christianity. In spite of all, however, Jamaican historians had rightly taught that over 68% of their people are descendants of Ibo slaves and much higher percentage of Ibo slaves are now Haitians.

Indeed, the Rastas in Jamaica, a mostly Ibo-slave community, are classified as Jews although their social characteristic and theology significantly differ from others in that category.

When William Saunders Crowdy founded the first American Black movement, little did he know that he was being used as an instrument of honour in the hand of the Almighty for the eventual reintegration of the Black Jews the world over into the World Jewry. Crowdy thought that Africans descended from the lost tribes of Israel and as such were Jews; but he did not go further to prove his case by giving evidences and making references to the Holy Books of Israel to link the Black Jews with Israel and to say why they initially left Israel, the promise of return and restoration for all Jews in exile, and so on, as has done the author of this book. One interesting thing about the story about Black Hebraism in America is the belief of some of the Black teachers of the black superiority similar to those being expounded by the nations of Islam. Wentworth Matthew, for example, thought that the era of white ascendancy will soon come to an end and that the true "Back Jews" will be restored to their rightful position of world leadership (Wynia, 1994). Actually, a case of Black Jewish superiority can be made right from the time of Moses to a certain point in history of the Jews, when Moses, finding it difficult to rule the children of Israel in the wilderness was advised to go for the acquisition of a superior knowledge of governance of God's people at Median in African, from where he (Moses) also married, to meet the black Jews there, descendants of Abraham from his black wife Keturah whom he married after the death of his wife Sarah, but who returned to Africa with her children after the death of Abraham.

Another Jewish Black writer F.S. Cherry taught that God is colored or black and that he created colored or black people originally (with color of the earth, not white, having molded the first man, Adam, from the earth-sand) and that white people descended from some one (maybe Lucifer, the beautiful rebellious angel) who has cursed.

Some of these beliefs, strange they may sound are not be too far from the truth, considering the conclusion in Chapter Nine of this book, which also traces the legitimacy of the black race in Jewish state to the nucleus

Jewish families of Abraham through his black wife Keturah and Moses through his black wife Zipporah,

and the other Jews who married "cushite" or colored/black women during their 400 years period of slavery in Egypt.

Ironically, the "regular" Jews – the Ashkenazim and Sephardim who essentially constitute the World Jewry – do not recognize any of the African-American groups as legitimately Jewish although they recognize the existence of Black Jews in Africa and the fact that the Jews "include those whose skins range from the lightest to the darkest in colors" (Donin, 1972:8).

For today's World Jewry, the standard position has been that to be Jewish one must have a Jewish mother or be formally converted by a rabbi with appropriate standing. This precludes most Blacks from being Jewish. And this raises another unanswered question: 'What happens to the descendants of the children of the black wives of Abraham, Moses, Solomon and other Jews throughout history till date too numerous to mention particularly during the days of slavery in Egypt?

The problem of Israel and the "regular" Jews is not that they have no knowledge of their historical past in terms of their blood relationship with some Blacks stems from their European connection, culture, and attitude. Modern Israel was born as a result of the troubles of Europe, which were characterized by intolerance, discrimination, pride and prejudice. The "regular" Jews translated these social traits into action in their dealings with their colored Jewish brothers. Israel's problems were created in Europe by Europeans and should have been solved in Europe by Europeans. In looking at the current division or problem between the colored Jews and the "regular" Jews, an important aspect in the history of both people is unfortunately forgotten. A search through the history will reveal that though there was some discrimination with regard to the color of the skin, there never was any deep-seated hatred among Jews of different colors living together as a people, just as the Almighty God of Israel designed it. The Almighty actually demonstrated His disapproval of discrimination amongst Israelites on the basis of color of the skin when He reacted angrily against Aaron and made Miriam leprous on account of their opposing the marriage between Moses and his "cushite", black, woman called Zipporah.

It is my opinion that in choosing the discriminatory postures of the "regular" Jews against the Black Jews who were the strength of Israel in the early years of the nation, today's Israelis are making the greatest mistakes in their history – a mistake that can cost the nation the most reliable "internal" force and ally and some "regular" Jews their salvation in the last day, in the last World War (should I say 3rd World War?). When all the Euro-American allies whose arrogance and discriminatory attitude the "regular" Jews have copied, will suddenly join the powers of the Arabs and the East to march to Jerusalem with a view to destroying Israel for ever, when the irate world powers, led by Russia and China together with all the Moslem Arab nations and suddenly supported by the Euro-American allies will match on to Jerusalem with hundreds of thousands or millions of soldiers in a last desperate and determined effort to destroy Israel in retaliation to the destruction of the Palestinians by Israel. And then shall come the predicted "God's own army", the second coming of Christ, the intervention of the great Messiah of Glory to save Israel and all true worshipers of the LORD Almighty, God of Israel from the other nations of the earth, the "spiritual Israelites" from defeat and honor His word and His holy name. The Stone (the Messiah, the Christ) will then appear from heaven to smite the image on the toes and the entire image (world powers) will collapse.

Dr. Phillip and Dale Emeagwali. The Internet Inventor.

Cardinal Francis Arinze

Cardinal Arinze has worked extensively in the United States. Here, he presides over a dedication of the St. Vincent Archabbey Basilica in Latrobe, Pennsylvania.

CHAPTER TEN

THE JEWS AND THE GENTILE CHRISTIANS; MY DILEMMA AND ISSUES ARISING

Over the years, the "goyim" (the Hebrew word for Gentiles) who were converted into Christianity had referred to the Jews as "Christ killers". As a result, the knights of the Crusades descended on the Jews with the cross/Bible in one hand and a sword in the other. It will be recalled that before the Gentile Christians, were converted by the early Jewish Christians (Paul and the apostles) there were already thousands of Jewish believers won to Jesus by Paul and the apostles.

Thou seest, brother, how many thousands there are among the Jews of them that have believed (in Christ); and they are all zealous for the law (Acts 21:20).

Before the destruction of Jerusalem in 70 A.D., the first thousands of early Christians were in vast majority the Jews, and "they were all zealous for the law". This means that after the death of Jesus Christ many thousands of Jews became Christians, the Christians of the very early church, practising Christianity and still obeying the Law (the Ten Commandments of the Almighty God of Israel) and the Prophets (the utterances and prescriptions of the holy prophets of Israel - from Moses to Malachi). For Jesus Christ had told his disciples while he was alive:

Do not think that I have come to abolish the Law or the Prophets; I have not come to abolish them but to fulfil them. Verily I say unto you, until heaven and earth disappear, not the smallest, not the least stroke of a pen, will by any means disappear from the Law... Anyone who breaks one of the least of these commandments and teaches others to do the same will be called least in the kingdom of heaven. (Mathew5:17-19).

In fact, it was in view of this that Apostle Paul accepted to pay the expenses and join in a certain purification rites so as to prove that there was no truth in the accusation levelled against him before the Jewish elders of the early church. The accusation was that he was teaching "all the Jews who live among the Gentiles to turn away from Moses, telling them not to circumcise their children or live according to the customs" of the Jews. (see Acts 21: 17-26). However, the early Jewish Christians decided to modify or simplify some of the laws for the non-Jews newly joining the Christian fold, ignoring Christ's injunction regarding "anyone who breaks the least law and teaches others to the same". Even at that, the modification for the Gentile believers was in the areas of the other laws of Moses, not in the Ten Commandments. And in this book we are talking of the Jews now living in Israel and in the Diaspora, including the Ibos of Nigeria.

Even at the crucial point in 70 A.D. when the destruction of Jerusalem was completed in fulfillment of the prophecy of Jesus Christ, the Jewish believers or rather Jewish Christians were still very much a part of the Jewish community, obeying the Law and the Prophets as well as the early Christian tenets. They therefore harkened to Christ's prophecy concerning the destruction of the Second Temple in Jerusalem in the Gospel according to Luke, and so when they saw Jerusalem surrounded by Roman armies, before the Roman armies completed their task of destroying Jerusalem, thousands of these Jewish Christians had fled the city, remembering as it were the prophetic injunction of Jesus Christ to them: But when ye shall see Jerusalem compassed with armies, then know that her desolation is at hand. Then let them that are in Judea flee unto the mountains; and let them that are in the midst of her depart out; and let not them that are in the country enter therein (Luke 21:20-21)

For some historical accidents or in fulfilment of God's plan, after Jerusalem was destroyed and the Jewish warlord, Rabbi Akiva, who rose at the time and led the Jews against the Roman invaders and whom the Jewish believers saw as a non-Christian prophet, was killed by the Romans, Jewish anger ironically grew against the Jewish believers rather than against the Roman invaders. The believers were considered as saboteurs, deserters and traitors of Israel. Actually, many of the believers had come to regard the Jerusalem event as a fulfilment of the word of God rather than a calamity for the Jews, and as a strengthening of their belief in Jesus Christ whose prophecy had come to a fulfilment and as the Messiah who by his death and resurrection had fulfilled the prophecy of Isaiah regarding the "everlasting" New Covenant that would liberate the Jews from the rigorous 613 rules and regulations of Moses under the Old Covenant. This is without prejudice to the Law and the Prophets, to the Ten Commandments of God as stated in the book of Exodus. And so the Jewish believers were to be ostracised for non-involvement in the war, and had remained so ever since.

Meanwhile, while the Jewish believers, were still in this state of disapproval and denial by their kith and kin, Christianity was being properly established and growing in leaps and bounds throughout the entire Gentile world. Hundreds and thousands of Gentiles became believers whereas the number of Jewish believers continued to dwindle or at best became stagnant. Before long the Gentiles finding themselves in the vast majority began to do away with certain Jewish customs in the Christian religion. For instance, whereas the Jewish believers wanted the resurrection day of Jesus Christ to be celebrated on the third day of Passover, that is, on the 17th day of Nisan (latter part of March and early April), the Gentiles wanted to fix a date that had no meaning in the Jewish calendar. There were the other Gentile decisions which produced doubtful Easter day, Sunday worship instead of the Sabbath worship as contained in the Ten Commandments of God which Christ said he had not come to destroy but to fulfil; Christmas day tallying with a day for a fetish celebration in Rome besides its being celebrated on a questionable date for the birth of Christ, and so on. Many Jewish believers who protested against the said anti-Jewish practices in Christianity were attacked and killed by the Gentile Christian authorities in Rome. At one time thousands of Jewish Christians who refused to worship in the church on Sunday and insisted that the worship day for the Christians should be on the Sabbath day, which is on Saturday, were killed. Soon those Jews who could not continue to bear the numerous ant-Jewish practices in Christianity went back to their original practice of Judaism. Soon with the exit of the Jews, the Church began to even forget that it had Jewish roots until the deadly blows of the Crusaders, the Inquisition, the pogroms and the "final solution" to the Jewish question in the concentration camps of Nazi Germany during the Second World War. And in each occasion of the Gentile face-up with the Jews, the latter were murdered and raped and pillaged, all in the name of 'Christianity'. For instance, during the Inquisition in Spain in 1492 any Jew who refused to convert to Christianity was killed. However, those Spanish Jews, the Maranos, who converted to Catholicism publicly in order to save their lives and those of their families still maintained their Jewish identity in the privacy of their homes, and taught their children about Jewish ways of life. The terror of the pogroms, the vicious attacks on the Jews, and unimaginable manners of man's inhumanity to man, all of it put a deeper mark on the separation between the Jews and the Gentiles and caused more distrust and suspicion, hostility and fear, anger and hatred. Then came the Second World War, the Nazi concentration camps in Germany, a "self-labelled"

Christian nation, and the establishment of the state of Israel in 1948. There was the reunification of Jerusalem under Jewish control after the Six-Day Desert War in 1967, which marked a decisive change in relationship between the Jews and the Gentiles, the people of the other nations who now began to see the hand of God in the affairs of Israel; and ushered in a period of peace moves, peace accords such as the Camp David Peace Accord between Israel and Egypt, and Pope John Paul 11 going to the Wailing Wall in Jerusalem to worship God and apologising to the Jews for the Church's insensitivity to the plight of the Jews during the Nazi occupation of Europe. All these have worked together to fulfil God's word regarding the "mystery" of reconciling the Jews with the Gentiles who had had so much hatred for each other (Rom. 11; Ephesians 3).

The actualisation of this "mystery" in today's world is manifest in the fact that more and more exiled Jews are returning to Israel with a new notion of Jesus and the Christians, and a new attitude that can be appealing to the orthodox Jews and help to change the Jews' hatred for the word 'Christian' and for the name 'Jesus'. Yes real hatred, and a well-founded one too – a hatred with good reason. Imagine the atrocities committed against the Jews in the name of Jesus during the Dark Ages, during the Inquisition in Spain in 1492, the 1st World War and the 2nd World War. Not only did people continue to commit hideous crimes against the Jews in the name of Christianity in Russia in particular in the years after the Dark Ages and in various other nations of Europe and Middle East, in more recent years, within the very last generation or so, the so-called Christians in Germany, Poland, Rumania and even in England and France have acted as the real Satan against the Jews. They falsely accused the Jews of all manners of crime, calling them provocative names such as "Christ killers"; "drinkers of Christian blood"; "witches and wizards", etc. Several accounts in this book talk of the brutalities against the Jews before and during the Second World War, in Hitler's gas chamber and British and German concentration camps.

With shame and great worry all true Christians and all true worshippers of God must admit the role the Pope in Rome played against the Jews during the Second World War. In the last World war, after openly receiving the Pope's blessing, Hitler reportedly slaughtered millions of Jews and turned their bodies into fertiliser. In Russia, Poland and other Christian countries, thousands of Jews were brutally massacred and many burnt in pogroms. Branding the Jews "Christ-killers" as an excuse, even their cemeteries were plundered. Many dead Jews buried within two months or less were dug up and "the putrid and mangled corpses thrown on the dooryards of their families". Any wonder, therefore, why the surviving Jews so much hate to hear about Christians and Jesus. Who else finding himself in the place of a Jew whose parents or grand parents and relations passed through all these ordeals in a living memory would have behaved otherwise? Herein lies the root of what the Apostle Paul foresaw and called "Israel's blindness" and prejudice against Jesus.

For I would not, that ye should be ignorant of the mystery, lest ye should be wise in your own conceits, that blindness in part is happened to Israel, until the fullness of Gentiles come in (Rom. 11:25).

Before the First World War, the "blindness" and prejudice were alarmingly dense; but after the war, from 1917 onwards and particularly after the Second World War, remarkable disappearances of the blindness and prejudice began to be noticed. And today, although only about 5 percent or less of the Jews who live in Israel are Christians, most of them (Jewish Christians and non-Jewish Christians alike) think very favourably of Jesus, referring to Him as a Holy Man of Israel, a most marvellous reformer and the greatest of Israel's prophets. The works of some Jewish scholars like Stan Telchin who wrote on the problems and prospects of today's Christian Jews, Dr. Klansner who wrote on the life of Jesus in very complimentary terms, though not seeing him as the Messiah, Delitzsch, Ginsburg, and others are now widely read in Jewish circles and through them "Israel's blindness" and prejudice are gradually but surely removed.

Actually, thousands of years of blindness and prejudice cannot be removed overnight; but the said works and the efforts of Jewish Christians who have returned to Israel from exile [many are yet to return] have cleared ground for the complete disappearance of the Israel's blindness and reconciliation of the Jews with the Gentiles. The end of the times of the Gentiles began in 1914, the date that some religious analysts erroneously regard as the end of the times of the Gentiles. But what may appear to a casual observer as the predicted fullness of the time of the Gentiles, the full end of the time of the Gentiles when Israel's blindness would see its final end was in 1967 after the Six-Day Desert War, when virtually, the whole of Jerusalem, was liberated by the Israeli army (see Alaezi, 1999). Even at this, the full end is yet to come because the Palestinians are still occupying a part of Jerusalem.

For Jesus Christ said "Jerusalem shall be trodden down of the Gentiles, until the times of the Gentiles be fulfilled" (Luke 21:24). Indeed, in the fullness of time, when the times of the Gentiles will be fulfilled, the whole Jerusalem, not part of or divided Jerusalem, will belong to Israel and it will serve as the capital of the country for the Almighty had said so through the Prophets, "out of Zion shall go forth the law, and the word of the LORD from Jerusalem (Isaiah 2:3), and "At that time they shall call Jerusalem the throne of the LORD. (Jeremiah: 3:17).

What may be deceiving some analysts to think that the full end of the time of the Gentiles has come with the end of the Six-Day Desert War is that since 1967 till date, not even a single Christian nation the world over will like to offend Israel in any way, and, indeed, the sweetness of the name of Jesus has become the same in the ears of both Israelites and the Christians of the other nations.

As has been said earlier, not only did Pope John Paul 2 tender some unreserved apologies to Israel for the role the Church played in the War against Israel but also owned up the false propaganda against the Jews during the Second World War.

Nonetheless, Israel has made a lot of astonishing progress in agriculture, commerce, industry, and so on. And other events in the Middle East now point to the truth in the Scriptural prophecies of the last days and the conclusion that the anticipated end is in sight. Let this not deceive us, for the total liberation of Jerusalem from the hands of the Gentiles, which will tally with the end, is yet to take place. It will surely take place during the soon coming 3rd World War as would be explained later in this book. Furthermore, the name Jesus is a Greek name, another name for Joshua or Jehoshua (Numbers 13:16), which means Jehovah's Deliverer. The name Christ is derived from the Greek equivalent for the name Messiah. Any Jew in Judaism who is rightly informed about the teachings of Christ is bound to respect him and his earliest followers as among the holiest Jews that ever lived. They should not be judged according to the so-much adulterated teachings of prosperity and liberty from all kinds of diseases and afflictions by a vast majority of today's Christian leaders, teachings of revenge through 'dangerous' prayers with the book of Psalms, separation and hatred in the name of Jesus, not the teaching of love of God and one's neighbour or doing to others, in everything, what you would have them do to you, "which sums up the Law and the Prophets" (Mathew 7:12) that Jesus gave his followers as the greatest of all the laws. However, there are, in the Christendom, some true worshippers of God, who worship Him in truth and in spirit, among whom are also the Jews particularly those like the Nigerian Jews (or Ibos) living in exile among the Gentiles. With this category of Jews, the "mystery" of reconciling the Jews with the Gentiles through Jesus Christ or the removal of the blindness of Israel to see and recognise Jesus as the great Messiah of Glory sounds more of a reality.

115

And the Prophet declares that it will be after the return of the exiled Jews to Israel and after the Time of Trouble which is now upon Israel and the world as a whole and upon today's few true Christian churches that the Jews will recognise that the great Messiah, the great Michael of Daniel 12:1, for whose Kingdom they (the Jews) have been waiting is no other one than the very one of the Jewish race (Isaiah 7:14, 9: 6,7) - the very crucified Jesus. Believe it or not, part of the mystery of the reconciliation of the Jews with the Gentiles and the removal of Israel's blindness is that the least expected breed of Jews will play the most significant role in the reconciliation exercise. My prediction is that this will be the Jews living and already fully integrated with the Gentiles, the Jews of the lowly "darkest in color", the Nigerian Hebrews (Ibos) who much more than any other breed of Jews in exile are very much integrated into the Gentiles' way of life, and are also virtually all Christians albeit mostly idolatrous Christians.

Today, the Ibo Christian leaders are very much in the forefront of the spread of Christianity in Nigeria and Africa south of Sahara, and their own brand of Christianity is (unlike that of the 1st Century European Gentile Christians) in complete sympathy with Israel, and many of them are tilted towards a return to Sabbath worship as a panacea for true Christian worship of God of Israel, God Almighty the Creator of Heaven and Earth. This category of Jews in Africa together with other Christian Jews outside Africa, the vast majority of whom are yet to return to Israel are most likely to be the champions of Jesus' New Covenant arrangement through which the whole of mankind will receive their own blessings of Israel by compliance with the New Covenant Law. Hence in this same wise again the Holy Scripture declares:

I say then: Have they (the Jews) stumbled that they should fall? God, forbid; but rather through their fall salvation is come unto the Gentiles, for to provoke them (the Jews) to jealousy (Romans 11: 11).

God is extremely definite and orderly in His dealings with Israel as with other human races, for He is the God of all mankind for whom nothing is impossible to do (Jeremiah 32:27). He humbles the pride of people and raises his instruments of operation from lowly places least expected by man. For instance, the LORD Almighty promises to humble the pride of Israel by restoring the Sodomite and the Samaritans - peoples whom Israel detested as inferiors and sinners. He declares that when He would bless Israel again, He would also bless these other peoples in their midst.

When thy sisters, Sodom and her daughters, shall return to their former estate; and Samaria and her daughters shall return to their former estate ...

116

Nevertheless I will remember my covenant with thee in the days of thy youth, and I will establish unto thee an everlasting covenant... and I will give them (Sodomites and Samaritans) unto thee for daughters, not by the covenant (not under the Old Law Covenant given to the 12 tribes of Israel at Sinai; but under the New Law Covenant of the future) and I will establish my covenant with thee... that you mayst remember, and be confounded, and never open thy mouth any more because of thy shame, when I am pacified toward thee for all that thou hast done (Ezekiel 16:55-63).

I predict that this new and better Covenant is to be facilitated by human actions of a lowly breed of Jews, most probably the Nigerian Hebrews (Ibos) or the like whom the World Jewry have hitherto failed to identify (or when identified to respect), just as they failed to identify the Mediator of the New Covenant, the great Jesus Christ who was born in Bethlehem in Judea where the early Jews believed no good thing could come from. But in the fullness of time, in due course of God's own time, He will open their (the Jews') spiritual eyes of understanding, and so as the Prophet Zechariah declares:

They shall look upon me whom they have pierced (Zechariah 11:10)

My prediction that the Almighty will use African-oriented breed of Jews to facilitate this "mystery" in the last days is not far-fetched when one remembers that God has in the beginning used Africa to accomplish His most crucial divine designs for His people, Israel, and the whole world. Consider these facts in the Holy Scriptures of Israel. Moses was taken to and raised in Africa (Egypt) for the initial deliverance and the foundation governance of Israel. God had sent Moses to Africa, specifically to a priest of Midian, "a descendant of Abraham through Keturah" to help him (Moses) fulfil his ministry and obtain the inheritance of the children of Israel (Exodus 18: 1-27; Numbers 10: 24-32).

In order to accomplish the dreams of Joseph and save lives, God allowed Joseph's brothers to sell him into slavery in Africa (Egypt). When Herod wanted to kill the infant Jesus, he was, on the instruction of the angel of God, taken to Africa (Egypt) for safety. When Jesus Christ was to be crucified for the redemption of mankind and he (Jesus) could no longer continue to bear the cross to the Calvary, it was an African, a man from Cyrene in Africa, called Simon, that the Roman soldiers saw and forced to carry the cross for Jesus to the Golgotha so that the God's planned end for Jesus will be fulfilled. Earlier on, when there was the great seven-year famine in the whole of Middle East, the children of Jacob had to go to Africa (Egypt) in search of food and ended up settling there even with their old father Jacob (or Israel). Therefore, it is logical to predict that God will also use the Jews living in Africa as exiles, or rather His people based in Africa, to accomplish His last days' plan for Israel and the rest of mankind just as He had used Jews like Joseph and Moses living in Africa to begin His plans for Israel and the world at large. And many analysts believe that the Ibos of Nigeria will form the nucleus of this category of Jews living in Africa to be used for the Almighty's eventual purpose or final plan for Israel and mankind.

My Dilemma; Issues Arising

As I write this and see myself as a branch of Jacob, a Jew of Nigerian nationality, I am faced with a dilemma. Virtually all Ibos, myself inclusive, have been brought up in Gentile or Gentile-oriented Christian homes where many realities of Jewish way of life are pitifully lacking, and where, when they exist, have been polluted sometimes beyond recognition. But once these Ibos hear of the overwhelming similarities in their tradition and culture and in their share of pogroms, hatred, slander, persecution, etc., by their neighbours of the same nationality, they develop a tremendous hunger for roots. This is evidenced in the unanticipated mad rush for my first book on the Jewish origin of the Ibos titled Ibos: Hebrew Exiles from Israel... They want to know more and more about their identity as Jews and about other things Jewish. When the news is on Israel, whether for good or bad, most Ibos feel very involved and often

turn instinctively to one another with a certain expression of peculiar understanding even in the presence of fellow Nigerians from other ethnic groups.

As in the pattern of the Jews in the early Christian faith or the present Jewish Christians in Europe and America, the questions to pose regarding the Ibos as partakers in Jewish hopes, though resident outside Israel, are: (1) How are the Ibos or Nigerian Jews to function in an absolutely Gentile country? (2) In our worship of God of Israel, how do we function in an apparently anti-Jewish Christian churches? (3) Should we strive to evolve a new way of Christian worship in line with the early Jewish believers with due respect to certain Jewish traditions like the Sabbath worship instead of Sunday worship, the Passover Feasts, etc.? (4) Will this not bring us into conflict with the Nigerian Gentile Christians? (5) How are we to include our Jewishness or Hebraism into Christian way of life under the New Covenant of Christ the Messiah rather than the Old Covenant of Moses with its heavy 613 rules and regulations?

The issues arising from the above questions are not universal. These may not be real issues in Israel itself and in some other Jewish communities of America, Europe and Russia. There, the vast majority of Jewish Christians were and still are not threatened by any loss of their Jewish identity as in the case of the Nigerian Hebrews or Jews, the Ibos. They [the Middle East Israelites and European/Russian Jews] knew that they were Jews and no amount of Christianity with anti-Jewish practices or any other form of religion could take their Jewishness or Hebraism from them.

In Nigeria as in other Jewish communities of the world where there has been a remarkable loss of Jewish identity, there cannot be any positive treatment of the said issues unless the whole level of the awareness of the Jewishness of the people can be raised. This requires the planning and development of Jewish studies within the framework of a multi-cultural and multi-ethnic group of Jewish people with different languages and dialects but from one ancestral and historic origin in Israel.

The various issues in this Chapter can be summed up as a socio-religious change issue. Success in this direction can only come through a process of a systematic awareness campaign and growth involving a sustainable research, education and organisation of the particular Jewish people in question. In all essentials, however, for the average Jew in exile, the country of exile notwithstanding, what is important is the level of awareness of his ancestral origin and his preparedness to change, to accept the proposal, for a Jewish cultural rebirth with a focus on the worship of one and only God, the Almighty God of Israel, whether in Christianity or in Judaism.

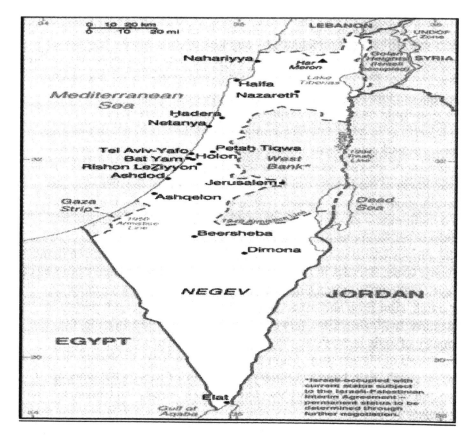

Map Of Israel

CHAPTER ELEVEN

THE GENESIS AND CHRONICLES OF THE IBOS: HEBREW EXILES FROM ISRAEL

Genesis of Ibos: Hebrew Exiles from Israel
Black Jews in America trace their heritage back to those Jews who fled from Jerusalem into Africa after the destruction of the First Temple 2,500 years ago... there are about a quarter million Jews of African decent living in America today. (Rabbi Capers Funnye (1999) - The Jerusalem Post, April 2, 1999 page B4).

The movement into Nigeria of the exiled Hebrews from Israel referred to in this book as the Nigerian Hebrews or Ibos following the curse of God upon the ancient Israelites, their ancestors, for disobeying Him began about 718 B.C. when King Salmanzar V of Assyria defeated Israel and drove away the inhabitants after rendering the entire land desolate. The Assyrian King brought in a large number of pagans from Assyria to occupy every inch of the land of the scattered Jews so as to blot out their identity, as a people of God. However, two tribes, Judah and Benjamin, out of the twelve tribes of Israel remained untouched by the Assyrians, Greco-Persians and Babylonians. And so only two tribes, of Israel were left behind in their original places until the advent of the Roman Empire. In AD 70, the Roman General, Titus, drove away the remaining two tribes of Israel and the remnants of the Hebrews or Israelites from their homeland, Israel, "into the four corners of the earth" in final fulfilment of the God's curse, on them (see Deuteronomy 28 Ezekiel 23).
- 1 will disperse you among nations and scatter you through the countries and 1 will put an end to your uncleanness (Ezekiel, 23:15).
- 1 will scatter them with a whirlwind among the nations they have not known (Zechariah 7:14).
With the last scattering exercise by the Romans about 700,000 Hebrews found themselves back to Egypt as a people in a renewed trouble. From Egypt they moved to Tunisia, to Syria, to Iraq, Morocco, Libya, Sudan and then to sub-Saharan Africa, settling in their largest numbers in Nigeria that was then not yet occupied by any Gentile power as in the countries of the Middle East and North Africa.

The then Nigeria was therefore safer in terms of freedom of religious practice. The Kwas, the Allokoos and the Pigmies who had no organised or established religion per se, (not Arabs) only inhabited Nigeria then. This was the most cogent human reason for the choice of Nigeria for final settlement in such a large number by the scattered Hebrews who more than any other thing wanted a safe place for their practice of Judaism/monotheism, worshipping the Almighty Creator of the Universe, the God of Abraham, Isaac and Jacob as the only God. But God's own reason for the choice of Nigeria for the scattered Jews in such a large number has just been known almost 2,500 years after the divine choice was made. There is oil and other mineral reserves second in quantity to that in the Middle East in the places where the Nigerian Jews, the Hebrews (Ibos) were forced to settle for the fulfilment of the Almighty's promise of restoration in the last days "after His great anger on the Hebrews should have been turned away".

As has been said earlier, given the large number of Hebrews (Ibos) in Nigeria, it is not likely that Israel as at now, "too small for the inhabitants", can contain any significant number of the Ibos, and in fact any other Jews now in the Diaspora. In fact, it is clear that not all the millions of Hebrews in the Diaspora including the Ibos will go back to settle in Israel before the soon coming 3rd World War because of the smallness of the land. But to show the holiness of His great name, to honor His words, His promise of material and spiritual restoration will get to all Hebrews wherever they may be in the world during the last days, even before the final gathering back of all the exiled Hebrews to the Land, as has been indicated in the previous chapter, will be increased very significantly following the final swift recovery of the "mountains of Edom, the mount of Esau, Philista. Ephraim and Samaria. Gilead and Zarephath" (Obadiah v. 18) - now referred to as south Jordan, Gaza, the West Bank, north Jordan and south Lebanon - every inch of the land now occupied by the Palestinians and the Arabs in the aforementioned places. In Nigeria, the God's grand plan for the last days' restoration of His people the Ibos is just too obvious now. Besides settling them in the oil rich areas of Nigeria, the LORD Almighty had blessed them with abundance of agricultural products (e.g., palm produce in big commercial quantity) besides their intelligence, dynamism and great ability for hard work. But what is happening to the material resources found in the Ibo areas of Nigeria is as if it is in fulfilment of this particular God's curse on the Jews:

People that you do not know will eat what your land and labour produce, and you will have nothing but cruel oppression... you will have olive trees throughout your country but you will not use the oil... (Deuteronomy 28:33.40).

Actually, the oil wealth in particular from Iboland is certainly not with the Ibos but with those from the other places where the oil is not found. However, it is believed that in God's own time, all that is due to the Ibos in Nigeria will get back to them. By "Ibos" here we mean all those in the Heebo (Ibo) nation of Nigeria irrespective of their present Nigerian or Gentile tribe or tongue - the Kwa and Ibo (Kwa-Ibo or Qua Ibo) groups in the core Ibo states, in the Rivers and Cross River States, in the Delta and the Nok culture areas of Benue/Plateau who accept their Hebraism (Iboism) and are willing to come to terms with the Almighty God of Israel and keep His commandments. Fo the Almighty has so much punished the Hebrews "for the sin of the father to the third and fourth generation of those who hate (Him)", He will show mercy and "love to a thousand generation of those who love (Him) and keep (His) commandments" (Exodus 20:6).

Chronicles of the Ibos: Hebrew Exiles from Israel.

The movement of the Hebrews (Ibos) from Israel to North Africa and then to Chad Basin of Nigeria and from there to the other parts of Nigeria where they are found today may have taken quite a long time. An estimated number of 400,000 out of 700,000 Hebrews who left Israel via Egypt arrived the apparent safe territory of Nigeria within the first hundred years of their forced journey. Ezeala (1992:14) holds that it took them eighty years twice the period of the Exodus from Egypt to move from Israel to Nigeria. According to Ononoju (1996), "The sufferings, regrets and groaning" that faced the Hebrew (Ibo) exiles in this period of movement and uncertainty are too many to mention. In fact, it has been noted by many writers (e.g., Basden, Purkiser) that whereas some of them (the Hebrews) repented and sought their God in line with the Torah, others re-examined their relationship with God in line with the tenets of the new religions championed by the Gentiles that they came across in the course of their movement whereas others forgot their God entirely and resorted to idol worshipping, sorcery, witchcraft, inter-marrying with the Gentiles, human killings and sacrifices, etc. even after they had moved into their permanent places of settlement. Here are the specific stages of the movement of the exiled Jews into Nigeria, of Ibos: Hebrew Exiles from Israel in the years that followed as revealed to the author:

1. The Nigerian Hebrews (Ibos) camped first at Chad Basin in North Eastern Nigeria, from Israel after the destruction of the First Temple about 2500 years ago, passing through Egypt, Libya and Sudan.

2. They left Chad Basin and camped around Zaria area including the Nok culture areas.

3. Some left Zaria/Nok culture areas of Benue/Plateau and camped in the neighbouring towns of Igala and Idoma. Some went as far as to Cameroon to settle.

4. The vast majority left Zaria/Nok culture areas for Southern Eastern Nigeria and settled en mass in Caleb Arbar (Calabar) where they first found salt water. The second place where salt was found was named Uburu (an almost perfect imitation of Hebrew). The salt from Uburu was from a salt lake in a dry hinterland and therefore, was more natural than the salt water from the sea in Calabar. So both Calabar area and Uburu became two first permanent places of abode for the exiled Hebrews, with Uburu attracting a vast majority of them because of the availability of the more natural salt and the relative dryness of the place.

5. From Uburu an overwhelming large section of the Ibos, following the already mentioned dispute left and moved towards north, south, east and west of the town in tribal and family groupings, naming each of their new area of settlement after the father or founder of the particular Israeli tribe from where they originated (e.g. Ozubulu, a town in Anambra State, after "Zebulun" the father of the tribe (Zebulun); after a prominent son of the tribe or family (e.g. from "Eri", the fifth son of Gad, the father of the tribe of Gad: Agulu-Eri, Ora-Eri Mbi-Eri, Umunne-Eri or Umuleri, Oweri or Owere or Owerri, Nkwo-Eri or Nkwere Ikwerre, etc. or from "Arodi", the sixth son of the Gad: Aro or Aro Tshuku or Chukwu); from "Attai" (pronounced as Atta): Atta Oweri, Uratta, Aguatta (Aguata), Umuatta (Umuata), etc; from an event surrounding the place of settlement (e.g., Awka from the Hebrew world "or'cha, meaning travelling caravan); from combined Hebrew words (e.g. Abam from the Hebrew words "ab", bush and "am", people or community; or from words coined from Hebrew and Kwa/Allokoo/Gentile words (e.g. Ama-Igbo or Igbo community; Aho-Igbo, Afigbo or Afikpo meaning the belly that gave birth to Igbos or the motherland of the Igbos). In most of these new areas, they established very formidable communities or kingdoms. Examples: Eri/Igboukwu kingdoms; Arochukwu kingdom; Igala kingdom, etc., even when they are in the minority.

6. From Eri and Igboukwu areas, some of the Eris moved to Onitsha and then later went across the Niger to Benin on a special spiritists assignment for an Oba of Benin and then back covering such Delta Ibo areas as Ibuzo ("Buz"), Asaba ("Asa Abba"), Isubuzo ("Hi-Sug Buz"). Agbo ("Abor"). Others who chose not to go back to Onitsha went southwards and passed through and settled in parts of today's Delta, Bayelsa and Rivers States. Some of the Nigerian Hebrew exiles in Eri as in Aro, Itam or Item, etc. had so much exhibited great mystical powers that were greatly patronised by both Jewish and non-Jewish nationals of Nigeria. Indeed, there is the popular legend that one of the descendants of Eri who first settled at Onitsha, at the bank of River Niger, near the domain of his relatives from the descendants of Zebulun (Ozubulu in Anambra State) had to travel across the Niger to the ancient Benin City or kingdom to prepare war medicine, talisman or charm for a prospective contender to the stool of Oba of Benin.

The people of Onitsha are purely Hebrews or Heebos (Ibos) of Eri stock from the tribe of Gad.

Another section of the fleeing Eris left Benin and moved southwards towards the sea and went to settle in some parts of the present day southern Delta, Bayelsa and Rivers States. After the Benin massacre of Eri descendants some went to settle in the riverine areas of now Delta, Bayelsa and Rivers while others found themselves back to the Ibo hinterland with each group making a tremendous impact in the lives and history of the people they went into their land to settle. These Hebrews from Benin were later to be joined by their kith and kin from Uburu at Bonny or (Ubani) after "Bani" (see Ezra 10: 29) now Opobo areas of Rivers State; at Amok after "Amok" (see Neh. 12:17), at Bonny under the leadership of Amakri after "Micri" (see 1 Chr. 9: 8), at Ahoda after "Judah" spelt and pronounced as 'Yehudah' in Hebrew, and so on.
7. Again from Uburu another small section of the Ibos mainly from the tribe of Judah who are not of Eri stock left and settled in Ahiara ("Ahira"), Abayi/Ahaba ("Ahab"), Ahiazu, Aba-na-Ohaz ("Ahaz"), Umuahia (of "Ahiah") i.e., now Mbaise/Ngwa/Umuahia areas; Ohazara (of "Azariah"), Iza "Izhar", Uzzi ("Uzzi") i.e., now Ebonyi/Enugu areas; in Item (Itam), after the Hebrew name "Etam" the tribe of Judah, in Etinan after "Ethnan" also of the tribe of Judah (see 1 Chronicles 4:3,7); in Anan of Levi (1 Chronicles 2:46); in "Caleb Arbar", Calabar (1 Chronicles 2:46).

It is in this rough and ready manner that the Ibos scattered themselves among the Gentiles in Nigeria, compromising their rich, ancient and noble Jewish heritage and inheriting the Gentiles' way of life and their worship of many gods, reminiscent of one of the God's curses on the Hebrews: "the LORD will scatter you among all nations, from one end of the earth to the other. There you will worship other gods - gods of wood and stone, which neither you nor your fathers have known". (Deut. 28:64). The different Hebrew (Ibo) tribal leaders that led their people into exile in Nigeria eventually became kings first in the manner of kings of Israel but before long some of them degenerated into the Nigerian Gentile demigodism after the manner of, for example, the Gentile King or Oba of Benin. According to Adams (1975:229):

The King (Oba) of Benin is fetish, and the principal object of adoration in his Dominions. He occupies a higher post here than the pope does in catholic Europe; for he is not only God's vice regent upon earth, but a god himself, whose subjects both obey and adore...

This type of rulership imitated by the Ibo kings which included instant capital punishment "coup de tete" which terminates instantly both his (erring subject's) life and sufferings... "was more in Eri Kingdoms of Delta areas and Onitsha who have had to live in Benin for reasons narrated above and so copied the fetishism and punishment methods of the Oba of Benin than in the other parts of "Ibo kingdoms". However, with the arrival of the missionaries in Nigeria in about 1842, with the striking assertion by Dr. Basden of the Anglican Mission (1861) that the Ibos are "a branch of the Hebrews" and so their history and origin should be concealed to them or else their practice of ancient Judaism could dwarf the spread of Christianity in (Heebo) Ibo nation of Nigeria and the incidental clashes and wars between the Ibo kings/leaders and the white people - in Aro Chukwu led by the Aro king, in Bonny led by the Bonny king, in Item, in Mbaise, in Abam and so on. In some of these places, there were incidences of beheading and sometimes eating of the flesh of the white people. Therefore the British decided to deal drastically with the entire Ibo (Heebo) nation, destroying both their kings and kingdoms, replacing them with warrant chiefs (solely chosen to serve the interest of the British, not of the people), carrying away their artefacts and deliberately erasing their history, and particularly their Jewish identity.

The impact of the defeat of the kings and the appointment of detestable or unacceptable warrant chiefs by the British was so tremendous that today the generality of the Ibos continue not to have any regard for their kings or leaders.

Hence the practice of republicanism for which the Ibos are now associated with in Nigeria. Besides, there is the consequent big dislike of Ibo culture and language particularly by the westernized or educated Ibos, bordering most of the times on Ibos hating their fellow Ibos in preference to non-Ibos. In fact, the "self-hatred" among the Ibos is so much that, for instance, the Ibos of Rivers, the Ikweres, despite their indisputable Ibo identity in all respects, their Ibo names and Ibo dialect, their Ibo culture, etc., publicly deny their Iboism; the Delta Ibos say they are not Ibos but Ika Ibos, the Onitshas say they are Onitshas not Ibos, and so on. But ironically when Ibos are attacked in Nigeria, as in the case of the Biafran War, all of them are attacked without discrimination. Writing on this issue in the Vanguard, Wednesday, August 19, 1998, Page 8, Ikpenmarom alleges that:

The Igbo refugees that fled Port Harcourt (during the Biafran War) returned only to discover that Port Harcourt indigenes (including Ikwere Igbos) had seized their landed property and tagged them "abandoned properties". Attempts to recover the properties only deepened hostility. In the option of the victimised Igbos of the central communities, such

An act, especially by their Port Harcourt Igbo speaking brethren, came to be regarded as void of brotherly sympathy. Because of this development, the Ikweres of Port Harcourt came to be marginalised psychologically, culturally and politically by other Igbos. Soon cultural and political marginalisation widened to attract tribal self-marginalisation. Some Igbo communities in Rivers State recently made attempts to change their names both of towns and persons to be free from Igbo identity. Thus, it is not surprising to hear that "Obigbo" is now called "Oyigbo", "Umueme" now "Rumeme". "Umumasi" now "Rumumasi "Umuokoro" now "Rumuokoro", etc. Influenced by this disaffectionate attitude towards their kinsmen, today it is not difficult for modern man or woman from some of these self-marginalised Igbos to deny that he or she is an Igbo. Most of them now feel strange when called Igbo.

In his own version Ralph Okoro, in the Hallmark National Newspaper, June 6 - June 12, 2001, page 9, asserts thus:

Some Igbos, wish to be more Nigerian than Nigeria itself. They are like a people who feel as if they should render a passionate if not national apology for being Igbos. Some of them would give anything to derobe themselves of all Igboness. If they had the opportunity they would like to tear out their Igbo names. Some would like to deface their Igbo appearances. Others would like to yank-off even their Igbo souls.

Perhaps there should be a national proselyte programme, to exorcise some of their Igboness.

With the Biafran War raging and ravaging many Ibo towns and villages, many Ibos, particularly those in the riverine areas, in the present day Rivers and Bayelsa states, were compelled to seek for ways of escape from the Biafran or Ibo enclave, where life had become practically unbearable, and join in the eventual share of the spoils of the war against their own brothers and sisters. For example, one notable Ibo man from Ikwere Ibo of the present Rivers State replied to the war time situation in which his kith and kin were the unfortunate victims by denying his Iboness, although his first and last names, his first and surname, including every aspect of his culture, language inclusive, point to the fact that he is an Ibo, through and through and nothing more. This Ibo man, the author of Sunset in Biafra, who confessed his bias in the following words: "my mind was filled with misgivings which I could not get rid of" (Amadi, Sunset in Biafra, 1973:77) was all out to "yank-off" his very Ibo soul and change or deform everything Ibo about himself and about his native Ibo town, Ikwere. In his own distorted version of the history of the Ibos in the riverine areas of today's Rivers and Bayelsa States, Amadi states:

Some thirty years ago the Ibos began to move in to trade in the riverine areas. Eventually many settled and by sheer force of numbers began to dominate the smaller tribes. Igbo came to be so widely used that certain tribes practically lost their mother tongue. It is a fact that one or two riverine tribes can hardly speak their own language now, and have to make do with a peculiar Igbo pidgin highly amusing to the Ibos. A determined effort is now being made to remedy the situation. In some areas this cultural imposition was very pronounced. Igbo was officially taught and spoken in schools. It could hardly be otherwise, since most of the teachers were Ibos. Gradually many local languages eroded... (Amadi, Sunset in Biafra, 1973:21)

The efforts of certain Ibos, whose actions and writings are religiously illogical and historically false, have touched the soul of the Ibo nation and led to, in no small measure, the promotion of disunity among the Ibos. This appears to be in line with the divine plan of the Almighty or rather His own way of fulfilling the aspect of His curse of lack of "singleness of heart and action" on the scattered Hebrews - a curse that fortunately will be repealed in the last days that we are now living in:

Behold... I will bring them back... I will give them singleness of heart and action. For thus says the LORD (Jeremiah 32:39).

Furthermore, from time immemorial, the history of the Jews or Hebrews has always repeated itself in Nigeria among the Ibos, particularly in the area of punishment through pogrom or war or destruction of property by other Gentile tribes, and the fulfilment of ancestral blessings at the end of each God's permitted disaster on them even when all hopes seem to have gone. Good examples are found in the incidences of the massacre of the Ibos and destruction of their property by the Hausa-Fulani of Arab descent in 1954, 1966, 1967 and mid 1980s in various parts of Northern Nigeria; and the 1967-1970 Biafran War following the killing of over 30,000 Ibos in the North and other parts of Nigeria.

After each sad event, after each organised killings of the Ibos and the looting and destruction of their property, they (the Ibos) reassemble, and go back to the places where, not long ago, they were the unfortunate victims. There they quickly recover their losses and progress even more to "the shame and disgrace" of their attackers or enemies. Observers maintain that this is as if the Ibos in Nigeria are deliberately being used as a cosmic playback to the following blessing of Almighty God of Jacob (Israel) and his seeds from the various chapters of the Holy Scriptures.
"All who rage against you, will surely shamed and disgraced
I will strengthen and help you.
I am your God; I will never forsake you.
I will always be with you irrespective of your sufferings,
No weapon fashioned against you shall Prosper.
You shall not be consumed, you sons of Jacob.
I will bless the works of your hand."
The story of quick social and economic recovery of the Ibos after wanton attacks on their lives and property is strikingly the same with the other world Hebrews - the European, American, Russian, North African, and so on. It is an indisputable fact that the World Jewry has produced for this planet earth, the greatest scientists and artists, greatest religious leaders, wisest men, greatest political leaders and richest people. As one of the seeds of Jacob or "a branch of the Hebrews", the Ibos are bound to enjoy all the blessings of Jacob. For instance, the Ibos of Nigeria have produced one of the world's best computer scientists, and the best among the black people of the world. An Ibo man, Philip Emegwali, produced the world's fastest computer; he was, as a result, invited by the then President of U.S.A., Mr. Bill Clinton, to the White House and honored accordingly. Indeed, the Ibo people's intellectual exploits, too many to mention here, in Nigeria and elsewhere in the world, in Britain, America, etc. are interestingly astonishing.

The Ibos may still have external and internal problems even among themselves, yet "God will never forsake them", for the ancestral blessings as well as the curses will follow "all seeds of Jacob wherever they are, even in the most distant part of the earth". Little wonder, therefore, why the Ibos of Nigeria are so oppressed and blessed at the same time. In fact, doing away with Ibos tantamount to doing away with the most prominent groups of the Nigeria's greatest scientists, greatest artists, greatest religious rulers, greatest rulers, greatest sportsmen and women, etc. The Ibos are the most scattered Ethnic group in Nigerian. Living as strangers or non-indigenes, the most prosperous stranger elements wherever they find themselves, the most dynamic and fearless group and the most positive contributors in terms of the development of the area of their residence whether as indigenes or non-indigenes. The Ibos, according to the famous British journalist, David Reed (1969), are "the people of Africa's most industrious and educated tribe. The industrious Ibos have boundless ambition..."

Conversely, when the words or the curses of God on the Hebrews are reviewed, one may think that they are specifically being directed to the Ibos in Nigeria:

"I will scatter you among the nations.

Your neighbours shall hate you.

Other tribes will hate you.

Your children will go into

slavery, with iron yoke on their necks'.

Your carcasses will be food for all the birds of

the air and the beasts of the earth."

At one time or the other in the history of Nigeria, the Ibos have these calamities singularly or severally as a result of the ancestral curses from the Almighty, not as a direct result of their own offence. In Nigeria of yester years, the Ibos far more than any other groups in Nigeria were carried away into slavery "with iron yoke on their necks" to America, with Ibo leaders and traders themselves playing the key role in the illegal dirty trade. Actually, in the past, God had always raised a wicked king in the land of Israel to fulfil His curse on the people of Israel, His chosen people, and after came His forgiveness and great blessings.

"Captain Adam's figure of 370,000 Ibo slaves sold in the Delta markets over a period of twenty years - equal to about one-quarter of the total export from all the African ports" - gives an idea of the number of Ibos sold as slaves to European slave traders for the American markets (Hodgkin, 1975:49).

130

For four hundred years this trade in human beings flourished!

By extension of this fact, it may be correct to assume that over one-quarter of all African Americans are of Ibo descent. The Ibo slaves exported in such alarming large numbers left behind them a Nigerian Hebrew (Ibo) nation in decay.

There was the psychological impact of slavery that it undermined the entire traditional Jewish system of life among the Ibos, and there was the corruption that spread with this breakdown of the time-honored tradition, coupled with the new opportunities for individual advancement at the cost of others. Some of the Ibos felt it better to sell their services to the European slavers and helped capture their fellow Ibos so that they themselves would not be caught. The result was the rise of a tiny but powerful class of Ibo slave dealers such as the Aros, the Amaigbos, to mention the best known examples, followed by a rapid and terrible degeneration of many of the Jewish values that had existed in Iboland before this time. The scramble for survival, which had once been a social matter, typical of a Hebrew society in exile, became an individual matter and greed coupled with inhumanity spread particularly among the new breed Ibo slave dealers. The new rich and powerful Ibo slave dealers with all their new tricks and fetishism of the Ibini-ukpabi in some cases prospered for a while, but only outwardly. They, particularly the Aros, became so proud and arrogant that they attracted the jealousy of the British colonial masters. The Aros, for instance, boasted very openly and caused it to be broadcast that, with their long juju or Ibini-ukpabi, they were invincible. Even when slavery was made illegal in Europe and America, the Aros refused to give up slavery. They attacked the British for refusing to allow them continue as middlemen in the new lucrative trade in palm oil and palm kernel. For these and other reasons outlined by Onwukwe (1995), the British vowed to destroy the Aro Empire, and to put a final end to Aro opposition to their rule. In 1912, the Chukwu, Ibini-ukpabi was destroyed and those who were implicated in its obnoxious activities were sentenced to death by hanging. As for Eze Kanu Okoro, the Eze Aro, he was sent into exile like the earlier "stubborn" Ibo leaders of Bonny ('Bani') and they all died in exile.

So, the success and prosperity of the Aros soon became the seeds of their own downfall and that of their fellow Ibos. A lot of punitive measures were instituted against the now demoralised and leaderless Aros. For instance, new roads were deliberately built away from the old Aro trade routes. In this way the Aro settlements were cut off from Aro

homeland. Business dried up and the economic life of Aro society collapsed. For the entire Ibo nation, the Aro mayhem destroyed their essentially ancient Jewish form of government, just as it destroyed their essentially Judaic traditional economy. Ibo unity and togetherness built up right from their time in Israel broke apart, just as families broke apart, seeking protection and succour from the smaller gods and witchcraft of the aborigines of Nigeria, and so monotheism as in Judaism, which many of the Ibos were merely managing (in the face of the earlier cultural erosion from the Gentile neighbours) to sustain, received yet another fatal blow and many important aspects of the Ibo Jewishness became a tragic myth. The desired Jewishness, as in the case of the Ethiopian Jews of North Africa, that would have been the Ibos' had it not been for the slave trade is unimaginably enormous, but at least many of it was transplanted with the slaves and continues to thrive today in South and North America where these ex-slaves are predominant, giving rise to the present generation of American black Jews. Indeed, according to Rabbi Capers Funye, the only black Jew sitting on the Chicago Board of Rabbis:
There are about a quarter-million Jews of African decent, living in America today.
The experience of black Jews in the United States is one of the best-kept secrets of the American, Jewish   community" (Rabbi Caper Funnye, 'Black and Jewish in America' in The Jerusalem Post, April 2, 1999, P.B4).
The killings of the Ibos during the Biafran war (1967-70) and the sight of their dead bodies littered all over the places for birds and wild beasts to feed upon reminds one of the curse: "your carcasses will be food for all the birds of the air and the beasts of the earth" (Deuteronomy 28:26). The taking away of Ibos "with iron yoke on their necks" and eventually selling them as slaves in open markets in America after a tortuous journey from Africa to America in ships, reminds one of the other God's curse on the Hebrews: "The LORD will send you back in ships to Egypt (this time, Hebrews (Ibos) in Nigeria to America) on a journey 1 said you should never make again. There you will offer yourselves for sale to your enemies as male and female slaves" (Deuteronomy 28:68).
The fact that the Ibos are found in all the nooks and cranny of Nigeria far more than any other language group in Nigeria or that they (the Ibos), are hated by their neighbours of other tribes is not any news to anybody in Nigeria; the fact is too obvious. As it was with the Hebrews in Israel in the days of king Ahab, Jeroboam and Ahaz who led Israel to the worship of other gods like Baal and brought calamities on the land, so it was with the

132

Hebrews in Nigeria (the Ibos) in the days of king Obi Ossai, Anna (Anan) Peppel, Jaja, the Aro-Chukwu slave traders, and the unknown Ibo kings and/or leaders (whose memory and names have been wiped out from the annals of history by a grand British design as punishment for their insurrection against the European traders and missionaries). These Ibo kings and leaders led the Ibos into all sorts abominations and hardships, so much so that in the end true Judaism (omenala Igbo) among the Ibos was slightly practised and the people "waver between two opinions" (1 Kings 18: 19,20) as in the case of other disobedient Jews in exile, and finally abandoned the faith.

Let it be noted here once again that the trouble for the Hebrews, especially when it has to do with God's curses on them, has always been brought about and perpetuated by fellow Hebrews themselves. In the Nigerian case, the slave traders who sold the Hebrew (Ibo) slaves to the European slaves masters were all Ibos - the Aro-Chukwu slave traders through the manipulation of Aro-Chukwu oracle in the hinterland and the Amakris, the Anna Pepples, the Jajas and others in the riverine areas of Ibo nation. It was horrible; but God's words of blessings or curses must be fulfilled in order to maintain His holiness.

In fact, one cannot convey a better description of the fulfillment of God's curses on the Hebrews (or in this case the Nigerian Hebrews or Ibos) regarding being taken away into slavery with "iron yoke on their necks" than by quoting the exact words of John Adams (1975):

This place is the wholesale markets for slaves as not fewer than 20,000 are annually sold here, 16,000 of whom are natives of one nation, called Heebos (Ibos), so that this single nation has not deported a less number of its people, during the last twenty years, than 320, 000; and those of the same nation sold at New and Old Calabar, probably amounted to 50,000 more, making an aggregate amount of 370,000 Heebos. The remaining part of the above 20,000 is composed of the natives of the brass country called Allokoo and also of Ibibios or Quas (Ibibio Kwa). Fairs, where the slaves of the Heebo nation are obtained, are held every five or six weeks at several villages, which are situated on the banks of the rivers and creeks in the interior...

Other exiled Hebrew descendants (e.g., Judah and Zebulun) are not as many and have been swallowed up by the Eris. Besides, Judah or the Jewish exiles bearing the tribal names of Judah (of the family or tribe or descendants of the third son of Jacob), who ought to have been considered before Gad (of the seventh son), has his descendants cut across Efik/Ibibioland, Igboland, Rivers, Benue, and so has no prominence or

133

logical claim to rulership in Igboland, where comparatively only a small number of his descendants live as minority.

Actually, the place of restoration of the fortunes of the exiled Jews is specifically Israel in the Middle East

- And I will bring back the captivity of my people Israel, and they shall build the waste cities, and inhabit them; and they shall plant vineyards, and drink the wine thereof... and they shall no more be plucked up out of their land which I have given them, saith the LORD thy God (Amos 9:14-15).

- I will bring them out from the nations and gather them from the countries, and I will bring them to their own land (Ezekiel 34:13)

The "land" can also be a symbolical term for any Jewish occupied territory outside Israel in any part of the world (e.g., Ibo nation of Nigeria) where the Jewish exiles may have found themselves, for the LORD Almighty had also said to the Jews through the Psalmist:

Ask of me, and I shall give the nations for thine inheritance, and the uttermost parts of the earth for thy possession (Psalm 2:8).

I am glad indeed that some of the Ibo-Jewish origin researchers have now discovered the second version of God's promise of restoration to the Jews, and are now saying that Israel's blessings can also get to all Jews wherever they are in the world, not necessarily when they get back to settle in Israel. If settlement, in Israel is occasioned, well good. If not, Israel's last days' blessings will surely get to all Jewish returnees in Israel as well as Jewish exiles located even at "the uttermost parts of the earth" (e.g., Ibo nation of Eastern Nigeria), especially if they, for one reason or the other, pray God to allow them remain in the place of exile, than go back to Israel to settle.

My interviews with a reasonably large number of Ibos on the subject of this book reveal that the prayer of many Ibos in this regard would be something like this: 'Oh God of our forefathers, God of Israel, after integrating us into the World Jewry, give us all the blessings of the promised restoration as unto all the other Jews the world over - restoration of fortunes, of singleness of heart and action, freedom from idol worshipping, etc. - but allow us to continue to remain in Iboland as our permanent homeland and indeed as a second homeland of any other Jew or group of Jews who may so desire in line with your above quoted words in Psalm 2:8.

In the light of the above, I hold that the thrust of our Ibo-Jewish origin research should not be to go to settle in Israel. Rather it should be on proper identification of the Ibos as part and parcel of the Jewish stock;

on a universal Jewish rebirth of the Ibos; and on international brotherhood of the Ibos in Nigeria with Jews anywhere in the world. This would provide a psychological cushion against which all Ibos in Iboland and in the Diaspora can sit and effectively operate in national and international politics, in commerce and industry.

The aforementioned, especially the case of some Rivers Ibos versus their brothers in the other parts of Iboland and the different versions of Jewish claim of the Ibos suggest that the Jewish rebirth of the Ibos and their gathering back into the World Jewry can be problematic if proper care is not taken to deal with basic erroneous assumptions on ethnic differences, self-perceptions and fallacies regarding the Ibos that have over the years permeated their life style in their various places of exile in Nigeria.

Needless to over-emphasise the fact that adequate and proper treatment of these assumptions and problems by way of research and publications should be made by the local intellectuals, not by their foreign counterparts, since they (the local intellectuals) have better knowledge of the local realities in their country, of the political, social, religious and ethnic differences among the Nigeria Hebrew exiles which can make their integration into the World Jewry or their "singleness of heart and action" difficult. But their foreign counterparts in Israel or America, for instance, are more knowledgeable about the organization and systematization of knowledge and experience besides their better financial and material standing. It is from this last standpoint that foreign help and co-operation may be needed. Prominent among the erroneous assumptions, fallacies and problems in question that require serious consideration are the following:

Ethnic, political and sometimes differences among the different Nigerians that now claim to be Hebrews in exile (e.g. Ibos and Ibibios; Rivers Ibos and upland Ibos) are so deep rooted that they can never live and work together as one community.

Hebrews, are light-skinned. Therefore, it is wrong to talk of Nigerian Hebrews since there are no original white or light-skinned Nigerians. Hebrews or Jews in Israel have no regard whatsoever for dark-skinned people whether they have genuine claim of Jewish blood or not.

The story of dark-skinned Hebrews like that of Zipporah, the African wife of Moses or the descendants of Moses who are dark-skinned or black women married to Hebrews like King Solomon and others in the Scriptures is a fallacy.

The idea of Hebrews in Nigeria connotes automatic rejection of all other religions (Christianity, Islam, etc) in favour of Judaism.

Religious facts (e.g., prophecies in the Old Testament Bible or the Torah) that relate to Israel as a people but have not been repeated or modified or changed in the New Testament Bible or the Quar'an cannot hold true, and should be ignored.

What the Nigerian Hebrews need most is that their children should become responsible, self-reliant adults with good intelligence and technical know-how to continue with popular traditional roles of their people, not knowledge of Israelis' affairs or of Jewish way of life. Jewish way of life, their methods of production, the pattern of consumption, the systems of ideas and values that suit the relatively affluent and educated world Hebrew community are unlikely to suit poor, semiliterate Nigerian Hebrews. Poor peasants and semiliterate people cannot suddenly acquire the outlook and habits of sophisticated people of the Jews in the West and Middle East.

There is no solutions to the problems of Hebrew exiles in Nigeria, unless the whole level of traditional and Western education of the different Nigerian Hebrew exiles or communities in Nigeria can be raised so that each Nigerian Hebrew area can afford different rich systems of ideas and values (as in Israel) for its members to choose from.

The various issues in this book can be summed up as a social change issue. Some form of magic produced by religious activities, scientists, and economic or educational planners cannot obtain success in this direction. It can come only through a process of growth involving research, education and organisation as well as the discipline of the people involved. For the people, the level of awareness of their ancestral origin and their preparedness to change, or for a Jewish cultural rebirth cannot be taken for granted.

For proper and well deserved treatment of the Nigerian Heebo (Ibo) nation in the community of World Hebrews, due and mature investigations and considerations are needed in the areas of these assumptions, fallacies and problems. Already, the Nigerian Hebrew Renaissance with Headquarters in Nigeria led by the author and Center for Igbo Roots & Culture with Headquarters in Tel-Aviv, Israeli, Prince Okonkwo-Uzor and other Hebrew groups in Nigeria or elsewhere in Africa, such African Hebrew Organisation have started some good work in these areas. For instance, the Nigerian Hebrew Renaissance in collaboration with the Centre for Igbo Roots and Culture in Tel Aviv, Israel, carried out the 2002 research visit to Agulueri as reported earlier in this book.

136

Dr. Nnamdi Azikiwe, Nigeria's First President.

CHAPTER TWELVE

HEBREW WORDS AND NAMES IN IBO VOCABULARY

Introduction

In the previous chapters of this book, one can find enough evidence to show that the Ibos of Nigeria (some of whom are now of permanently located in non-Ibo speaking areas and speak languages of those other Gentile tribes as their mother tongue) are of Hebrew descent. The evidence in words and names contained in this chapter is merely an embellishment. However, this evidence has the extra advantage of leading us to the knowledge of the tribes of origin of the exiled Hebrews in their ancestral home, Israel.

Hebrew Names and Words, in Ibo Vocabulary.
Among the Nigerian Hebrews (Ibos) and World Hebrews names given to children are selected from the immediate or extended family circle. For both stocks of Hebrews or Jews, these names are selected from among the living and dead relatives - father, mother, grandfather, grandmother, uncle, nephew, cousin, and so on, or sometimes someone every dear to the father or the family as a whole, his family of origin notwithstanding. This explains why the Ibos of Nigeria like any other Jews raise eyebrow or ask questions if, on the day of circumcision and christening of their male child, which in a traditional Ibo society, is usually on the eighth day of birth, a non-family based name is given to the new-born child. For instance, when John the Baptist was born and the name John was announced by the mother Elizabeth, on the eighth day being the day of the boy's circumcision and christening according to custom, the Hebrew neighbours and relatives present at the ceremony were surprised and pointed out to her that "there is no one among your relatives who has that name" (Luke 1:6). It is common among the Ibos, particularly of the old Bende Division of Eastern Nigeria to answer not only ones relative's names but even also one's father's name. Hence they answer names as Kalu Kalu, Eke Eke, Agwu Agwu, Anyim Anyim, Imo Imo, etc. Some first-born males and their children have borne no other name other than the family name, particularly when the family is a famous one. Hence we

find the spread of such Jewish family names among the Ibos as "Ishi" (Isi or Ichi). "Agur" (Agu), "Attai" (Atta), "Abia" (Abia). "Eder" (Ede), "Naarah" (Nara), "Ara: (Ara), "Ezer" (Ezer), and so on. Ishi, for example, is a Hebrew or Jewish name that is found in virtually all parts of Iboland - Anambra State (Ichi, Ichi Nnewi, Amaichi); in Imo State (Amaichi Etiti; Umu-Isi Mbano. Inyishi Atta Ikeduru...); in Abia State (Ishi-Osu, Okoko Item; Umu-Isi, Igbere), in Ebonyi State (Ishiagu), in Rivers State (Isiokpo), and so on.. 'Ishi' is pronounced as 'ichi' in Anambra Ibo, as 'Ishi' in Enugu and Ebonyi Ibo, and as 'Isi' in Abia and Rivers Ibo. The same is true with the Hebrew name "Attai" pronounced as 'Atta' - Aguatta or Aguata, Imo State; Umuata, Atta Ikeduru, Uratta ("Hur Attai") in Owerri, Uratta Ngwa, in Abia State, etc. The other Hebrew or Jewish derived names in Iboland have been outlined in the Table below.

Ibo as well as Jewish names are also given in remembrance of events, name of the day of birth, certain circumstances surrounding the birth and so on. Hence we have with the World Hebrews such names as Emmanuel* (God with us); Moses* (drawn from water - Pharaoh's daughter drew him from the water); Gershom (alien - the father of Moses reminds himself that he has become an alien in a foreign land: Exodus 18:2); Eliezer (God is my helper, for the father of Moses affirms at his birth: 'my father's God is my helper - Exodus 18:2); Achan (troubler, Achan troubled Israel); Isaac (laughter, for Sarah laughed when the birth of Isaac was prophesied to her by the Angel); Jabez (sorrowful, for Jabez was born in sorrow, etc.). In the same manner, Nigerian Hebrew (Ibo) names have circumstantial meanings too. They include Okonkwo, Okafor, Okorie, Okeke, (because the child was born on any of the market days: Nkwo, Afor, Orie or Eke); the same explanation goes for other Ibo names: Nwankwo, Nwafor, Nwaorie, Nweke or Mgbokwo, Mgbafor, Mgborie...

Other circumstantial names among the Ibos include: Nwaogu (a child born during war time); Amara (a child seen as a special grace or charity from God); a child destined to bring God's blessing to the family).

---

*This is the English derivation of the name in Hebrew as recorded in the English version of the Holy Scriptures, but the concept of circumstantial evidence of the name, which is our major concern, is the same. Such

English version of the Jewish name as John, James, Peter, Stephen, etc., that abound in the new Testament Bible are not included at all in the Table presented below.

Onwuchekwa, Onwubuiko or Ndukwe (plea for long life for the child); given because there had been previous cases of premature deaths before the birth of the child).

In the first edition of this book, I tried to show that Ibos of Nigeria named their towns and children after certain famous people in Israel from where they came to Nigeria (e.g. Kings like "Asa" (Asa Ngwa, Abia State; "Ahab" (Ahaba, Isuikwuato, or Ahiaba Ngwa, Abia State); Ahira (Ahiara Mbaise) or after prominent people like "Eri" (e.g., Agulueri); "Uzzi" (Uzzi Ossa Umuahia; "Naarah" (Nara Enugu State); "Izhar" (Izza Ebonyi State); "Ono" (Ono, name of person in Enugu State); "Ahlai" (Alayi), "Asa" (Asa); "Abiah" (Abia);"Anan Arba" (Ananaba). Others include "Ishi" (Ishi or Ichi); "Eder" (Ede); "Nob" (Nnobi); "Ezer" (Eze); "Eker" (Eke); "Lod" (Lodu); "Nebo" (Nebo), "Dan" (Adani). Examples of such names that occur in Israel and Iboland with the same spelling and similar or the same pronunciation abound and only the best known, are outlined in the Table that follows:

Ibo (Igbo?) Names of People and Places	Equivalents in Hebrew
Aba (Ibo town in Abia State, Nigeria). Refer to: -Abagana (Abba Gana), Anambra State; -Abala (Abba Ala), Abia State; -Abala Osimili, Delta State; -Abaomega (Abba Omega), Ebonyi State;	"Abba", father popular name of person in Israel and Arab world; or from the name "A(r)ba, forefather of Anak of the tribe of Judah (see Joshua 15:13
-Abakiliki (Abba kaliki) Ebonyi State; Umukalila, Obingwa, Abia State;	of "kalika", Hebrew word for winding,...
-Abatete (Abba Hetite), Anambra State; -Abaukwu, Aba Ngwa, Abia State;	of "Hetite", one of the mighty men of David (2 Samuel 23:39)

140

-Abara (Abba Ara), name of person in Item, Abia State; Umuara, Osisioma Ngwa, Abia State; Abanta, Amaokwe Item, Abia State; -Amaba (Ama Abba), Amokwe Item, Abia State	of "Ara", one of the grand sons of Asher (11` Chronicles 7:33) or of "Arah" (see Ezra 2:5).
Abba, town in Imo State, Anambra State. Abali (Ibo name, Rivers and Abia States)	of "Obal" (see 1 Chronicles 1:22).
Abam (town in Abia State)	from two Hebrew words, "ab", bush and "am", people of; community of people living in a bushy area (as of the early times).
Abayi (town in Abia State). - Abayi Ngwaukwu; - Abayi Umuocham; - Abayi Nchokoro; - Abayi Umuokoroato; Abayi Aba Ngwa;	of "King Abijah" of the tribe of Judah – (see 2 Chronicles 13:1 – pronounced as Abiya, corrupted as Abayi in Ngwaland and as Abiayi in Item, Abia State. In Hebrew, 'j' is pronounced as 'y', and so, for example, Jesu (Jesus) is written as Jesu but pronounced as Yeshua. In the same vein 'Jah', the attribute name of God, Yahweh, is pronounced as 'Ya'. Hence 'Ale le Jah' is pronounced as 'Ale le

Ya'. So, in effect,
'Tonu Ya' in Ibo is
simply a corrupt Hebrew
of 'Tonu Jah' or praise
be to Jah. Indeed
whenever the Ibos greet
or shout 'Kwenu!' to
elicit the response 'Ya',
they are merely trying
(as did their forefathers
in ancient) to invite the
presence of the
Almighty God of Israel
in whatever they are
doing. In Judaism, the
religion of the Jews, it is
forbidden to pronounce
the revealed name of
God. Hence the use of
attribute names of God
instead. Some of these
attribute names include:
Hashem, Elohim, Adoni,
Eloheaka, Eloheenu,
Hoseenu. And with the
advent of the Gentiles or
Gentile believers in
overwhelming majority
in Christianity, Bible
translators, or rather
Gentile Bible translators,
ignoring the non-calling
of the revealed name of
God of Israel, as other
Jewish customs in the
early Christian church,
began to add the full
revealed name of God of
Israel, Yahweh,
corrupted as Jehovah, to

	the name attributes resulting into such names of God among the Christians as: -Jehovah Mekaddishekem (Exodus 31:13), instead of Mekaddishekem only as instead of Mekaddishekem only as in the Torah; Jehovah Tsidkenu (Jeremiah 23:6); Jehovah Nisi (Genesis 14:18); JehovahEl Elyon (Genesis 14:18); Jehovah Shanmmah (Ezekiel 48:35); Jehovah El Gibbor (Isaiah 9:6-7); Jehovah Sabaoth (1Samuel 1:3); Jehovah Rohi (Psalm 23:1); Jehovah Rapha (Psalm 103:3); Jehovah Shalom (Judges 6:24); Jehovah El Shaddai (Genesis 17:1). Actually, the discredited form, Jehovah (from Jahveh) for YAHWEH, was unknown till an erring scholar coined it in the sixteenth century. "Abba", (common Hebrew name in Israel

Abba (name of town in Anambra and imo States)	and in all Middle East, including Arab nations).
	"Abijah", (pronounced as 'Abiya' as 'j' in Hebrew is pronounced as y') name of one of the sons of King Solomon; also name of the second son of Samuel (1 Chronicles 6:28; 7:8).
Abia (town in Ohafia, Abia State; town in Udi Enugu State).	
- Obikabia (town in Abia and Imo States);	
- Ebiabi (Ebi Abia), Amokwe Item, Abia State;	Prophet "Abaye" one of the minor prophets of Israel.
Abiaeye (name of person in Item, Abia State; also in Rivers/ Bayelsa Ibo areas).	"Abor", Hebrew word for 'cross over'. During the early period of the Ibos: Hebrew Exiles from Israel from Israel to Nigeria, and from one place in Nigeria to another, the name (usually Allokoo or Kwa) of the final settlement area was joined with the Hebrew word 'Abor' to indicate that there was a cross over of usually a river or something like a big gully or so before the final settlement of the people in the area. Example: Abor or Aboh-Mbaise, etc. 'Abor' alone was used to stand for the name of a town.
Abor or Agbor, town in all Iboland (e.g., Agbor, town in Delta State). Abor-Mbaise, Imo State; Abor-Achi, Enugu State; Abor-Enugu-Agu, Anambra State, etc.	

	The group of Eri descendants who were forced out of Benin and went to settle at Agbor saw themselves as having made a successful cross over from the danger zone in Benin to a new place of safety and freedom across the big river between Benin and Agbor and so they called the place 'Abor", now pronounced as 'Agbor'.
Ada (name of person, usually the first daughter in an Ibo family); a popular common name for any female child in an Ibo family	"Adah", name of the first daughter of Elon (see Genesis 36:2).
Adani (town in Enugu State).	mimicry of the Jewish name, "Dan" (2 Chronicles 30:2).
Adiele (name of person in Abia, Imo and Rivers States)	"Adiel" (1 Chronicles 27:25; 4:36).
Afra (town in Umuahia, Abia State). Afra Atta Ibeku, Umuahia; Opara or Okpara or Okpala, (name of person in all Iboland, usually the first son of the family)	mimicry of "Ophra", first son of Meconothai of the tribe of Judah (1 Chronicles 4:13, 14). - variations of "Ophra" .

145

Aham (name of town, person in all Iboland); Aham, a popular Ibo name is pronounced as 'Afam' in northern Ibo nation and as 'Aham' in southern Ibo nation. Afam, name of Ibo town, Obigbo or Oyibo, Rivers State. Actually in some Ibo areas 'f' is pronounced as 'h'.	"Ahiam" (see 1 Chronicles 11:35).
Agu (name of person in all Iboland). Aguata (Agu Atta), town in Anambra State.	"Agur" (Proverb 30:1).
Agulueri (Agulu Eri), name of town in Anambra State.	"Agur Attai" – "Attai" of the tribe of Judah is pronounced as 'atta' in Hebrew (1 Chronicles 12:11). "Eri", the fifth son of Gad of the tribe of Gad (Genesis 46:16). 'Agulu' is Allokoo word for namesake. When combined with the name 'Eri', it means the namesake of Eri, a name to be borne only by a son of Eri.
Ahaba (town in Abia State, pronounced as Ahab in Isuikwuato, with 'b' almost exactly as in as in Hebrew, or as Ahiaba in Ngwaland. Ahiaba Ngwaukwu; Ahiaba Ubi Ngwa; - Ahiaba Okpulo " Amaba (Ama	"King Ahab" of the tribe of Judah (1 Kings 19:1).

Ahaba)Isuikwuato Amaba Alayi; Amaba or Amabo Okoko Item; Amaba (Ama Ahaba) Ugwueke, etc. Ahiara (town in Mbaise, Imo State). Ahukam (name of person in Imo State). Akabo (town in Owerri, Imo State). Akanu (name of person and of town in Abia, Enugu, Ebonyi States. Of person:- Akanu Ibiam, Kanu Nwankwo, Kalu (different from Kamalu, name of an idol). Of town:- Akanu Item; Akanu Ohafia; Akanu Ngwa; etc. Nkanu (corruption of Akanu) Enugu State; Umunakanu (pronounced as Umunakano) Mbano, Imo State. Akaeze (town in Ebonyi State).	"Ahira" (see Numbers 7:28). "Ahikam" (see Jeremaiah 41:1). "Acbor", son of Micaiah of the tribe of Judah (2 Kings 22:11). "Akan" (see 1 Chronicles 1:42).

Alaezi, Alezi (name of person in Abia State), of the shrine of god, Alaezi, mimicry of Elieazer, considered by the ancient Hebrews exiled into Nigeria (just Moses (Amusu), Elisha (Olisa), Paul, and other ancient prophets of Israel) as a god.

Alayi (town in Abia State)

Ama (Ibo word for compound, community of, people of..) Used before a name or people, it means people of or community of the aforementioned. Therefore, Amaigbo, for instance, means people or community of the descendants of Igbo. Note that Igbo is the famous (notorious?) relation of Eri.
-Amasiri, Amaeke, Amakahia

Amiri (town in Abia, Imo, Anambra States). Amiri, Uturu Abia State; Obomiri, Imo State; Ekwulumili, i.e., Ekwulumiri, Anambra

"Eker Ezer" of the tribe of Judah. "Eker" (1 Chronicles 2:27; "Ezer" (Nehemiah 3:19; 1 Chronicles 1:42).

mimicry of Hebrew name, 'Elieazer', the priest in the days of Moses (see Numbers 32:2).

"Ahlai" of the tribe of Judah (1Chronicles 2:31).

State; Mgboko Amiri, Obingwa, Abia State.	"King Omiri", king of Israel (1 Kings 16:21).
Amorka or Amoku (town in Abia, Anambra, Rivers States). Amoku, Alayi, Abia State; Amoku, Rivers State; Amorka, Anambra State.	
Anaeke or Aneke (name of person in Enugu, Anambra, Ebonyi States).	"Amok" of the tribe of Levi (Nehemiah 12:7; 12:17).
Anaiah or Anagha (name of person in Abriba, Abia State – Anagha Ezeikpe)	
Anyiam (name of person in Ebonyi State), literally meaning 'Overcome'). Anyim (name of person in Abia and Ebonyi States – e.g., Anyim Pius Anyim);	"Anak" (see Joshua 15:13). "Anaiah" (see Nehemiah 10:22).
Ariam or Ariama (town in Abia State). Umuariama Ngwa; Umuariam, near Umudike Umuahia; Ariam Usaka, Obingwa; Ariam Usaka, Ikwuano Umuahia. *Osoka (corruption of	"Aniam" from the half-tribe of Manasseh (1 Chronicles 7:19); "Ayin" is the 16th Hebrew Alphabet, literally meaning

Usaka), name of person in Item, Abia State.	'aliyah' or overcomer
Aro, Arodi, Aro-Chukwu (town, name of person in Abia, Anambra, Ebonyi and Imo States) Arodi Izuogu (logically corrupted as Arondizuogu).	"Aram Issachar" – "Araam" (1 Chronicles 7:34); "Issachar" (Genesis 46:13).
Atta (town in Abia, Imo and Anambra States).	
Aguata (Agu(r) Atta) Anambra State; Atta Ikeduru, Imo State; Umuatta, Atta Ikeduru; Atta Nkwere Isu, Imo State Amata (Ama Atta Ishiagu, Ebonyi State; Amata, Uburu, Ebonyi State; - Amatta, Ikeduru Oguta (Og Atta), Imo State;	"Arodi", the sixth son of Gad of the tribe of Gad (Genesis 46:16).
Uratta (Ur Atta) Owerri, Imo State; Uratta Isiala Ngwa, Abia State; Atani (Ata Ani) Arochukwu; Atani Uburu, Abia State Atanko (Atta Nko), Amaokwe Item, Abia State.	"Attai" (pronounced as 'atta' in Hebrew) – see 1Chronicles 2:37. of "Agur" (Proverb 30:1)
Afra Atta (Ophra Attai)	

Ibeku, Umuahia	
Awka (town in Anambra State). Awka Etiti (Awka Hetite) Anambra State; Okigwe (Awka Igwe) Imo State; Dioka (Ndi Awka), Mabano, Imo State.	of "Og" (see Deuterenomy 3:13). of "Ur" (see 1Chronicles 11:35). of the word, "ani", Hebrew word for land; prosperity. Therefore, 'Atani' means 'Land of Atta or Attai.
Awa (name of person in Item, Ohafia, Abia State; also name of town in Oguta Imo State). Ndiawa, Arondiziogu, Imo State; Umuawa, Ohuhu Umuahia, Abia State; Umuawa, Isialangwa, Abia State; Umuawa or Umuowa Orlu, Imo State. Aya or Eya (name of person in Rivers and Enugu States); in Abriba, Abia State, it is pronounced as Eye, also	from Hebrew name "Ophra" (pronounced as Ofra or corrupted as Afra), first son of Meconothai of the tribe of Judah (1 Chronicles 4:13). "or'cha" (awka), Hebrew word for travelling company, caravan. Maybe referring to a group of Ibos who first found themselves in that particular settlement area, referring to themselves as settled

name of person. Ogboaya, popular name in Opobo, Ubani ("Bani") Ibo area of Rivers State.	travellers – one of the circumstantial names adopted by the Nigerian Hebrews for themselves.
Asa (town in Abia State). Asa Umunteke (or Asa Umu Tekoa); - Asa Nnentu; Asa Umukalika; Asaba (Asa Abba)	from Hebrew word, 'avva', desire, longing… 'v' is pronounced as 'w' in Hebrew.
Asaga (town in Abia State). -Asaga Ohafia, Abia State; - Asaga Akholo, Okoko Item	
Azumini (Azumiri) Abia State. - Nzimiro, name of person in Imo State	"Aija", pronounced as Aya since 'j' in Hebrew is pronounced as 'y'. (Nehemiah 11:31, 35; Ezra 2:33).
Ebe (name of person in Abriba, of town in Item, Abia State; first settlement area of Itam, Item ("Etam") people before Potopo, mimicried as Opobo in the present Rivers State. Ebe, Udi, Enugu State; Ebenebe, Enugu, Anambra State; Eberiomuma, Rivers State; - Ndiebe, Amaogudu	from "King Asa", king of Judah, of the tribe of Judah (1 Kings 15:8). "Tekoa" (see Nehemiah 3:27).

Abriba.	
Edda (town in Ebonyi State)	- from Hebrew word, "saga", to grow, expand, become large. Adopted name for a Nigerian Hebrew town with expansionist tendencies, like Asaga Ohafia. Mimicry of "Zimiri" (1 Kings 16:15) Corruption of "Zimiri".
Ede (name of Ibo person and/or town). Ede (name of person in Enugu State); Ede Ede or Edede (name of person in Abriba, Abia State); Nede (town, Anambra State); Umunede (town, Delta State); Amaede (town, Isialangwa, Abia State); Egede Udi, Enugu State.	"Eber" (see 1 Chronicles 1:18).
Eleke (name of person in Item, Abia State). Umuoleke (or Umu Eleke), Isialangwa , Abia State.	"Eldaah" brother of "Abida", descendant of "Keturah", second wife of Abraham (Genesis 25:4). *There is an Ibo community next to Abaukwu in Aba, Abia State, called Obida (corruption of 'Abida').
Eketa or Ekenta (name of town and of person in Ite and Ngwa, Abia State). Eketa Isialangwa; Ekenta Okoko Item; Keita (name of person in Akwa Ibom, part of Ibo	from Hebrew name, "Eder" (see 1 Chronicles 23:23)

nation).	
Eke (name of person in all Iboland; also of town in Enugu State).	"Helek" of the tribe of Judah (Numbers 26:30).
Eke (town in Enugu State);	
Amaeke Item, Abia State;	
Amaeke Ishiagu, Ebonyi State;	
Ugwueke, Abia State; Abueke (Aboeke), Ihiteuboma, Imo State; Umueke Umuoba Isiala Ngwa, Abia State.	from Hebrew name "Kelita" (Ezra 9:23).
Ekennia (name of person in Mbaise, Imo State).	
Enam (Unam) – name of person in Item, Abia State.	"Eker" of the tribe of Judah (1 Chronicles 2:27).
Ete (name of person in Item, Abia State; attribute name for an elder in Bende areas of Abia State and in Akwa Ibom and Cross River States).	
Obete (Obrete, Obingwa, Abia State); Mgboko Obete, Obingwa, Abia State; Akwete Ndoki, Abia State;	
Ogbete Enugu, Enugu State	
	"Elkannah"

Epele (name of person in Abia, Ubani ("Bani") Ibo ares of Rivers State and Delta States.	(1Chronicles 6:25). "Enam" of the tribe of Judah (Joshua 15:34).
Etinan (name of town in Abia and Akwa Ibom States).	"Ether" of the tribe of Judah (Joshua 15:42)
Eze (name of person in all Iboland). Ndieze Akholo Okoko Item; Umueze; Ihodimeze, Imo State; - Udumeze (of Royal family in Ohafia, Abia State. Ihodimeze, Owerri, Imo State	
	"Elpelet" of the house and family of David (see 1 Chronicles 14:5). "Ethinan", a clan of Judah (1 Chronicles 4:7)
Eri (of town and person in all Iboland). Of towm:- Agulueri; Umuleri; Oraeri; Mbieri Of person:- Nwaneri; Erinma.	"Ezer", son of Joshua (Nehemiah 3:19; 1Chronicles 1:42).

Ezike (town in Enugu State). Enuguezike, Enugu State. Ezinifite, (town in Anambra State); Ezinihite, (town in Imo State).	- "Dumah" "Ezer"; "Dumah" (1Chronicles 1:30). Actually, "Ezer" was the son of Mispah (Nehemiah 3:19). In ancient Israel that name symbolised good leadership and tody among the Nigerian Hebrews, the Ibos, Eze (Ezer) also symbolises good leadersip or rulership, and it is also simply given to a child destined or expected to be a good leader in future. From the Hebrew name, "Eri" (Genesis 46:16).
Ibuzo (town in Ibo area of Delta State) - Obuzo (town in Ngwaland, Abia State); Obuzo, Ukwa West, Abia State. Iheaka (name of person in Item, Abia State)	Corruption of "Hezekiah", king of Judah. - from the Jewish word 'Ibrit' (or Hebrew in English), pronounced as Ivrit, corrupted as Ifrit or Ifite, and then Ihite for those Ibos that pronounce 'f' as 'h'. The word 'Ibrit' stands for Hebrew or emigrant.

	Ezinihite or Ezinifite means community of Ibrit or Hebrews, another version of Oraifite, as 'ora' and "ezi" in Allokoo/Igbo language means 'compound of' or community of'.
Ihite or Ifite (names of towns in Anambra and Imo States). Oraifite (town in Anambra State); Iiteukpo (town in Anambra State); Ihite (town in Imo State); IhiteUboma (town in Imo State); *Abridged version of Ihite in the parts of Iboland where Ifrit or Ifite is pronounced as Ihite is 'Ihie'. Hence we have these other variations of Ifrit or Ifite as Ihie Ngwaukwu, abis State; Ihieoma orlu, Imo State; Ihiembosi, Anambra State; Ihiechiowa, Abia State; Ihieala (Ihiala) Anambra State.	from "Buz" of the tribe of Gad (1 Chronicles 5:12).

"El heaka", one of the attribute names of God of Israel. The other attribute name of God that has been used as a name of a town, though, is "Nissi". Hence the name, 'Enugu Nise (Nissi) or Nise Enugu. |
| Ika Ibo (name of a group of Ibo people in Delta State) | from the Hebrew word 'Ibrit', pronounced as 'Ivrit', 'Ifrit' in some parts of Iboland, corrupted as 'Ifite' or 'Ihite' in those parts of Iboland where 'f' is pronounced as 'h'. The original Hebrew word 'Ibrit' means emigrant, a nickname for Abraham |

	who God commanded to migrate to Canaan, for eventual establishment of the state of Israel. Today, the name 'Ibrit' is so respected by the Nigerian Hebrews (Ibos)
Ikenazi (name of town in Obowu, Imo State)	that in some parts of Iboland, precisely in Owerri area, whenever there is an apparent
Ishi, Isi or Ichi (of towns in all Ibo nations of Abia, Anambra, Delta State, Ebonyi, Enugu, Imo, Rivers ...) Ichi, Anambra State; Ichi Nnewi, Anambra State; Amaichi, Imo State; Ishi Agu (Agur) or Ishiagu, Ebonyi State; Umuisi (Umu Isi or Ishi) Igbere, Abia State; Osuisi (Osu Isi or Ishi) Amabo Okoko Item; Isieke Okai Item; Isiegbi Ozuitem; Isingwu Ohuhu Umuahia, etc	mishap or abnormality or even an abomination, the Ibo person at the spot quickly dissociates himself and reaffirms almost instinctively his Hebraism or Jewishness which abhors such abnormality by shouting 'Ihiemo' or 'Ihiemkwa', which means, 'I am still Ibrit (i.e., Ifite, Ihite or Ihie), I can, therefore, not be part of this abnormality.
Isu (name of town in Abia, Imo and Delta States) - Isuikwuato, Abia State; - Isuochi, Abia State; - Isubuzo (Isu "Buz") Delta State; - Isunjeaba, Imo State. Item , Itam (name of	from Hebrew word "ikkar", meaning ploughman, tiller. In those early days tilling of the land is a very noble profession and so anybody referred to as ika (ikkar) regards such appellation with pride. "Kenaz" of the tribe of Judah (1Chronicles 4:15).

town in Abia and Akwa Ibom States; also name of person). - Item, Bende LGA Abia State; - Ozuitem " " "; - Itam, Itam LGA Uyo, Akwa Ibom State. Izza (name of town in Ebonyi State). Izzi or Uzzi (town in Abia, Imo and Ebonyi States) Uzzi Ossai Umuahia, Abia State; Uzzi, Imo State; State; Uzzi, Imo State; Lodu, near Uzuakoli (town in Abia State). Maduka (name in all Iboland). Mbieri (town in Abia State). Naka (town in Enugu State). Nara (town in Enugu State). Naze (town in Owerri, Imo State). Nekede (town in Owerri,	"Ishi" of the tribe of Gad (see 1 Chronic les 4:20). from Hebrew words, "hi", lamentations, and "sug". To go back – (Hisug or Isu). "Etam" of the family of Zorathites of the tribe of Judah (1 Chronicles 4:3; 4:32); also name of ancient city in the city of David; person's name in

Imo State)	Israel, e.g., General Etam of the current Israeli army.
Nebo (town in Anambra State).	
	"Izahar" of the tribe of Levi (1 Chronicles 6:2).
Neri (Ner), Neni or Nenu (name of towns in Abia, Anambra and Imo States).	"Uzzi" of the tribe of Levi (1 Chronicles 6:5).
- Nneri (Ner) Isiala Mbano, Imo State; - Neni, Anambra State; - Nenu Obingwa, Abia State.	
Nnewi, town in Anambra State	
	"Lod" (1 Chronicles 8:12); Nehemiah 1:35).
Nobi – town in Anambra State.	"Mordecai", pronounced as Mordka in Hebrew. (see Esther 5:9).
	of the descendants of "Eri" of the tribe of Gad (Genesis 46:16).
Nise (name of Ibo town) Nise, Enugu State Nise, Isialangwa South, Abia State.	from Hebrew word, naka, to turn away. "Naarah" (1 Chronicles 4:6)
Nkwere – Nkwo Eri, corrupted as Nkwere – (town in Imo State).	from Hebrew word 'naza', to cause to start.
	"Nekoda" (Ezra 2:48).
Nsukka (town in Enugu State).	
	"Nebo" (Ezra 2:29).
Nzimiro (name of	

person in Imo State). Obosi (town in Anambra State).	"Ner" (1 Chronicles 8:33).
Obuda (town in Aba Ngwa, Abia State).	Nineveh (pronounced as Nineweh, for 'v' is pronounced as 'w' in Hebrew) – 2 Kings 19:36).
Offia (name of person, part name of town in Abia and Anambra States) Ohafia, Abia State; Nofia, Anambra State; Isuofia Aguata; Ofiavu Okoko Item, Abia State.	"Nob", name of town in ancient Israel (see 1 Samuel 21:1; Nehemiah 11:32). "Nissi" (Jahvey Nissi) one of the attribute names of God of Israel.
Opara (Okpara or Okpala) – name of person in all Iboland, particularly the first male child in the family.	of the descendants of "Eri", son of Gad of the tribe of Gad (Genesis 46:16). from Hebrew word, 'succha', sweepings,...
Onam (name of person in Abia State)	"Zimiri" of the tribe of Judah. (1 Kings 16:15).
Ono (name of person in	from Hebrew word, "chobesh", to envelope,

Abia and Enugu States)	to enclose,… The difficult ch gluttoral sound in chobesh makes it sound like Obosi when pronounced in Hebrew.
Onitsha (Onicha) – town in Abia, Anambra , Delta and Enugu States. Onitsha (Onicha) Anambra State; Onicha Ngwa, Abia State; Onicha Ugbo, Delta State.	corruption of "Abida", brother of Eldaah (Edda), one of the grand children of Keturah, the black woman that Abraham remarried after the death his wife Sarah. (Genesis 25:1-4).
Oraeri (Ora Eri) – name of town in Anambra State. Oraifite (Ora Ifite) – name of town in Anambra State.	"Ophrah" (pronounced as 'Ofra', and in many Ibo towns corrupted as Opara or Okpara), the first born of Meonothai,of the tribe of Judah. (see 1 Chronicles 4:14).
Ossa or Ossai (name of person and of town in all Iboland) Oshimiri (or Oshimili) – name of town in Delta and Anambra States.	Third generation corruption of "Ophrah", the first son of Meonothai of the tribe of Judah.
Oti (name of person in Abia State) – e.g., Sonny Oti, a famous Arochukwu musician)	"Onam" of the tribe of Judah (1 Chronicles 1:40). "Ono" (11 Chronicles 8:12; Nehemiah 7:37; 11:35).

Otolo (Otoro) Nnewi, Anambra State.	from Hebrew word, 'oni', oppression, affliction, and 'sha'a', to become desolate, to be laid waste.
Owelle or Owele (name of person and of town; title in Iboland – e.g., Owelle of Onitsha, Owelle Ndigbo) *Okwelle is the corruption of Owelle; Okwelle, Imo State.	
Ozubulu (town in Anambra State).	Of the descendants of "Eri", son of Gad (Genesis 46:16). 'Ora' is Allokoo/Kwa Gentile word for community of; people of. Therefore Oraifite means community of
Ubani (name of person in Abia and Imo States; collective name for Ibos in the Opobo areas of Rivers) *Bonny is the corruption of 'Bani' or Ubani.	Ifite (Ifrit corruption of Ivrit or Hebrew). "Hosah" (1 Chronicles 26:10).
Udi (town in Enugu State)	"Shimiri", one of the sons of "Hosah", mimicried as Ossa by the Nigerian Hebrews,
Uduma (name of person in Ohafia, Abia State).	Ibos (1 Chronicles 26:10).
Udumeze (Udumeze)	"Hothir" from the group of singers, of the tribe of Levi (1 Chronicles 26:10).
Umuara (name of town in Abia State)	from Hebrew word, 'ataroth', of several

Umuariam or Umuariama (town in Abia and Imo States) Umuariam Obowu, Imo State; Umuariam Umuahia, Abia State; Umuariama Obingwa, Abia State.	towns. from Hebrew word, 'ohele', family tent, congregation, habitation.
Umuleri; Umueri (town in Anambra State) Umuhu (town in Abia and Imo States) Umuhu Abam, Abia State; Umuhu Ngor Okpala, Imo State.	"Zebulun", the sixth son of Jacob or Israel or the father of the tribe of Zebulun (Genesis 46:14; 1 Chronicles 6:63). "Bani" (see Ezra 2:10).
Usua (name of person in Item, Abia State). - Umuasua (Umusua) Isuikwuato.	
Uz (of town and person in Abia State). Of town:- Uzuakoli, Abia State; Uzuabam (Ozuabam), Abia State; Uzitem (Ozuitem), Abia State. Of person:- Uzunma	from Hebrew word, "ud", to attest, to assure. from Hebrew word, "Dumah" (1 Chronicles 1:30). "Dumah Ezer" – "Ezer" (see Nehemiah 3:19). of the descendant of "Ara", the son of Jether (1 Chronicles 7:38). "Aram" (1 Chronicles 7:34)

	of "Eri" (Genesis 46:16).
	of "Hur" (1 Chronicles 2:19).
	From Hebrew name, 'Joshua', pronounced as Yosua, mimicried as Osua or Usua by the Nigerian Hebrews (Ibos).
	"Uz", the first son of Nahor (Genesis 22:21); also name of a Hebrew town (see Genesis 36:28).

One striking observation in the choice of names that the exiled Hebrews (Ibos) gave to many of their places of settlement is that they connote curse(s) when then do not describe events or circumstances. This is very likely because they fully realised that they were there following God's curses on the Jews generally as a result of their own or their parent's disobedience to God's command, that they (the Hebrews) had been forced to fall from grace in the beautiful Zion in Israel to grass in the most underdeveloped places, jungles and bushes of Nigeria. Before they left Israel, the Holy Scriptures had made the prophecy clear:

Because you did not serve the Lord, your God… Therefore, in hunger and thirst, in nakedness and dire poverty, you will serve the enemies the Lord sends against you. He will put an iron yoke on your neck until he has destroyed you (Deuteronomy 28:47-48).

Therefore, the names chosen for their various places of abode in the awe-inspiring jungles and bushes of Eastern Nigeria reflected their thoughts about their situation their mood and disposition. And so the Hebrew words like "O1", yoke, servitude, from where the name of the town 'Orlu', was derived. or "Ad" and "Ani", perpetuity, oppressed, afflicted, poor, wrecked from where the name of the town 'Adani' was derived, or the Hebrew words "Oni" and "Sha'a" to become desolate, to be laid waste, from where we get the name of the town, Onitsha, etc. are all indicative of the sorry state of the minds of the Nigerian Hebrew exiles then, of their insensitivity to good things of life and life itself, since the LORD Almighty has promised them such terrible calamities, "the sight of some of which …will drive them mad" (Deut. 28:34), without any hope of their ever ending in their life time.

The other striking thing is that with the passage of time and the aculturisation and merger of Hebrew (Ibo) language with the local Kwa and Allokoo languages into the modern Igbo language, some of the Ibo names have come to assume new meanings that can sometimes be logically explained away in the modern Igbo language, a concoction of Allokoo/Kwa/Ancient Hebrew. One good example is Ahia ("Ahiah", see Neh. 10:26), from where we have Umuahia. But today, the name 'Umuahia' has been given many strange but logical meanings by both the indigenes and strangers alike, in and outside Umuahia. Some say it is 'Umu ahia' (community of traders) and others say it is 'Omo ahia' a place for trading or a trade post, and that it is the white man that mispronounced it as Umuahia, ignoring the fact that Umuahia is a pure Allokoo+Hebrew name which means community or people of Ahia. The other example is Adiel (as in 1 Chron. 4:36) pronounced as Adiele, in modern Igbo language with strange but logical meaning of 'looking unto God' and borne as a name in many Nigerian Hebrew (Ibo) communities. What is referred to as Arondizuogu today is nothing but Arodi Izuogu. Arodi is the junior brother of "Eri" the fifth son of Gad (see Genesis 46:16). On leaving Uburu, the first port of call of the exiled Hebrews in Eastern Nigeria, the Arodis or Aros journeyed far and wide. They established their presence and trade posts in areas east and west of the Niger, in Yorubaland and Igalaland. In lgalaland, history has it that the (the Aros) found the other Hebrew exiles from the lineage of Eri who had earlier settled there on their way back to Onitsha from Benin.

Offia (corruption of Ophra - (1 Chron. 4:13) is given a corrupt Ibo meaning of bush and so 'oha ophra' or Ohafia is said to mean community of bush people instead of the original Hebrew meaning of community of people of Ophra. There is also Afara (Ophra) Ibeku. Uz is a Hebrew name (see Genesis 22:21 - Uz, the firstborn of Nabor). In the same vein, Uz Item, Uz Abam, Uz Akoli ... is logically but wrongly said to relate to ozu or Ozuzu (resting place) so that Uzuakoli, for example, is used to mean a resting place for the people of Akoli; so with Item and Abiam instead of the original Hebrew connotation of community of the first born of Akoli or Item or Abiam. For "Uz" and "Ophrah" (Afra, Opara, Okpara) are names normally borne by the first male child of the family just as "Ada" by the first female of the family in ancient Israel.
Similarly, the same confusion surrounds the Hebrew name, "Abor" in Abor Mbaise, Abor Achi, Abor Enugu Agu, etc., as the word 'abor' has lost its original meaning in Hebrew of 'cross over' or crossing over' or 'place crossed over', and is given all sorts of strange interpretations in modern Igbo language. However, these Hebrew words and names in Ibo vocabulary with strange interpretations are not many; they are the exception rather than the rule. The rest of the other names as contained in our table have maintained their original Hebrew sounds and sometimes spellings as evidenced above.
More intriguing examples with names and words including concepts and ideas abound. For instance, "uja", meaning fluid and/or its container is the same in Ibo as in Hebrew with the same sound, same pronunciation, "oria", a word in Hebrew meaning insensibility, unseemliness of mind, body or skin equally the same in Ibo as in Hebrew with the same sound, same pronunciation. "Sof", a Hebrew word meaning 'to vanish' is the same in Ibo. "Sofuo" in Ibo means vanish or disappear. "Sofu", or "Sopu" means to vanish or to disappear, to run away from, in Ibo. Similarly, 'nuf' in Hebrew language means to cause to move. Likewise in Ibo it is 'nufu' or 'nupu' with the same meaning, 'to cause to move'. Also, the fruit called 'udara' in all Ibo land and Akwa Ibom/Calabar areas Heebo (Ibo) nation is also called 'udara' in Hebrew language. Indeed, virtually all Ibo words

that end in 'ara' originate from Hebrew: Ara, Nara, udara, Anambra, Umuara, etc.

Besides, Ibo word order in sentences is much the same with that of Hebrew. It is true that the entire words and structures now differ tremendously. This is a common feature in many languages that now have their old (in living memory) and new versions, such as the Old English and Modern English. Therefore the many differences between modern Hebrew and ancient Hebrew (from where modern Igbo language originated) cannot be held as a point of argument against the Jewish origin of the Ibos, moreso when, despite the long period of transformation and metamorphosis or transformation of ancient Hebrew into modern Igbo language in Nigeria can be linked to that of Saxon or Old English into modern English language, with very little to account for structural similarities. The Ibo case in this regard is even better because of the abundance of the similarities in words, names and concepts. Take for instance the first three lines of this poem in Old English:

Hwaet, we GarDena in
Geardagum peodeyninga Prym
Gefrunon, hu oa aepelingas ellen fremedon
In modern English language, this is almost saying:
Hail! We have heard of the
Greatness in days past of the kings
Of the Spear-Dans, of how
The nobles did mighty deeds

Notice the difference in the pattern and structure of the two versions of the same poem within a period of just 1000 years or so. In the same manner, the ancient Hebrew spoken by the forefathers of the Nigerian Hebrews (Ibos) before they left Israel for Africa (Nigeria) about 3000 years ago have more or less unbelievably different structures and yet strangely enough, with a more striking similarities in words, names and even in structure still in existence. Example. The expression in ancient Hebrew dialect: "Talitha koum", (see Mark 5:41) spoken by Jesus Christ to the daughter of Jairus is akin to today's Hebrew (Ibo) expression, "Telita kumo", both of which when translated into English from ancient Hebrew, "Talitha koum" and the modern Hebrew (Ibo) language, "Telita kumo", have the same meaning: 'Get up' or rather 'Get up and breathe'. In King James Version of the Bible, the expression, "Talitha koum", is translated as "Little girl... Get up!"

Furthermore, the concept of one God, Almighty, popularly referred to as God of Abraham or God of Abram by the Hebrews is exactly the same in Ibo. The corruption of Abram in Ibo is 'Abiama'. Hence to the Ibo man Chukwu Abiama is the same thing as Almighty God of Abram. Tshuku is the name of the famous Aro Chukwu oracle, which the Aros manipulated to succeed in slave trade. As has been mentioned earlier, it is actually from the famous oracle, 'Tshuku', pronounced as Chukwu by the Ibos, that Aro-Chukwu derived its present name when the white missionaries arrived in Iboland and there was need to translate the Bible into Igbo. Tshuku was used to translate God for want of a better word. To distinguish Tshuku the oracle and Tshuku the God Almighty, Abram or Abiama was used for the latter, leading to the Ibo name 'Chukwu Abiama' for God of Abram or God Almighty the Creator of the Universe. Among the Ibos of Rivers State Nigeria, Chukwu is still being pronounced as Tshuku. However, modern Ibos prefer to say 'Chineke, God the Creator, for God Almighty to 'Chukwu Abiama', although the two names can be used interchangeably without any ambiguity for God Almighty the Creator of the Universe.

Besides Chukwu Abiama, the Jewish attribute name for God, 'Ya' the short form of Yahweh is still being used by the Ibos of Nigeria to refer to the LORD God Almighty. For instance, the Ibo sentence, 'Tonu ya', means 'Praise be to God, with the word 'Ya' standing for or used as the short form of Yahweh, the revealed name of God to the Jews, which is normally never fully pronounced by the Jews unless at a very crucial point of one's death. The Ibos also often use the word 'Oliya' as an expression of congratulations when a difficult achievement or an achievement that is clearly impossible without the help of God takes place. Used in this sense 'oliya' is rightly translated as 'Praise be to God who has made the achievement possible'. Hence the Ibo sentence, 'Oliya, inwetawoya, nyemaka' which is correctly translated as 'Praise be to God, you've got it, give me a handshake'. 'Oliya' is just the corruption of the Hebrew expression, Alu le Yah, which means 'Praise be to God' As had been said in the above table, whenever the Ibos greet or shout 'Kwenu!' to elicit the response 'Ya' they are merely trying to invite the presence of Ya, short form of Yahweh, the Almighty God of Israel.

Again the Ibos have other ways of calling God by name or other names for God, instead of using the revealed name of God and falling into the sin of breaking the seventh commandment of the Almighty; namely: "Thou shalt not take the name of the Jehovah (Yahweh) thy God in vain (misuse the name)." (Exodus 20:7). For example, the name Aliezi or Alaezi or Alezi

the name of Eleazar son of Aaron, was used to refer to a place in the family compound or village where the high priest performed his priestly functions. The high priest occupied the highest position among the three orders of priesthood in Israel. "Its origin, is traced to Eleazar, son of Aaron" (Crim, 1975; 307 ff.). Long after the days of such priestly functions the original place designated for such functions known as Alezi is still being regarded as a holy place where no person's blood more especially a relation's blood can be shed, no crime of any type can be committed, no person who has defiled him- or herself can go and stand or stay, no person whatsoever can stay and make false declarations or tell lies or speak vain words under oath without bringing damnation to himself. However, whereas some Ibos, the females (in Aro Chukwu, Abia State) bear the name Alezi or Alaezi with reference of the name of a holy place for priestly functions within the family compound or village, others, the males, (in Item, Abia State), bear the name simply as a mimicry of Eliezer the priest, son of Aaron or Eleazar, son of Moses (see Exodus 18:4). There were other Hebrew names that were treated with such great respect or even used to symbolise God. Amusu or Moasi (Hebrew) or Moses (English) was used for any person who was able to perform great mystical fits like Moses. However, with the passage of time, the name assumed a negative dimension and is now being used to refer to a witch (wizard in modern Igbo language. Olisa is the mimicry of Elisha the prophet. For another example of the ancient Israeli prophets who were called "gods" by the Hebrews and treated as such refer to Psalm 82:6-7: "I said 'you are gods'; you are the sons of the Most High. But you will die like mere men". Consider this too. In the New Testament Bible, Jesus answered thus,
Is it not written in your law, I said, 'you are gods'? If He called them gods, to whom the word of God came (and the Scripture cannot be broken), do you say of Him whom the father sanctified and sent into the word, You are blaspheming…?' (John10:34-36).
Therefore, that the Nigerian Hebrews or Hebrews in exile in Nigeria call Elisha (Olisa) god is in keeping with their ancient Jewish tradition. Today, they (the Ibos) use the word, 'Olisa' to also to refer to God Almighty. Other names used by the Ibos to refer to God Almighty include Chukwu, Chukwu Abiama, Chineke and Obasi who lives in Heaven, and so, like their counterpart World Jews, any ruler over the Ibos in the traditional Ibo society is regarded as a direct representative of God, a God's Regent. Hence the Ibo title, of 'Igwe' for a titled chief, or ruler in many parts of Iboland.

Interestingly, however, the conceptual difference in both ancient Hebrew and Nigerian Hebrew (Ibo) - so far as my studies have revealed - does not exist in any significant manner. Indeed, the concept of brotherhood, business, warfare, discipline, work and service, to mention only a few examples, is virtually the same for the Nigerian Hebrews (Ibos) as for the World Hebrews. For instance, Abram (called Abiama by the ancient Ibos) gave the Hebrews an ideal of true brotherhood and its demands. For instance, when "The invaders took Lot, Abram's brother's son... And when Abram heard that his brother was taken captive, he led forth his trained men" (Genesis 14:12. 14). Although Abram was formally separated from Lot, he was still knit closely to him by natural and spiritual bonds of fraternity. He was moved by the thought of his brother's suffering and was in no way indifferent to his fate. In the ancient Ibo as well as other World Hebrew societies, the only protection for life and property lay in a man's willingness to defend his kinsmen and avenge the injuries done them. Every male relative, every man of the same tribe or people, was a brother to keep and protect. In the Holy Scriptures it was the thought of a brother in chains that stirred Abram's heart. In Achebe's Things Fall Apart, the great novel on the olden Ibo society, it was the same thought of his kinsmen in "chains of Christianity" that stirred the heart of Okonkwo the chief character of the novel. It is the same great ideal of Hebrew brotherhood which transformed Odumegwu Ojukwu, a peacemaker at beginning, just before the Biafran War (1967-1970), into a man of war, intense and ardent, swift to move and to smite, with a "brow of a noble cause" just as in the case of Abram, the Hebrew (Genesis 13:8).

Today, even as I gather materials for this book, it is the same thought of his Hebrew (Ibo) brothers in "chains of political and economic tutelage in Nigeria" that has led to the emergence of yet other young Ibo leaders, intense and ardent also and with a firm and new declaration like that of Governor Orji Uzor Kalu in Ohaneze Summit (Enugu, January 2001):
I (Dr. Orji Uzor Kalu) represent a new generation of the Igbo purged of the psychology and burden of defeat, conscious of the peculiar socio-political circumstances of the Igbo in our country and determined to forge a new identity and vision for our people in whichever part of Nigeria they may reside...
Or that of Arthur Nwankwo in Vanguard, Wed. Dec. 29, 1999, p. 11 who asserts:
There will continue to be problems (in Nigeria) until the Igbo nation finds accommodation in the country; when they are not just tolerated but accepted unconditionally.

In their own different versions, today's Ibo leaders like Sam Egwu, Chimaraoke Nnamani, Chinwoke Mbadinuju, Achike Udenwa, Anyim Pius Anyim, Joe Irukwu, Ojo Maduekwe, Kema Chikwe, Emmanuel Iwuanyanwu, Arthur Nwankwo, Arthur Nzeribe, Rochas Okorocha, Emeka Ofor, Vincent Obguluafor, Onyema Ugochukwu, Jim Nwobodo, Chekwas Okorie, Ben Nwubueze, to mention but a few, have taken a vow of practical sympathy which is willing to dare to seek the welfare and do things to protect the integrity of the Ibo man in Nigeria, although some of them see themselves as political enemies in the larger Nigerian political scene, with some of them unfortunately going to the extent of compromising their Iboness or Hebraism.

In work, the Hebrew concept of work is still very much alive among the Ibos. The way Joseph, the Hebrew, served and worked for his master in Egypt is similar to the way an average Ibo man or servant serves his master either under slavery or normal condition of life. This is confirmed in the statement made by Oluadah Equiano while writing on the slave trade era in Africa:

The West Indian planters prefer the slaves of Benin or Eboe to those of any other part of Guinea, for their hardiness, intelligence, integrity, and zeal. (Equiano, 1789).

Joseph did not subscribe to the opinion that idleness is the stamp of nobility. He was the next king in rank yet the busiest in the land. He was an honest incessant worker. These are exactly the same attributes that made Ibo servants the envy of all Ibos and non-Ibos alike and even the Colonial masters before the Biafran War, which ruined virtually all the Hebrew ideals among the Ibos of Nigeria. And, in fact, in today's Nigeria, the loss of their Hebrew ideals notwithstanding, any employer of labor in Nigeria (indigenous or foreign) desirous of a hardworking manager or servant/employee will be advised to look for an Ibo.

In business, the account of the transaction in the purchase of property that Abram bought of the sons of Heth at the gates of Hebron reads like a legal document (Genesis 23:17-18). The whole business was carried out with the same scrupulous care that today's World Hebrews including the Nigerian Hebrews (Ibos) carry out their day-to-day business transactions. In courtesy, in business, any person who had witnessed a bargain making with a Jewish businessman will agree that the Nigerian Hebrew or Ibo businessman depicts it to a nicety and totality. The typical Ibo seller like his Jewish counterpart will normally open up the transaction with very warm welcome greetings and speech, with the assurance that everything he has in his shop is yours and bidding you to take whatever you want. Even when you feel flattered and protest against such undeserved kindness, he continues to urge you to oblige him, until you succumb to his pressures. When you finally decide to enter into business, and he condescends to name a price, which he does in such a casual manner as if the affair is of no importance to him, it is sure to be three of four times the actual price; this is particularly so if he suspects that you have no idea of the price. With much manoeuvring, almost oblivious of time, the negotiation is sustained until it is concluded.

COMRADE (CHIEF) CORMAN C. AND LOLO GRACE C. NNOROM.
THE OHAMADIKE OF OBEAMA,
AUTHONOMOUS COMMUNITY, IMO STATE.
A FOREMOST IBO TRADE UNION LEADER IN NIGERIA.

CHAPTER THIRTEEN

THE GREAT SALVATION OF THE WORLD HEBREWS, THE WHITE & BLACK JEWS - POSSIBLE SET BACKS FOR THE IBOS?

How shall we escape if we ignore such a great salvation? (Hebrews 2:3) - Salvation of every one who believes: first for the Jew, then for the Gentile (Romans 1:16).

The promise of salvation, the restoration of the state of Israel and the gathering back of the Israelites, the Jews or the Hebrews to their homeland, Israel was confirmed to the Hebrews by the holy prophets of Israel who heard Him then. After Moses had pronounced the course of the Almighty God on the people of Israel, he also later told them that after God's furious anger and great wrath might have been turned away from the Hebrews the Lord would, in His own time,

will restore your fortunes and have compassion on you and gather you again from all the nations where He scattered you. Even if you have been banished to the most distant land under the heavens(Deut.30:3-5).

A clear image of the fulfilment of the curses of God in His fierce, burning anger on the Hebrews not only in Nigeria but elsewhere in the word is seen in the most horrible events of the second World War when, besides other calamities that befell the Hebrews, at a swoop, six million of them were killed in Hitler's gas chamber.

The LORD will bring a nation against you from far away, from the ends of the earth, like an eagle swooping down, a nation whose language you will not understand, a fierce looking nation without respect for the old or pity for the young. The sights you see will drive you mad. You will become a thing of harrow and an object of scorn and ridicule to all the nations... At midday you will grope about like a blind man in the dark. All these curses will come upon you (Deuteronomy 28).

Anybody who is familiar with the events of the second World War and the fate of the Hebrews during the said war - how "a fierce-looking nation", Germany, swooped down upon the Hebrews like an eagle in utter destruction, and other nations "from the ends of the earth" joined Germany to make the victimised Hebrews "a thing of horror and an object of scorn" - will quickly see the everlasting truth in the above quotations,

But thanks to the Almighty for His eventual change of heart to turn His anger away from them "for the fathers' (Abraham, Isaac, Jacob...) sake (Romans 11: 28) and for the sake of the holy name of God.

There is nothing whatsoever to suggest that the promise of restoration of Israel and its people is only for a section of the Hebrews, say the light-skinned at the exclusion of the dark-skinned Hebrews.
In fact, the Scripture has it that black or dark-skinned people such as the Ethiopian Jews, the Ibos of Nigeria, or the Tutsis of East Africa in Jewish lineage came to be even at the very inception of the Jewish race. The establishment of the Jewish race began when the LORD God Almighty chose Abraham because of his faith in God and called him out from his native country, Shem, in the present day Iraq, separating him from his kith and kin, and established him in the territory of Canaan, the son of Ham. Canaan was a mostly dark-skinned or black people's territory in the Middle East. Ham is the father of Canaan. Other sons of Ham include Cush (now Ethiopia), Mizrarn (now Egypt, Africa), Put (now Libya, Africa) and Canaan (Palestine) (see Genesis 10:6).
Now the LORD has said unto Abram, get thee out of thy country and from thy kindred and from thy father's house unto a land that 1 will shew thee... and 1 will bless thee... So Abram departed as the LORD has spoken unto him...and into the land of Canaan they came. And the LORD appeared unto Abram and said unto thy seed will 1 give this land (Genesis 12).

After the death of Abraham's wife, Sarah, the mother of Isaac in the new land, he was properly remarried to Keturah a black woman from Cush (a black country south of Ethiopia or between Ethiopia and Sudan, but no longer in existence now) who bore him other legitimate children among whom was Median who later went with his mother to settle in Ethiopia. Then again Abraham took a wife, and her name was Keturah. And she bare him Zimran and Jokshan and Medan and Midian and Ishbak and Shuah... And the sons of Midian: Ephah, and Epher, and Hanoch, and Abida, and Eldad. All these were the children of Keturah (Gen. 2.5:1-4).

It is interesting to note that the names of the sons of this black wife of Abraham are today prominent among the names borne by the Ibos of Nigeria. For example, Abida (corrupted as Obida in Aba, Abia State; Eldad (corrupted as Edda, the most populous town in Ebonyi State).

Midian, another son of Keturah was later to be used by God to establish the state of Israel through Moses. In Ethiopia, Midian being one of the sons of Abraham through Keturah zealously and faithfully applied the teachings in the book of Genesis and so raised his descendants to become priests and teachers of the word of God of Abraham. And so in the fullness of time, the Almighty God of Israel had to send Moses to Jethro a priest of Median, a descendant of Abraham through Keturah to help him (Moses) fulfil his ministry and obtain the inheritance of the children of Israel (Exodus 18:1-27. Numbers 10:24-32).

A more direct case for the black Hebrews in Jewish history can be made when we consider that two of the maids of Jacob's (Israel's) wives were given to him by his wives to bear children who actually became part of the twelve tribes of Israel that God chose for HIMSELF. These maids, Bilah and Zipali were all blacks and the Torah says that their (the black maids') children formed the nucleus of the tribes of Israel.
Bilah, the maidservant of Rachael begat Dan and Nephtai whereas Zilppah, the maidservant of Leah bore Gal and Asher.

Another case is that of Moses. Moses married a Midian woman called Zipporah. This is besides the earlier conclusion that some Jewish people were intermarried with the dark-skinned Cushites and Midians including some Egyptians who opted to marry some Jewish slaves during their 400 year long period of slavery in Egypt. Therefore, any Nigerian Hebrew (Ibo) that focuses his thoughts negatively on the colour of his skin in actualising his Hebraism is being unkind to himself; he is creating undue problems for himself and for others.

Hagar would have been the first link with or source of the black or dark-skinned race in Israel if only. Abraham had married her in the proper way as in the case of Keturah. Abraham's relationship with Hagar (Ishmael's mother) was based on a canal request made by Sarah who thought that she was too old to bear the Almighty's promised child of covenant, Isaac. But God's plan cannot change, nor can man hasten His time. Something had to happen for God's plan to take its normal course. And so, on getting her son Ishmael, Hagar began to despise Sarah and, wrongfully and unwittingly assumed the role of the mother of the heir to her mistress and consequently she (Hagar) was cast out with her son, Ishmael.
Wherefore she said unto Abraham, cast out this bondwoman (Hagar) and her son for the son of this bondwoman (Ishmael) shall not be heir with my son, even with Isaac (Gen. 21:10).

Of course, when Ishmael grew up his thought was that Isaac had taken his birthright away from him. But by God's divine promise it was not his but Isaac's. It hurt Ishmael all through his life on earth and had, until date, gone deep down into the minds of all the descendants of Ishmael (now the Arabs of the Middle East) and has adversely affected the psyche and thinking pattern of the Arab twelve princes concerning Jacob (Israel) and all its branches of which the Ibos of Nigeria are one, leading to the incessant disagreements and wars between the two people wherever they find themselves - between the Hebrews in the Middle East and the Arabs; between the Ibos of Eastern Nigeria and the Hausa-Fulani Arab descents of Northern Nigeria.

Pertinent to the treatment of the issue of salvation of the Nigeria Hebrews (Ibos) and their gathering back to Israel or integration into the World Jewry is the concept of individual and group preparedness for the salvation as well as the possible militating factors or set-backs. The first of such setbacks has to do with last days' offences that can be effectively handled by the preachers in the "houses of prayer"[e.g., the Churches]. They concern the abomination of the desolation, spoken by Daniel the prophet", men being "lovers of money, boastful, proud, abusive, disobedient to their parents ungrateful, unforgiving, slanderous, treacherous, rash, conceited, lovers of pleasure rather than lovers of God - having a form of godliness but denying its power" (2 Tim. 3:2-5). They also concern the earlier laws to the Hebrews summarised as follows: Let no debt remain outstanding, except the continuing debt to love one another, for he who loves his fellowman has fulfilled the law. The commandments, 'Do not commit adultery', 'Do not murder', 'Do not steal','Do not covet', and whatever other commandments there may be, are summed up in this one rule: 'Love your neighbour as yourself'. Therefore love is the fulfilment of the law (Romans 13, 8-10).

For these setbacks the preachers and the Churches in Iboland have achieved a very reasonable degree of success in sensitising people about them and making people turn away from them. Individuals who are caught pants down with such sins in the last day will only blame themselves. The other set of possible setbacks about which the preachers and churches in Iboland have woefully failed to handle has to do with idolatry and associated sins - the Osu-caste/Ahiajoku or Agwu or Kamalu or Ali (Ani) idolatrous practices. Writing on osu-caste system in Iboland, the preachers and the churches, Ezeala (1992:43): The priests of these Churches do not want to eradicate the osu-pagan abomination so as not to reduce the amount of eggs, chickens, goats and yams, which they take home on Sundays.

In brief, very regrettably, some Nigerian Hebrew (Ibos), either individually or as a group still live outside the law of idolatry, consciously or unconsciously dedicating themselves to some Kwa/Allokoo/Gentile idols and very notoriously "immersing themselves deeply into the osu-idolatry of the pagan" (Ezeala 1992), and abandoning monotheism, the only Judaic religion and tradition that can more than other factors help to identify them as a branch of Hebrews. Although the osu-caste system is now limited to Imo and Anambra and a few parts of Abia Ibos, the Osu stigma on the entire Ibo race is general. The Osu is a system of idol worshipping, sacrificing human beings to idols and obeying false signals and orders from the "gods of wood and stone". It is a clear rejection of the Almighty God of Israel whose name is Jealous (Exodus 34:14) and whose first law is: "You shall have no other gods before me" (Exodus 20:3). Therefore all Ibos who individually or collectively believe and/or practise Osu system are not Hebrews and cannot lay any claim to the promises of restoration or salvation of the Hebrews.

A thrilling parallel to the Osu-caste idolatrous practice of the Ahiajoku material and "academic" sacrifice. It is one of the most striking societal ironies of our time that the world acclaimed intellectual harvest of the Ibo race, the famous Ahiajoku lecture, is named after a false "god of wood and stone", a god that the almighty God of Israel had warned many times that we as a branch of Jacob should have nothing whatsoever to do with.

Having now known what Chukwu Abiama means as against Ahiajoku god or oracle, if, for instance, we say Abiama lecture, we would be referring to our forefather Abraham, the father of Israel rather than to a god of wood and stone. The association of the name Ahiajoku or any other cult or shrine with the famous Ibo lecture series is pitifully a reflection of what these idols stand for or of our rejection of the worship of one God as in our ancestral home Israel and therefore a rejection of our noble identity. Conversely, very interestingly, the first Ahiajoku lecture by Professor J.C. Echeruo began with the admittance of the loss of identity of the Ibos, declaring that, "the challenge we (Ibos) all face today is that of re-establishing our identity". That I criticise an appellation in the Ibo lecture series does not in any way mean an attack on the lecture series. 1 conceed that it is one of the best things that ever happened to the Ibos (Hebrews) of Nigeria.

Finally, there is the other possible setback that is psychological, having to do with the negative attitude of the Nigerian Hebrews towards their Hebraism. Those Ibos who have this type of problematic mentality often say: 'We can't believe this. Can a black man be a Jew?' Among them, there is the undercurrent fear of discrimination because of the color of their skin as evidenced in the case of the Ethiopian Jews in the recent past, although this very fear has been drastically reduced by knowledge and understanding that:

The universalism that permeates the faith of Israel, is reflected not only in its theological formulation and in its vision of the future, but in the very composition of its people... these people include those whose skins range from the lightest to the darkest in colors and within it a broad range of cultural diversity is represented (Donin, 1972:8).

Dr. Peter and Mary Odili
Dr. Peter Odili is a Surgeon and currently the Executive Governor of Rivers State of Nigeria while Mary Odili is a Judge.

DR. MARYAM BABANGIDA

Our most visible and effective daughter was born to the Okogwu family of Asaba and married to Former Nigeria's Military President, Ibrahim Babangida. As first lady, she achieved the creation of Abia State and Delta State with capital at Umuahia and Asaba respectively for the Igbos. She empowered the Nigerian women by creating and adequately funding the **BETTER LIFE FOR RURAL WOMEN PROGRAM**. The People's Bank was also a project she encouraged the husband to establish for the welfare of the poor.

ALAUDAH IKWUANO.

THE IBO FOUNDING FATHER OF BRITAIN'S BLACK POLITICAL MOVEMENT WRITTEN AS: OLAUDAH EQUIANO, IN HISTORY BOOKS.

Booker T. Washington

APPENDIX:

GLOSSARY OF IBO NAMES

Apart from family names, borne mostly by the first-born male in an Ibo family, about where there can be no choice, Ibos are extremely very careful in choosing a name for their new-born child because they believe that the name a child bears can sometimes change his destiny and affect his future positively or adversely. As can be seen on the Table in this book, many of these Ibo names are Jewish or Hebrew, of whose real meaning, today Ibo parents have no knowledge excepting that certain researches into the Hebrew origin of the Ibos (e.g., Alaezi, 199) have now pointed out to us in the Torah and the Bible, the holy Books of the Jews (e.g., Ahia, Nebo, Adiele, Onoh, Ada, Ahira (Ahiara), Eri, Ede, Ete, etc.). It is to be noted that only very few of today's Ibo people's names are Jewish. This is in sharp contrast to the fact that over 90% of the names of all Ibo towns and villages are Jewish (see Table in this book). Names of places diehard and many live for hundreds and thousands of years, e.g., Egypt, Israel, Syria, Lebanon, Rome. But people's names easily change with time, space and current culture.   M   In all essentials, however, every Ibo name has a deep-rooted scriptural and/or social meaning, often expressing and exalting the name of God Almighty, Chi or Chukwu or Chukwu Abiama (corruption of Abram) in the life of the child. This is particularly so with all Ibo names starting or ending with the names of God, Chi or Chukwu (e.g., Chibueze, God is king, Chukwuebuka, God is mighty, Ikechukwu or Ikechi (shortened as IK or Iyk), by the power of God. The following are some selected Ibo names and their meanings:

Aba* (of "Abba, Arba") (m)
Abba (of "Abba")
Abayi (of "Abia, Abijah")
Abiayi (of "Abia, Abijah")
Aboaja – basket for sacrifice; a rejected basket but very useful for disposal of sacrifice meant to save life (m)
Achi – a type of timber tree of great value (m)

183

Achike – an achi tree, strong, mighty and useful (m)

Ada - name usually borne by the first daughter in a family- (of "Adah" first daughter of Elon")

Adaka Guerrilla (a child desired to be as strong as a guerrilla in future. (m)

Adaku – daughter destined to bring wealth to the family (f).

Adeze – princess (f)

Adanna – father's preferred daughter (f)

Adanne – mother's preferred daughter (f)

Adaora – daughter of the people (f)

Adibe –[short form of Adibenma], A prophet is not honored in his hometown—difficult to please, ones kindred. [m]

Adiele--Angel (of "Adiel") (m)

Adikwuru – lived long enough to see the arrival of the child; a child born at old age or after series of child bearing mishap (m)

Adidimekwe – agreement with God; a covenant child (m)

Adindu – once there is life, there is hope (m)

Afuekwe – seeing is believing (f)

Agbeze – look before you leap; approach life with caution (m)

Agbai – notwithstanding…(m)

Agbara – of the shrine of a god called agbara, holy and respectful   (m)

Agomuo – of a shrine's high priest (m)

Agha – war like --a child born during war time (m)

Agina (Aguina) – counted; I have been counted as one of the father's in the land (because of the birth of the child) (m)

*(in italics, Ibo name of Hebrew origin). For more on such Hebrew-based names see Table in the book.

Agri - (of "Aggrey") (m]

Agordi or Ogordi [God's kindness is real] [m]

Agu – (of "Agur") (m)

Aguiyi – a crocodile (child desired to be as strong as a crocodile) (m)

Aguwa – razor (a child desired to be as sharp as a razor in action and intelligence) (m)

Agwabunma – beauty is all about good manners, not physical appearance (f)

Ahamefula (Aham) – may my name not be forgotten (m)

Aham - (of "Ahiam") (m)

Ahia - (of "Ahiah") (m)

Ahukanna –father never saw this; son born after the death of the father (m)

Ajaero – people can have double standards – praise and hate at the same time (m)

Ajunwa – arrival of a child in the family, no matter what, is
a welcome event (m)

Ajuzieogu – positive words during the pouring of libation bring
blessings (m)

Alaribe—A Philanthropist; [Father wishes the child to become a
Philanthropist] [m]

Aka – a hand, a very important member of the body (m)

Akagha – scars of war (m)

Akachukwu – hand of God; finger of God is on the child (m)

Akubueze – wealth is royalty (m)

Alaka – branch

Akanu (corrupted as Kanu) – (of "Akan") (m)

Akanwa-- Short form of Onyekanwa or Ginikanwa
,[What is greater than a child?]

Akaotuonye – the making of one individual (m)

Akosim – no more abuses because of childlessness (m)

Ama – Street (of "Am") (m)

Amuta – I have got a child like others (m)

Amunike – nobody can get a child by his own strength without
God's own making (m)

Amuzie – of no defect during birth (f)

Anaele – looking on to God (m)

Anario or Anayo – praying/looking on to God

Anorijebe – wish of long life and good health (m)

Anosike – wish of good health and good stay on earth (m)

Anya – eye, a very precious member of the body (m)

Anyele – looking on to God and people (m)

Anyamele – I am looking on to God (m)

Anyadike – eye of a warrior (m)

Anyalewechi – looking on to God (m)

Anyanso – holy eye (of God) (m)

Anyaogu – eye for war; a child desired to be a warrior (m)

Anyaoku – hot eye, eye of a warrior (m)

Anyiam (of "Ayin", 16th Hebrew alphabet, literally meaning an
overcomer,
the same meaning as Ayiam, corruption of Anyim
or"Ayin" (Hebrew) in Ibo) (m)

Anyim – ("Ayin, 16th Hebrew alphabet") (m)

Anyawoke—[A child that is expected to reason aright at all times] -the eye
of a man [m]

Anyanwu --sun; {Always upright and fair } {m}

Arinze – of a noble/priestly birth (m)

Arisa – remembering the goodness of God (f)

Ariwodo – the unexpected has happened (m)

Asiegbu – may the gossip of enemy not kill or harm the child (m)

Asonye – whom shall I fear, none but God? (m)

Atowa – let's be in good terms (m)

Awa – (of " Avva", Hebrew, pronounced as "awa") (m)

Aya – (of "Aija", pronounced as 'Aya', Hebrew) (m)

Azikiwe (Azukaiwe) – behind one's back are many adversaries (m)

Azubike – those who act or argue for you when you are not there are your strength (m)

Azubuine – those who act or argue for you when you are not there are your pride (m)

Azuka - those who act or argue for you when you are not there are more important (m)

Azuonye – what happens behind a person determines his faith; question of what is behind us (m)

Chekwa (Chekwas), short form of Onwuchekwa) – may God protect the child (m)

Chetachi – remember God in all one's dealings (f)

Chiamara – gracious God's (m)

Chibueze – God is king (m)

Chibuisi – God is supreme (m)

Chibuzo – God is first (m,f)

Chibuko – God is my pride (f)

Chidera – what God has written or sanctioned must be upheld (f)

Chidiadi (Chidia) – God is real (m)

Chidiebere – God is merciful (m/f)

Chidinma – God is good (m,f)

Chidi – God is real (m/f)

Chidubem – may God lead me (m)

Chidozie or Dozie—May God control and direct the life of the child [m]

Chiedozie – God has perfectly arranged or kept it (m)

Chiemena – God has done it, it is of God's making (m)

Chiemezie – God has perfectly done it (m)

Chigaemecha – God will accomplish (f)

Chinwe – it belongs to God. (f)

Chigozie- may God's blessings follow the child (m.f).

Chijioke- God has destiny in his hand (m)

Chinarekele – To God be the glory. (f)

Chioma– Good God (f).

Chika – God is the greatest. (m.f is my companion. (m/f)

Chikadibia – God is greater than any physician {witch doctor). (m}

Chisom- God is my companion

Chisom- God is my companion

Chisomeje (Chisomje) – God is my companion.(m/f)

Chikaodinaka or Odinaka-- he/she is in the safe Hand of God. (m/f)

Chituru – the divine will of God. (f)

Chizoba – God save.

Chikaodiri – surrender to God. (f)

Chukwumba—Boasting is not strength, all power belongs to God. [m]

Chukwuebuka , Ebuka,) – God is great .(m)

Chukwuemeka (Emeka) – God has done it. (m)

Chikerenma – beauty comes from God. (Chukwunyere—God's gift [m/f]

Chikezie – expression of belief in God's will to create well. (m)

Chikwe – if God permits. (m)

Chima – God knows all. (m)

Chimaobi – God knows the heart of people. (m)

Chimaroke – God alone knows what he has in stock for us (m)

Chimuanya – God sleeps not (m/f)

Chimdi – My God is alive, God is real. (m.f)

Chimsom – my God is my companion. (m/f)

Chinagorom – God pleads for me. (f)

Chinasa – God answers prayers. (f)

Chinatu – God overrules. (m/f)

Chinaturum – God dictates for me. (m.f)

Chinazurum – God is my provider. (m)

Chinedu – God leads (m.f)

Chineme – God determines. (m)

Chinedu – under God's care.(m)

Chinenye – God gives. (f)

Chinyere – God's gift. (m.f)

Chinomso – My God is near. (m.f)

Chinonye (Nonye) – God be with me (m.f)

Chinwe – all belongs to God (f)

Chinaraekele – to God be the glory (f)

Chioma – good Lord (f)

Chisom – God is my companion (m,f)

Chisomeje (Chisomje) – God is my companion (m,f)

Chituru – the divine will of God (f)

Chizoba – God saves (f)

Chukwueme (Emeka) – God has done it; it is the Lord's making (m)

Chukwuebuka (Ebuka) – God is great (m)

Chukwuma – God knows everything (m)

Chukwumerije – God's prepared destiny or God made the way (m)

Chukwubunna - God is our father (m)

Chukwunonye (Nonye) – God with us (m)

Dibia – physician, a witch doctor of high repute (m)

Dike – mighty man of war (m)

Dimgba (Dim) – a wrestling champion; a warlord (m)

Diribe - live to help others (m)

Dozie—Short form of Chidozie [m]

Ebere – Mercy (m,f)

Ebo – a noble man (m)

Ebogu – a noble man of war; a great warrior (m)

Echebelem—My stress seized with the birth of this child. [m]

Ede - (of "Eder", Hebrew) (m)

Edozienu (Edozie or Edo) – a wish of perfect arrangement from
    Heaven (m)

Efuribe – a sin-bearer for all (m)

Egbo – saved from the agony of childlessness (m)

Egemonye – to whom shall I listen, if not God (m)

Egeonu – trust not to gossips; avoid gossipers (m/f)

Egesi – listen not to gossips (m)

Ejikeme – not by the strength of man (m)

Ejike – short form of Ejikeme) (m)

Ejinkonye – to whom are we indebted, if not to God? (m)

Ejiofor – protected by the staff of righteousness of the shrine god (m)

Ejimofor --protected by the staff of righteousness of the shrine god (m)

Ejiogu – protected by the staff of office of the shrine god (m)

Ejiseke – none is sure of what Destiny has in stock for him (m)

Ejim – I have (God) (m)

Eke – (of "Eker", Hebrew) (m)

Ekebuisi – matter of destiny (m)

Ekechukwu - destined or planned by God (m)

Ekekwachi – Destiny is according one's god's design (m)

Ekeleme – Destiny is real (m)

Ekennia – Father's destiny (of "El kannah", Hebrew) (m)

Ekeoma – a child of good destiny (m)

Ekere – Strong, useful twine from raphia palm; a child desired to be as strong and as useful (m)

Ekwe - a gong a powerful and useful instrument used for public announcement ; a child destined to be so useful. Broadcaster. (m)

Ekwueme – living up to one's words or promises always (m)

Ekezie—[Good destiny is wished for the child] [m]

Elechi – looking on to God (m)

Elekwachi - looking on to God (m)

Elele - looking on to God (m)

Eleme –I'm looking on to God (m)

Elendu – expecting long life for the child (m)

Elemadu – expecting that the child will not be destroyed by man (m)

Eleke – Observing destiny (of "Helek", Hebrew) (m)

Eleweke – looking on to Destiny (m)

Elezuo – waiting till the end to see what Destiny or God has in stock for the child; patience (m)

Elochukwu – God's will (m)

Elom – according to my desire; just as I want it (m)

Eluwa – of the mother earth (m)

Emeka – see Chukwuemeka (m)

Emenike – not by might (m)

Emezuo – it has been accomplished (m)

Enemchukwu - I am looking on to God (m)

Enechukwu – looking on to God (m)

Enyinnaya – his father's friend (m)

Enyioha – a friend to all (m)

Enyioma – good friend (m)

Enwereji – a wish of steady bumper yam harvest (m)

Esonu – listen not to gossips; do not listen to what people say against whatever good thing you want to do (m)

Ete – (of "Eter", Hebrew) (m)

Etim - (corruption of "Etam", Hebrew) (m)

Eto—Corruption of 'Eter'[An Ibo name of Jewish origin—see 'Ehter' of the tribe of Judah. [Joshua:15:42]

A child that is expected to make progree in life - [m]

Eye (corruption of Aya) – (of "Aija", pronounced 'Aya', Hebrew (m) Eze – (of "Ezer", Hebrew) (m)

Ekennia (of "El kannah", Hebrew) (m)

Ekeagwu—Destiny derived from the small god of justice. [m]

Ekeji—Title name for a wealthy yam farmer [m]

Ekeke (Okeke) – a male child born on an eke market day (m)

Ezeala – of goddess (m)

Ezealor – the king has come back (affirmation of the dead king's reincarnation) (m)

Ezeani – priest of earth goddess (m)

Ezejelue – the kingship has come to stay/is with us (m)

Ezeji – god of yam (m)

Ezenwa – a royal child, a prince (m)

Ezeogu – a child desired to be like a warlord, a warrior (m)

Ezeigbo,(Ezigbo)- a head in an Igbo family. (m)

Ezewuiro--Royalty attracts envy/enmity [m]

Igbokwe – may Igbo (regarded as powerful or respected as a god) allow him to live long (m)

Ezinne – sweet mother (f)

Ezinwanne – beloved brother/ sister, (f,m)

Febechi – continue the worship of God. (f,m)

Ginika – what is of more value than life? (m/f)

Ibe – one's compatriots, (m)

Ibeabuchi – compatriots are not One's destiny. (m)

Ibeji – compatriots hold a lot for an individual [m]

Ibeka – the will of compatriots is supreme, (m)

Ibekanma – compatriots are better (m)

Ibekwe – my compatriots allows him

Ibem – my own compatriots (m)

Ikechukwu, Ike, Iyk – power of God (m)

Ibeneme – of the compatriot's making (m)

Ibenna – father's compatriots (m)

Ibegbulam – may compatriots not kill me (m)

Ibezim – let others teach me; willingness to
    learn from others (m)

Idam (of ''Adam'', Hebrew) (m)

Ifeanyi – nothing is impossible to God (m)

Ifeoma (Eefee) – good thing (f)

Ifeyinwa (Eefee) – there is nothing like a child [f]

Igbe (Igbeaku) – box of wealth (f)

Igbo – Allokoo name given to one of the sons of Aguleri; Igbo is one of the founding
fathers of Ibo race in Nigeria after their arrival from Israel via Egypt (m)

Igwe – Heaven is real (m)

Iheaka – (of ''El heaka'' , Hebrew (m/f)

Ihechi – belonging to God. (m)

Iheke – belonging to Destiny (m)

Iheme – may evil depart from him or us (m)

Ihemegbulam – may my good action not turn into death [m]

Ihemekwala – may evil not befall him /us.(m/f) Ihuoma – good luck. (f)

Ijeoma ,– safe journey, (to husband's family when she is married). (f)

Ike – (Iyk; Iyke) – power, (m)

Ikechi – power of God. (m)

Ikechukwu, – God's Power. (m)

Ikerionwu – man's strength cannot overcome death (m)

Ikejiaku (Ikeji) – might is wealth.(m)

Ikodia – husband's concubine (a wish of sweet relationship with one's
   husband } (f)

Ikonne – mother's lover (m/f)

Ikonna – father's lover.(f)

Ikoro – wooden musical instrument carved out from a very big iroko
tree, used only on very great occasions mark of great elegance –
Mark of great elegance (m)

Ikpeama – Never guilty, Expected to be law abiding. (m}

Ikpechukwu – God's judgement, no appeal (m)

Ikpo – (nickname for Okereke). (m)

IIoh (Iro) – enmity between breathen, (not appreciated at all). (m)

Ilondu – enemy of life (m)

Irondi – enmity is exists (m/f)

Ireoma – sweet tongue (m/f)

Irechukwu – tongue of God (m)

Iroakazi – your enemy will never talk good of you (m)

Iroanya – show of hatred by sight (m)

Irobiko – may enemies allow the child to live (m)

Iroecheta – may he not be remembered by an enemy (m)

Iroha – my enemies spare his life (m)

Irohum – let my enemies live long to see my prosperity (m)

Irokansi – enemity is worse than poison (m)

Irokwe (Ironkwe) – if only enemies will spare his life (m)

Irole - let my enemies live long to see my prosperity (m/f)

Isiguzo – may his head continue to stand on his neck (a wish of long
life for the child) (m)

Isikaku – one's head is greater than wealth (m)

Item – (of "Etam" of the tribe of Judah, Hebrew) (m)

Iweha – annoyance or anger against a brother should seize (m)

Iwuala – the commandments of the goddess of earth (m)
Iwuanyanwu – the commandments of the god of sun (m)
Iwuchukwu – the commandments of God Almighty (m)
Iwuh—Short form of Iwuji, Iwuchukwu, Iwuoha—
A child expecte to grow as a law abiding citizen [m]
Iyama, Ayiam, Ayim—6th Hebrew alphabet [m]
Izuegbu – negotiation/dialogue rather than war pays (m)
Kanu (of "Akan", Hebrew) (m)
Kalu – of the shrine of the shrine of Kalu, holy, respectable and
dependable (m)
Kalunta –Young Kalu (m)
Karibe – Announce the good news to others (m/f)
Kelechi – thanks be to God (m,f)
Madu—(Person— Name given a child expected to be great, at birth) [m]
Maduabu – man is not God (m)
Maduako – may people of substance not lack us (m)
Muodi (Mordi) – Spirit (of God or Evil) is real (m)
Muokelu – The Spirit of God has created…
Nkoro – a cricket, beautiful and smart insect, useful to farmers (m/f)
Njoku—Price of harvest and plenty. Highly honored in ancient Ibo land
and only given to the male child of a wealthy yam farmer [m]
Ngozi – blessing (m,f)
Nnabugwu – a father's pride of the family; father has honour (m)
Nnanna – a reincarnation of one's dead father, or grandfather (m)
Nnadi – a reincarnation of one's husband's father (m)
Nnado, Nnadozie—Same as Chidozie (m)
Nnaji – father is handy or wealthy (m)
Nnamdi – my father liveth (m)
Nnemeka (Emeka) – it is of God's making, thanks be t God (m)
Nnaji—kin, A child expected to be the pride of the father [m]
Nneji – mother is handy (m)
Nneka – mother is supreme (f)
Nnenna – father's mother; the reincarnation of the father's mother (f)
Nnorom – Self Preseration, wishing that the child will live (m)
Nwachukwu – Son of God (m)
Nwadike – strong child (m)
Nwadinobi – a child after our heart (m/f)
Nwafor - a child born on an afor market day (m/f)
Nwaka, Nwakaibeya and Nwakaego-- child is better than anything
else(money) (m,f)

Nwakaego – a child is more precious than silver and gold (m/f)
Nwalozie – a child of good destiny (m)
Nwagbara (Wagbara or Wabara) – son of the shrine of agbara –holy,
 Desirable and respectable (m)
Nwakudu or Nwakudo—Child of peace and joy [m]
Nwanna (Nwana) – he is his father's son; true to type (m)
Nwankpa – an important child destined to help solve problems;
a highly desirable child coming in time of need (m)
Nwankwo – a child born on an nkwo market day (m)
Nwaogu (when pronounced as Nworgu)a child born during the war (m)
Nwaogu – a child of a covenant (m)
Nwabugwu – a child that will brings honor and glory (m)
Nwabueze – a child valued as a king (m)
Nweke – a child born on an eke market day (m)
Nwakaibeya (Nwakibeya) – a child destined to tower above others (m)
Nwakanma (Nwakama, Wakama) -child is better than anything else(m)
Nwanjioji – child brings gifts, wealth (m/f)
Nwokoro – a male child (m)
Nwosu – a son of Osu god. Osu god never support anything evil,
is very holy, extremely respectable and feared by all. A child named
Osu is desired to have all the attributes of osu god (m)
Nwigwe (Wigwe) – Child of Heaven (m)
Nwulu – son of the second son in the family (m)
Nze -a titled man, next in hierachy to the king in some communities(m)
Obasi – an attribute name of God Almighty (from Kwa language) (m)
Obi – a child desired to be a head or a ruler (m)
Obia (corruption of Abia) – (of "Abija, Abiah", Hebrew) Visitor(m)
Obiageri – born to enjoy (f)
Obialor, Obilor – our mind is now at rest as a result of the birth of the
child to the family (m)
Obidike – a child desired to have the heart of a warrior (m)
Obike – a child desired to be strong willed, to have the heart of a
strong man (m)
Obilom - my mind is now at rest as a result of the birth of the child in
 the family (m)
Obioma – A cheerful heart (m)
Obioha - a child desired to always speak or act out the mind and wishes of
all (m)
Obisike – a child desired to be a source of encouragement (m)
Obiukwu - a child desired to possess big heart (m)

Ochiabuto – laughter is not love (m/f)

Ochonma – longing after beauty (m/f)

Odinaka - it is all in the hand (of God) (f/m)

Odoala-A royal land Title holder in ancient Ibo Land [m]

Odoemela (Odoemena) – may it not happen again (m)

Odus—Lion. Pet name for any Ibo called Odum [m]

Ofoegbu – may the child not die by a curse; vain curse does not kill(m)

Ofondu – blessings of life (m)

Ofoma – good blessings (m)

Ofoaku – showers of wealth (m)

Ogba – a go-gether (m)

Ogbajie – a go-gether of repute (m)

Ogbunabali – that which kills at night (is only comparable to a
     powerful god or goddess – a child desired to have the attributes of
     such a god or goddess (m)

Ogbenyalu (Alua) - a child that is not destined to be betrothed to a poor
     man, but if per chance she finds herself in a poor man's home, she
     will bring wealth to the family (f)

Ogbolu—Born for the good of all [m]

Ogbonnaya (Ogbonna) – father's namesake (m)

Ogbuagu - a nickname for a great hunter who once killed a lion, tiger;
     a child desired to have the attributes of such a hunter (m)

Ogbuokiri – nickname for a great hunter who once killed a specie of very
     strong monkey-like wild beast called "okiri"; a child desired to
     have the attributes of such a hunter (m)

Ogu, Ogo (of "Ogo", Hebrew) Convenabt of God (m)

Ogechi – God's time (is the best) (f)

Oguejuafor – quarrel or war pays not (m)

Oguamalam – may I not be involved in fights or quarrels (m)

Ohanaja—A child that will be praised by the people [m]

Ojimadu – whoever has this child has somebody; a child desired to be
     Reliable and great (m)

Ojukwu – a type of palm fruit, very oily, nutritious and medicinal too;
     Highly   prized; a child desired to be so highly prized (m)

Okadigbo – it's yet too early to judge or conclude or form any opinion
     Concerning   this child (m)

Okafor – a child born on an afor market day (m)

Okechukwu – a gift from God (m)

Okezie – wish of good destiny for the child (m)

Okereke, Okeke, Ekeke – a male child born on an eke day (m)

Okezie – wish of good destiny for the child (m)

Okocha – a fair complexioned child of good hope (m)

Okoji – a dark complexioned child of good hope (m)

Okonkwo – a male child born on an nkwo day (m)

Okorie – a male child born on an orie day (m)

Okoro – a typical male child (m)

Okpa – nickname of the high priest of the shrine of god of yam in
    Item, Abia State (m)

Opara (Okpara, Okpala) – (of, "Ophra", Hebrew – name of the first
    Son of Meonothai of the tribe of Judah) – name of the first male
    Child born in an Ibo family (m)

Okporaocha (Oparaocha) – a fair complexioned first son (m)

Okpo – a beautiful mud fish, powerful, very sweet, very nutritious and
    Highly prized: a child desired to be as highly prized (m)

Okwudiri – let it be as decreed by God; Speak not the word of God (m)

Okwu – the short form of Okwudiri

Ola – A ring. (gold or silver; a child desired to be as valuable as gold or
silver) (f)

Oleka – What is greater than (God)? (m)

Olisa – ("of Elisha, corrupted as Olisa, Hebrew) – attribute name of
 God in Ibo land – ancient Jews also refer to their revered prophet as
    god (m)

Olisamaka – God is good (m)

Olisakwe (Osakwe) – if it is the will of God; the child will grow to be
    Successful. (m)

Oluchi – the handwork of God (f)

Onunekwu—The people's spokesman [m]

Onuoha—The people's spokesman [m]

Onwuliri—By the mercy of death, this child will remain alive [m]

Onyeama – man of the people; a child desired, to be recognised
 outside his immediate community (m)

Onyema – who knows tomorrow, the plan of God for the future? (m)

Onyebuenyi – who knows who the real friend is? (m)

Onyedikachi, Onyekachi, Onyedika – who is like unto God? (m/f)

Onyekoro—Who is lacking with the arrival of this child? [m]

Onyemaechi - who knows tomorrow, the plan of God for the future? [m/f]

Onyemerekwe – One should own up his fault? (m)

Onyeamara – a child got by the grace of God (f)

Onyenaekeya – each according to his own destiny (m/f)

Onyenwe – to whom do we(things) belong? (m)

Onyinyechi – gift of God (f)

Omenazu, – post death happening, a child born after father's death. (m)

Omenuko – a man who gives to others or performs during scarcity(m)

Omenka – a man of great dexterity (m)

Onoh – ("Onoh", Hebrew) (m)

Onu – the people's mouthpiece or spokesman; a child desired to be the people's mouthpiece or spokesman (m)

Onukawa – let people say whatever they like concerning the child, the plan of God for him must stand (m)

Onudibia – an oracle (m)

Onunigwe – oracle of God in Heaven (m)

Onuoha - the people's mouthpiece or spokesman; (m)

Onwuegbuchulam – may I not die young (m)

Onwuka – death is supreme as it can terminate all plans concerning an individuals (m)

Onwukaike – the power of death surpasses all powers (m)

Opara (see Okpara) (m)

Oraekwugha – the voice of the people as whole is the voice truth (m)

Oriaku – a child born to enjoy life (m,f)

Ori – short form of Oriaku (m,f)

Orji – iroko tree -a very useful timber, a very valuable child.
    Osigwe – man of Heaven (m)

Ositadinma -Beginning from the day the child is born ,all is well (m)

Osita – short form of Ositadinma (m)

Osondu – life's race is not easy (m)

Oso – the short form of Osondu (m)

Osu, – of the shrine of Osu. Osu god never support anything evil, is very holy, extremely respectable and feared by all. A child named after osu is desired to have all the attributes of osu god (m)

Osuagwu – a smaller shrine called "agwu", which belongs to the bigger shrine of osu or to osu god. (m)

Osuegbu - may the child not die as result of an osu affair (m)

Osuji – of the high priest of osu (in this case, a high priest of the god of yam as decreed by the oracle of osu) (m)

Tochi – praise be to God (m)

Tasie – patience (m,f)

Uba – treasures of life (m)

Ubani – (of "Bani", Hebrew) (m)

Udeogu – a child desired to be noted for war exploits (m)

Udo – Peace (m,f)

Uduma – (of "Dumah", Hebrew) (m)

Udochukwu (Udo) – peace of God (m,f)

Ucha – a fair complexioned child (f)

Uchechi – God's will (m/f)

Uchendu – thought of life not of death (m)

Uchenna – the will of God the Father (m/f)

Uchechukwu – Go's will (m/f)

Uche – short form of Uchechi, Uchenna, Uchechukwu or Uchendu(m)

Ufomadu – the surviving child; a child destined to survive; survival of
human beings in the family is assured (m)

Ufonna – the surviving father (m)

Ugboaja – basket of sacrifice; a vehicle for conveyance of sacrifice
for the good of all (m)

Ugboma – a child desired to be a vehicle of honour in the hand of God
(m/f)

Ugbondu – vehicle of life (m/f)

Ugo – an eagle, smart beautiful and highly prized because of its
a child desired to be as highly prized as the eagle (m,f)

Ugochi – an eagle (in this case, a child of great value) from God (f)

Ugochukwu - an eagle (in this case, child of great value) from God (m)

Ugonna—An eagle's feather on the father's cap: pride of the father [m]

Ugunwa, Ugwunna – Father's dignity (m)

Ugu – the short form Ugunwa (m)

Ugorji – an eagle, the one that usually perches on top 0f thegreat iroko
trees; a highly desirable child (m)

Uka – discourse; dialogue, worship (m)

Ukachi – God's case, no appeal ; as God wishes (f)

Ukachukwu - God's case, no appeal; as God wishes (m)

Ukairo – issue of enemity (not desirable) (m)

Ukandu – matter of life (m)

Ukaoma (Ukoma) – good news (m/f)

Ukoji – the pride of a woman is the husband (f)

Ume (Umeh), – Barrenness as a result of a curse, or genetic disorder.
The Ibos believe that if you call a curse or sin by its name, it
will disappear from you. Hence the name, Ume, which is an
unwanted curse. Recently said to be sicle cell annemia. (m)

Uloaku (Ulaku) – a child desired to be an embodiment of wealth (f)

Ulu – the second son in the family (mf)

Umunnakwe – If his kinsmen will allow him to survive (m/f)

Uwadi – kingdom of earth is real (m/f)

Uzoma – smooth way of life – a wish that the child should always walk on the smooth way of life (m/f)

Uzodinma – one good path (destiny) is desired for this child. (m)

Uwadiogbu – the world is a complex place (m)

Uwaoma – good life (m,f)

Uzunma – a child of great beauty; a child as beautiful as Uz, the proverbial great grand parent of the Ibos from Israel (m/f)

Uzoamaka – the journey (of life) so far is good for me (f)

Uzubi – pathway to farmland; pathway to source of life itself (m)

MORE NAMES WILL BE ADDED IN THE SECOND EDITION.

ONYX STONE (Exodus 39: 6-7)

An Onyx Stone with the inscription of GAD in Hebrew was discovered by Mr. Yitzhad David Israel, the International Director of the King Solomon Shepardic Foundation, from Israel in 1997 at AGULERI (Ibo land), Anambra State, Nigeria.
(Above is a sample of an Onyx Stone)

REFERENCES

ADAMS J. (1975). "Bonny, and the Slave Trade,"
in Hodgkin,T., Nigerian Perspectives: An
Historical Anthology. London: Oxford
University Press

AFIGBO, A.E. (1974). "Religion and Economic
Enterprise in Traditional Igbo Society", in
Econonalyst, Vol. 1 No. 1.
- (2001). Igbo Experience - A Prolegomenon.
Okigwe: Whytem Publishers Nigeria

AMADI E. (1973), Sunset in Biafra. London
Ibadan Nairobi: Heinemann

ALAEZI (ELIEZER) 0, (1998). "The Nigerian Hebrew
Community: A Myth or a Reality?" lnternal Mimeo
- (1999). Ibos: Hebrew Exiles from Israel -
Amazing Facts and Revelations. Aba: ONZY
Publications
- (2000). "New Yam Festival; Its Significance
in Item". A Guest Speaker's Speech on the
Occasion of New Yam Festival Celebration
Organised by Item Union in Lagos on 16th
September 2000.
- (2001). "The Spoils, of the Ibos of Nigeria".
Internal Mimeo.
- (2002). Ibo Exodus - Revealed! Aba: ONZY
Publications

ARINZE, F,A. (1970). Sacrifice in Ibo Religion:
A Definition. : lbadan University Press.

BASDEN, G.T. (1938). Niger Ibos. London: Frank
Cass and Co. Ltd.

CHECHE, N.K.O. (1999). "The Cultural
Similarities Between the Israelites and the
Ibos". A Lecture on the Occasion of the
Launching of "Ibos: Hebrew Exiles from
Israel..."

CHUKWUKERE, R.I.S. (1985). The History of the
Igbos and the Chronology of Events as
Revealed to Innocent Okorie, the
Stigmatist by our Lord Jesus Christ...
Enugu: Cecta (Nig) Ltd.

COHEN, R. (1974). Labour and Politics in
Nigeria. London: Heinemann Education
Books Ltd.

Daily Champion Newspaper, 27th April 1999,
page 5. Lagos, Nigeria.

DONIN, H. H. (1972). To Be a Jew. New York. Equiano,
0. (1974). "Ibo Society in Mid-Century",
in Hodgkin, T. op cit.
EGBOKE, BONIFACE (2001). "Ohaneze-Ndigbo and
their debased environment", in Daily Champion,
Tuesday, September 11, 2001.

EZEH, P. J. (2000) "Not Yet Hebrew Exiles", in
ThisDay, Dec. 8, 2000. Vol. .6. No. 2056, p.37

EZEA1A, J.0.L. (1992). The Great Debate... Orlu:
Nnaji and Sons Press Ltd.

ILOGU, E.(1974). Christianity and Igbo Culture.
New York: Nok Publishers Ltd.

IMPE, J. C. (1 994). "America, Israel, Russia and
World War". Ontario: N9A6 YICA.

LEON URIS (1958). Exodus. London: Corgi Books,
   A Division of Transworld, Publishers Ltd.

MBITI, J.S. (1975). Introduction to African
   Religion. London: Heinemann Educational
   Books Ltd.

NWANKWO, ARTHUR (1999). "Igbo Nation and
   Sovereign National Conference". in Vanguard,
   Wed.. Dec. 29, 1999. p. 11.

OFILI, O. (2001). The Last Jew (Tears of the East).
   Lagos: Eternity Creations.

OGOLOMA, N.A. (1994). New Research on Igbo
   Nation. Onitsha: Nze Publisher.
OJUKWU, C.O. (1968). Excerpts of Ahiara
   (Biafra) Declaration . Ahiara Mbaise

OKORO, RALPH (2001). "Igbo Presidency.Ukiwe's
   View Is   Warped", in Hallmark National
   Newspaper, p.9, vol.3 No. 10. June 2001

ONONUJU. E. (1996). Igbos: A Missing Tribe in

Israel? Aba: Emancipation Books.

ONWUKWE, S. O. (1995). Rise and Fall of the Arochukwu Empire,
   1400-1902. Enugu: Fourth Dimension Publishing Co. Ltd.

ORAKA, L.N. (1983). The Foundation of Igbo

Studies: A Short History of the Study of Igbo
Language and Culture. Onitsha: University
   Publishing Co.
Present Day Events And their Meaning from the
   Bible. Australia: The Gospel Publicity League. Reed, D. (1969).
   Readers Digest. April 1969. Pages 157-162

Schon, J.F. and Crowther. S. (1974). "Iboland
and the Slave Trade", in Hodgkin, T. op.cit.
ThisDay Newspaper. May 3, 1998 page 3.   Reverend R. Walsh (1830)
."Chasing a slave ship", in Notices of Brazil. New York.
Zion's Fire. March - April 1994, pp. 11-15.
Photographs and map Wikipedia Encyclopedia.

MAP OF NIGERIA, UNIVERSITY OF TEXAS LIBRARY.

THE STAR OF DAVID IN SOLID BRONZE WAS DISCOVERED BY BRITISH ARCHEALOGISTS IN AGULU (IBOLAND), 500 FEET BELOW THE GROUND IN 1917. THE BRITISH LATTER ENGRAVED IT ON THE OLD WEST AFRICAN PENNY AND HALF PENNY COINS.

Star Of David

IGBO MEN AT A CONVENTION IN ATLANTA

Ida B. Wells Barnett

Dr. Ada N. Njoku, MD

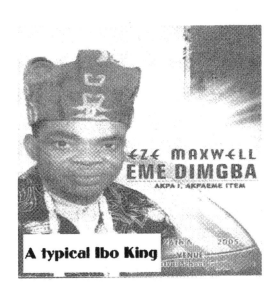

A typical Ibo King

Assembly of typical Ibo Chiefs

A TYPICAL VILLAGE WOMEN GROUP

ABIGBO DANCE BY MBAISE, ATLANTA

IBOS

Hebrew Exiles from Israel

For Distributor or Bulk Pricing email us at

ibosbook@gmail.com

Made in the USA
Middletown, DE
09 October 2023

40462061R10125